THE
BUSINESS
OF
PLATFORMS

THE
BUSINESS
OF
PLATFORMS

Strategy
in the Age of
Digital Competition,
Innovation, and Power

Michael A. Cusumano

Annabelle Gawer

David B. Yoffie

HARPER
BUSINESS

An Imprint of HarperCollins*Publishers*

HarperCollins books may be purchased for educational, business, or sales promotional use. For information, please email the Special Markets Department at SPsales@harpercollins.com.

FIRST EDITION

Designed by Nancy Singer

Library of Congress Cataloging-in-Publication Data has been applied for.

ISBN 978-0-06-289632-2

21 22 23 LSC 10 9 8 7 6

CONTENTS

PREFACE AND ACKNOWLEDGMENTS

This book brings together research, ideas, and experiences that the three authors have accumulated over the past thirty years. The initial motivation was to write a much-needed sequel to *Platform Leadership: How Intel, Microsoft, and Cisco Drive Industry Innovation* (Gawer and Cusumano, 2002).[1] Many companies and other organizations used that book to help them think about platform strategy and ecosystem innovation. It also laid the groundwork for additional research by ourselves and many other scholars. However, much time has passed, and there is much more to say about the business of platforms.

Platform Leadership introduced a framework that we called the Four Levers, intended to help managers at platform companies make key decisions with regard to strengthening their positions and ecosystems. Lever 1 dealt with how to balance the encouragement of third-party firms to innovate around the platform versus the decision to build your own complements. Our obvious example was a firm like Microsoft, which built both Windows (the platform) and Office (an essential complement). Lever 2 discussed how to design a platform that is accessible and modular so that external firms could more easily build their own complementary innovations. Lever 3 addressed initiatives to help ecosystem companies innovate around the platform, such as enabling tools, developer forums, and targeted venture funds. Lever 4 explored how platform leaders can organize internally to maintain some semblance of neutrality when they competed with their complementors and needed third-party firms to trust them.

In addition to the book, which focused on leadership principles for existing platform companies, we introduced two new concepts in a 2008 *MIT Sloan Management Review* article: *coring* and *tipping*.[2] "Coring" referred to how firms can become platform leaders in markets that have not yet introduced a platform. The strategy we suggested was to identify an industry-wide problem and then introduce a product, technology, or service as a "core" or essential solution (or key part of the solution) to this problem. The idea was to retain control over the technology and monetization opportunities but offer easy access to third parties, such as cheap or free licensing terms, and a modular design so other firms could easily connect to and build on top of the solution. Successful coring examples included the Intel x86 microprocessor along with DOS and then the Windows operating systems as solutions to the problem of how to build IBM-compatible personal computers. Another example was Google's free search tool bar as a solution for navigating the Internet. "Tipping" referred to a set of strategies to compete in markets with multiple platform contenders but none with a dominant position. Successful tipping examples included Google's use of a coalition (the Open Handset Alliance) to bring together smartphone manufacturers to compete as a group with Apple's iPhone. Another strategy was to subsidize a key side of the market, which Google did when it decided to give away the Android operating system for free. Apple also adopted a tipping strategy when it evolved the iPod music player into the iPhone by "enveloping" features and functions from products in adjacent markets.[3]

The current book incorporates these ideas but examines platform strategy in a much broader context. In particular, *Platform Leadership* only treated what in this book we call "innovation platforms." Now we discuss innovation platforms with many more years of experience, and we devote equal time to what we call "transaction platforms," which are far more common. In addition, we discuss "hybrid" companies and platforms, which include the most valuable firms in the world.

It took us three years to complete this book. We started in 2015, when Michael Cusumano and Annabelle Gawer began collecting data to see if platform companies did indeed outperform conventional businesses over long periods of time. This turned out to be the case. We also wrote up our initial thoughts on market dynamics and how business models and strategy differed for innovation platforms as compared to transaction platforms. David Yoffie joined the project after the publication of *Strategy Rules: Five Timeless Lessons from Bill Gates, Andy Grove, and Steve Jobs* (Yoffie and Cusumano, 2015), which included a detailed analysis of how platform thinking evolved at Microsoft, Intel, and Apple.[4] We then expanded the scope of this new book to examine common mistakes among platform companies, challenges for conventional firms trying to compete with digital platforms, platform governance and antitrust issues, and some emerging platform technologies that could greatly impact the future. Again, we hope to influence future research about platforms among our academic colleagues and students, but our primary audience has remained managers and entrepreneurs.

We are particularly pleased to work again with Hollis Heimbouch of HarperBusiness. Hollis was our editor for *Platform Leadership* when she was at Harvard Business School Press. She also was our editor at HarperBusiness for *Strategy Rules* (now translated into eighteen foreign languages). Her early interest in another book on platforms motivated us to finish the project and make the book as accessible as possible to practitioners. We also appreciated her suggestions on the manuscript.

Platforms are unique businesses driven by network effects and multisided market dynamics. Studying them was not a well-defined or popular topic among strategy and innovation scholars when we began our research and work with these types of companies in the late 1980s and early 1990s. In writing this book, not only have we moved considerably beyond our initial thinking, but we also have been able to build on a growing body of scholarship. Most notably, we need to thank our colleagues (in order of seniority) Richard Schmalensee, Thomas Eisenmann, David Evans, Geoffrey Parker, Marshall Van Alstyne, Andrei Hagiu, and Sangeet Paul Choudary for their many excellent books and articles. We cite their work numerous times.

We are indebted to several outside readers who provided detailed feedback on the manuscript. We are particularly grateful (in alphabetical order) to Pierre Azoulay, Donna Dubinsky, Nilufer Durak, Andreas Goeldi, Shane Greenstein, Andrei Hagiu, Mel Horwitch, Reed Hundt, Divya Joshi, Mary Kwok, Michael Scott Morton, Apoorva Parikh, Richard Schmalensee, Kiyoshi Tsujimura, Julian Wright, Nataliya Langburd Wright, and Feng Zhu. Peter Evans, working in part with Annabelle Gawer, also inspired us to create a comprehensive list of platform companies. Also providing very useful feedback from seminars and discussions about the data analysis were Carliss Baldwin, Robert Seamans, and other attendees at Boston University's Platform Strategy Research Symposium in July 2018. For contributions to the innovation and transaction platform framework, we thank Michael Jacobides and Carmelo Cennamo. In addition, Ganesh Vaidyanathan helped with the quantum computing discussion; Samantha Zyontz, as well as Gigi Hirsch and David Fritsche, helped with the CRISPR discussion.

Several research assistants helped with the platform company database and analysis. We thank Danny Nightingale, Damjan Korac, Georges Xydopoulos, and Ankur Chavda (who provided the most recent statistical analysis). We also thank David Yoffie's Harvard Business School research associates Eric Baldwin and Daniel Fisher for additional assistance with background research and editing as well as his faculty assistant, Cathyjean Gustafson.

Finally, we would like to acknowledge our spouses and families for their patience and encouragement. Michael Cusumano thanks his wife, Xiaohua Yang. Annabelle Gawer thanks her husband, David Bendor. David Yoffie thanks his wife, Terry Yoffie.

Michael A. Cusumano
Annabelle Gawer
David B. Yoffie
December 2018

THE
BUSINESS
OF
PLATFORMS

PLATFORM
THINKING

INTRODUCTION

HOW DID WE GET TO THIS POINT?

PLATFORMS DEFINED

PLATFORM BUSINESS MODELS
Two Basic Types

WHAT THE DATA SAYS

OVERVIEW OF THE FOLLOWING CHAPTERS

CHAPTER 1

It is a well-known story. In July of 1980, several executives from IBM visited a young Bill Gates, cofounder and CEO of a five-year-old company called Microsoft. Gates already had a reputation as the best source of programming languages for personal computers, a fledgling new market. IBM was planning to introduce a personal computer for businesses, and it wanted Microsoft to provide the operating system. At first, Gates demurred. He suggested that IBM speak with another start-up called Digital Research. Those discussions failed, so the IBM team returned to Seattle. This time, spurred on by employee Kazuhiko ("Kay") Nishi and cofounder Paul Allen, Gates decided to accept the job. Microsoft bought a crude operating system for $75,000, fixed it up, and named it MS-DOS, for Microsoft Disk Operating System.[1]

The less well-known part of the story is how Gates structured the deal with IBM. The basic contract was fairly routine: He charged IBM a development fee of $200,000 and as much as $500,000 for additional engineering work. Gates also gave IBM the rights to DOS and several programming language products it could bundle with the new computer. But—and this is crucial—Gates allowed IBM to use the operating system with *no additional fees or royalty payments* as long as Microsoft, and only Microsoft, could license the software to other manufacturers.[2]

What was Bill Gates thinking?

Gates was familiar with the "clone" industry that had emerged around the IBM mainframe during the 1960s and 1970s. The clones created a new but relatively small business around software and services for IBM-compatible machines. It occurred to him that, if the IBM PC became popular, then a new mass market would likely

3

emerge for the personal computer. If he alone had the right to license the operating system to companies that wanted to build compatible machines, then Microsoft would be at the center of a whole new industry.[3] Indeed, over the next several decades, this industry—today we would call it an "ecosystem"—attracted thousands of software and hardware companies, produced millions of "complementary" software applications and peripheral devices like printers, cameras, and game controllers, and today still counts more than a billion users.

Gates's decision to give away the basic software to IBM in return for the right to license it to other companies is now a famous and striking example of "platform thinking."[4] (This agreement was also one of IBM's *worst* strategic decisions.) But how would Microsoft make money if it gave away the software for free to its main customer? Gates realized there would be more than one "side" to this new market. His goal was not to maximize profits from the sale of DOS to IBM as a stand-alone *product*. Instead, the strategy was to make the operating system into an industry-wide *platform*—a foundation that many companies could use to build personal computers and compatible software applications. IBM seemed intent on controlling the PC market with production of its own personal computers, using Microsoft's software as a component. To Gates, however, encouraging many firms to invest in making IBM-compatible PC hardware and software applications would make the personal computer—and especially Microsoft's operating system—increasingly useful and valuable. Gates would soon enter the software applications business himself to grow the IBM-compatible PC market and take more of the profit, with Word, Excel, and PowerPoint. He did this first for Apple's Macintosh computer, introduced in 1984, and then for DOS and Windows PCs, bundled in the Office suite from 1990. To encourage other companies to help expand demand for PCs, Gates also decided to give away for free the software development kit (SDK) needed to build applications for DOS and then Windows.

By contrast, Apple cofounder and CEO Steve Jobs did not give away software development kits for free or try to build a broad applications market. Instead, he hired Microsoft in 1982 and paid Gates a $50,000 advance to write applications for the Macintosh personal computer, which was incompatible with DOS.[5] Jobs also charged hundreds of dollars to developers who wanted to build Macintosh applications on their own. The development fee was in addition to large expenses that programmers usually had to incur in order to design applications. Most expensive was the $10,000 Lisa, a failed predecessor to the Macintosh that nonetheless served as a software development platform before the Macintosh was available. Programmers also had to buy some programming language and database products.[6] But, Jobs reasoned, with an easy-to-use graphical interface, the Macintosh was going to be such a great product that companies *should pay him* for the right to build applications. Partly due to the resulting paucity of applications software as well as the high price of the hardware (about twice as much as an IBM-compatible PC, because Apple was the only manufacturer and there was no price competition), the Macintosh never garnered significant market share. Ultimately, PCs running DOS and then Windows—which mimicked the easy-to-use Macintosh user interface—captured roughly 95 percent of the market for personal computers.[7]

Microsoft was thinking platforms. IBM and Apple were thinking products.

The personal computer, like social media, online marketplaces, cloud computing, and smartphones in more recent years, turned out to be a *platform* business, not a *product* business. In the case of the personal computer, by this phrase we mean that, unlike in traditional businesses, success did not depend simply on the quality, price, or timing of Microsoft's operating system as a stand-alone product. Success depended more on complementary innovations that determined what users could do with the product—such as the number and quality of software applications or digital services produced by many companies. These "complements" added significant and even essential value to the core product, what we now call an innovation platform.

To turn its product into a platform, Microsoft also had to solve a critical "chicken-or-egg" problem: how to encourage other companies to build the software applications needed to stimulate demand for PCs. It turned out that broad and cheap licensing of the operating system facilitated the production of low-cost hardware by many companies around the world. Then the rising number of PC users using the same technology created demand for programmers to design increasing numbers of compatible software applications. Who won and who lost depended less on product quality or features and more on who could best bring multiple "sides" of the emerging market together and generate positive "feedback loops."

Fast-forward to April 2018. Mark Zuckerberg, cofounder and CEO of Facebook, was on the hot seat, testifying before the U.S. Congress. His company, established in 2004, started out by building a simple personal computer application accessed via the web. By 2018, Zuckerberg's free software and services enabled more than 2.2 billion people to send messages, share news stories or digital content like photos and videos, organize groups, send money, and do a myriad of other activities with friends, relatives, and acquaintances, as well as business partners and customers. In the initial stages of the company, Facebook users actively brought in their friends, and then friends of friends, and friends of friends of friends, weaving together a connected network of people that quickly spanned the globe. This network, aided by new features that Facebook enabled, made the social network increasingly valuable as a *transaction platform* for communications, electronic payments, and other purposes, as well as its core business—selling context-specific advertisements. In 2007, following the lead of Microsoft (which, not coincidentally, was a major investor in Facebook), Zuckerberg started to make Facebook's data on users and other functions available as an *innovation platform*—a kind of operating system for social media applications. This decision empowered outside companies and independent programmers to design games and other applications that soon came to number in the millions, and made Facebook an even more compelling experience.

But platforms do not always evolve in predictable ways, especially when they are able to add so many new functions from both inside and outside the firm. In 2014 a researcher at the University of Cambridge working with a small British consultancy named Cambridge Analytica (now bankrupt) built one of those millions of Facebook applications. Its main purpose was to track the preferences of users and their friends. The application provided data on as many as 87 million unsuspecting Facebook users in the United States and helped Russian hackers target particular users with fake news stories supporting candidate Donald Trump and criticizing rival Hillary Clinton.[8] The U.S. Congress called in Zuckerberg to explain how his seemingly harmless social media platform had become an instrument of such power for a foreign government. Zuckerberg explained in his written testimony:

> We face a number of important issues around privacy, safety, and democracy, and you will rightfully have some hard questions for me to answer. Before I talk about the steps we're taking to address them, I want to talk about how we got here.
>
> Facebook is an idealistic and optimistic company. For most of our existence, we focused on all the good that connecting people can bring. As Facebook has grown, people everywhere have gotten a powerful new tool to stay connected to the people they love, make their voices heard, and build communities and businesses. Just recently, we've seen the #metoo movement and the March for Our Lives,

organized, at least in part, on Facebook. After Hurricane Harvey, people raised more than $20 million for relief. And more than 70 million small businesses now use Facebook to grow and create jobs.

But it's clear now that we didn't do enough to prevent these tools from being used for harm as well. That goes for fake news, foreign interference in elections, and hate speech, as well as developers and data privacy. We didn't take a broad enough view of our responsibility, and that was a big mistake. It was my mistake, and I'm sorry. I started Facebook, I run it, and I'm responsible for what happens here.[9]

HOW DID WE GET TO THIS POINT?

For anyone who follows the world of business, it is now common knowledge that the most valuable firms on the planet and the first companies to surpass the trillion-dollar mark in value (albeit temporarily) are platforms. If we look at market values in late 2018, the top firms were Microsoft, Apple, Amazon, and Alphabet (the holding-company parent of Google since 2015). Also among the leaders were Facebook, Alibaba, and Tencent. Together, these seven companies at their peak represented close to $5 trillion in market value. Moreover, in a recent list of more than two hundred current and former "unicorns"—start-ups with valuations of $1 billion or more—we estimated that platforms made up between 60 and 70 percent. These were led by firms such as Ant Financial (owned by Alibaba), Uber, Didi Chuxing, Xiaomi, Airbnb, and other well-known private companies (several of which planned to go public in the near future).[10]

So, yes, Mr. Zuckerberg (and Mr. Gates)—*how did we get to this point?* How have a small number of companies come to exert such enormous influence over our personal, professional, and even political lives, as well as the world economy? There is nothing new about marketplaces; they go back millennia. But digital platforms that span the globe are new. How have they come to control the flow of information as well as such a large number of goods and services? In what ways are these new entities different, or similar, to the powerful corporations we have seen in the past? And are there limits to the market dominance and expansion of these digital juggernauts that can leverage user data as well as scale and scope economies in ways we have never seen before?

These are not simply rhetorical questions. The world is full of existing as well as emerging platform battlegrounds that will have great influence on our lives in the future. We can foresee a time when digital platforms and associated ecosystems will be the way we organize new information technologies such as artificial intelligence, virtual and augmented reality, the Internet of things, health care information, and even quantum computing. We can also see peer-to-peer transaction platforms replacing or competing with traditional businesses, especially as the "sharing" or "gig" economy expands and new technologies diffuse. Use of blockchains (distributed ledger technology that is extremely secure though not unbreakable) and cryptocurrencies (digital money, usually independent of banks and governments) may greatly reduce the need for many different services, from traditional banks to supply-chain contracts and monitoring.

Yet another hot topic as we write this book is increasing demand for governments to rethink data-privacy laws, antitrust laws, and other regulations that could rein in the most powerful platform businesses. Platform companies have faced antitrust challenges many times, and the incidents are likely to increase. The European Union fined Alphabet-Google $2.7 billion in 2017 and $5.1 billion in 2018 for anticompetitive behavior involving Google Search (which at that time had about 90 percent of the global market outside China and Russia) and its Android smartphone operating system (which accounted for about 80 percent of the global market).

In fact, Google Android has replaced Microsoft Windows as the most popular operating system in the world, with over 2 billion users. If we combine data from Internet searches with Google's Gmail (which has over 1 billion active monthly users) and Google's YouTube (which has close to 2 billion users), in addition to individual profiles that Google generated for targeted advertising, then Google probably has far more personal information than even Facebook could muster.[11] Another aggressive platform company, Amazon, was collecting vast amounts of data on its hundreds of millions of users and their transactions, and coming under rising scrutiny in the United States. With more than 500 million individual products for sale, Amazon has disrupted markets such as books, consumer electronics, digital music and video, cloud computing services, groceries, pharmaceuticals, and package delivery.[12] How should government regulators, as well as competing firms, respond to these new centers of power?

These are the questions we tackle in this book. For approximately thirty years, the authors have been studying and working with platform companies that emerged to build essential technologies and software applications for the personal computer, the Internet, and smartphones. Our books include: *Microsoft Secrets* (1995), *Competing in the Age of Digital Convergence* (1997), *Competing on Internet Time: Lessons from Netscape and Its Battle with Microsoft* (1998), *Platform Leadership: How Intel, Microsoft, and Cisco Drive Industry Innovation* (2002), *The Business of Software* (2004), *Platforms, Markets, and Innovation* (2009), *Staying Power* (2010), *Software Ecosystems* (2013), and *Strategy Rules: Five Timeless Lessons from Bill Gates, Andy Grove, and Steve Jobs* (2015). We have also written many articles, including a case study of Apple that, in multiple versions, has sold more than 1 million copies.[13] Most of our earlier work, especially *Microsoft Secrets* and *Platform Leadership*, focused on the ability of platform leaders to inspire complementary innovations from third-party firms. But the world has since adopted a much broader view of how digital platforms impact business, politics, and society. This book builds on our prior work (summarized in the Preface) and that of our colleagues. The goal is to help managers and entrepreneurs, as well as policy makers, better understand how to harness the power of platform thinking while avoiding some of the negative consequences.

Most people know the names of companies that shaped the evolution of platform strategies and business models. Intel (established 1968), Microsoft (1975), and Apple (1976), along with IBM (1911), made the personal computer a mass-market phenomenon during the 1980s and early 1990s. A second wave of firms from the mid-1990s built Internet software and services on top of the personal computer, led by Amazon (1994), Netscape (1994), eBay (1995), Yahoo (1995), and Google (1998), as well as Rakuten (1997) in Japan and Tencent (1998) and Alibaba (1999) in China. In the next decade came social media, pioneered by Friendster (2002) and MySpace (2003), and then Facebook (2004) and Twitter (2006). More recently, billion-dollar start-ups, such as Airbnb (2008), Uber (2009), and China's Didi Chuxing (2012), have brought great attention to the "sharing," or "gig," economy. They match smartphone and PC users with providers of rooms to rent or cars to ride as well as an almost unlimited number of other products and services. We now refer to all these firms as platform companies, even though they are not all the same.

Some people argue that the traditional rules of business no longer apply in this new age of digital competition. Woe to those who do not understand platform strategy and business models, big data analytics, artificial intelligence and machine learning, and what seem to be the new rules of the game. We believe there is considerable truth to this statement. However, we also believe there are several misunderstandings associated with the "digital revolution." In particular, the path to success for a platform company is by no means easy or guaranteed, nor completely different from what we have seen before. Why? Because many platforms today are not sustainable businesses. To succeed long term, all firms must ultimately perform better than the competition, whether the rivals are digital platforms or conventional businesses. They must be financially viable as well as politically and publicly acceptable lest they become crushed by debt obligations, social opposition, government regulation, or global trade wars. These observations are common sense, but, amid all the hype over digital platforms, a phenomenon we sometimes call "platformania," common sense is easy to forget.

The issues may be complicated but our argument is simple: Yes, managers and entrepreneurs in platform companies must understand the finer points of digital competition, innovation, and power. But they must also master the fundamental principles of business and good governance that apply in any company and in any era. Platforms will not generate profits simply because of adept use of digital technology, a clever "multisided" market strategy, or classifying all employees as gig-economy contract workers. If sales rely on large subsidies of one or more market sides, and the platforms continually operate at a loss, then the bigger they get, the more money they will lose. In short, managers and entrepreneurs in the digital age must learn to live in two worlds: the conventional economy and the platform economy. What this means and how to do this well is the subject of this book.

PLATFORMS DEFINED

Before we get into more details, let's clarify what we mean by "platform." In everyday conversation, we hear the word used in many contexts, and this often leads to confusion. Politicians compete on *ideological platforms*—ideas or policies that bring people together for a common goal. People catch trains on *physical platforms*—designated areas that bring people together to access a shared mode of transportation. Companies create *product platforms*—common components and subsystems that different engineering groups within the firm and its supply chain (such as automakers or aircraft manufacturers) can use to build "families" of related products more efficiently than building each product from scratch.

Platforms, in general, connect individuals and organizations for a common purpose or to share a common resource. Our main concern in this book is with *industry platforms* that emerged in the wake of the personal computer, the Internet, and mobile communications technologies. These industry platforms also create building blocks or common functions for use within and outside the firm. However, the platforms function at the level of an industry (or ecosystem). More importantly, *they bring together individuals and organizations so they can innovate or interact in ways not otherwise possible, with the potential for nonlinear increases in utility and value.*[14]

Later in this book we will give some concrete examples of "nonlinear increases in utility and value." Briefly, this means that the usefulness of an industry platform can grow with the power of the network: Each additional user, at least theoretically, can benefit from access to all the other users and innovations already available through the platform. What we have, then, is practical and economic value that can increase not by simple addition, as in adding one user or innovation at a time, which occurs in conventional business models. Rather, value with platforms can increase geometrically if each additional user can connect to all the other users or benefit from all the other innovative products and services already accessible to members of the network.

What are commonly called "network effects" are positive feedback loops that come from connecting different users and market participants to each other. The feedback loops can extend across entire ecosystems, which are broad linkages of producers, suppliers, users, business partners, and other stakeholders. We agree that building a business around network effects requires a different way of thinking about market dynamics and competitive strategy compared to conventional businesses. Platform businesses also have different ways of making money, since they may not directly sell a stand-alone product or service. At the same time, though, platforms do not all require "revolutionary" strategies and business models that did not exist before the digital age or that make conventional business logic obsolete.[15] Nor is it always useful to think of platform companies simply as "matchmakers" bringing different market actors together, although that is a common function for many platform businesses.[16]

We also have argued for many years that, in a platform market, having the *best platform* is more important than having the *best product*.[17] Look at the history of the Apple Macintosh. It was a better personal computer than the DOS or early Windows PCs in terms of ease of use and elegance of design. Despite its strengths, the Mac's market share remained stuck in single digits for the last thirty years because it was not the best platform. The Macintosh was too expensive and more difficult to build applications for, and Steve Jobs did not encourage mass adoption, such as with lower prices or licensing of the technology to other companies.

To be sure, not every industry lends itself to a platform strategy. Often, a stand-alone product or service is the best way to beat the competition or earn the most profits. However, a platform strategy should prevail over a stand-alone product strategy when (1) there are opportunities to tap the innovation capabilities of outside firms to enhance value; and (2) it is more economical to enable transactions rather than to own assets and deliver products or services directly. Managers and entrepreneurs need to understand how product and platform strategies and business models differ and when to use each approach. In many though not all industries, platforms can create significantly more value than conventional businesses and traditional supply chains. In some cases, such as personal computers, smartphones, video game consoles, or even social media, innovations from outside firms can *determine* the success or failure of the platform business. Here is a quick summary of what makes industry platforms unique.

ENGAGE MULTIPLE SIDES OF A MARKET

First, industry platforms deliver products or services by *bringing together two or more market actors or "sides"* (e.g., buyers and sellers, or an operating system maker with users, application developers, and hardware producers) that would not otherwise interact or easily connect. The platform company may begin by targeting one side, such as buyers or users. Over time, though, platform companies usually link actors who want access to another side of the market, such as sellers or producers of complementary innovations. For example, Facebook began in 2004 by connecting Harvard College students to their classmates. It expanded quickly as friends brought in friends and acquaintances. Fairly soon, the company identified another set of market actors: advertisers. These companies had goods and services to sell, based on what people were communicating about. Then Facebook opened up its platform to a third side of the market: application software developers such as game producers or companies seeking to understand user behavior like Cambridge

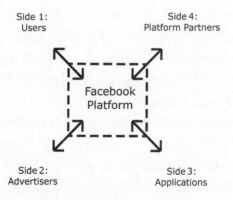

Side 1:
Users

Side 4:
Platform Partners

Facebook
Platform

Side 2:
Advertisers

Side 3:
Applications

FIGURE 1-1: **FACEBOOK PLATFORM AND ECOSYSTEM**

Analytica. And then came a fourth side: content providers, such as online newspapers, magazines, news sites, music sites, and others. (See Figure 1-1.)

GENERATE NETWORK EFFECTS

Second, as industry platforms connect users to other users or to other market participants, they generate *network effects*.[18] The unique feature of network effects is that the value one user experiences potentially *increases* as more people or organizations use the same product or service and as more complementary innovations appear.[19] Network effects can be strong or weak, positive or negative. When they are strong, the results are nonlinear increases in utility and value. These powerful feedback loops enabled Facebook to grow from two users to over 2 billion users in just a few years.

Network effects may sound like a vague concept, but we can explain how they operate with some concrete examples. With only one user of a telephone, fax machine, personal computer, or messaging app, these platform technologies generate no network effects and therefore have little or no value. Two people make these innovations more useful, three more so, and so on. More users encourage more users, which is a positive feedback loop. The user-to-user attraction is also an example of what we call a "direct" or "same-side" network effect. Similarly, a new smartphone operating system that has only a few users is not likely to attract many advertisers or developers of complementary software applications. However, more advertisers and developers are likely to appear if the number of users grows.

These examples illustrate why economies of scale are intimately related to network effects. In addition, negative network effects, such as declining user numbers or poor user ratings or too much advertising, can lead to increasingly rapid declines in usage. Friendster and MySpace in social networking as well as Nokia and Black-

Berry in smartphones all experienced negative network effects and rapid declines in their businesses.

When one side of the market, such as users, attracts another side of the market, such as sellers or developers of complementary products and services, we refer to this type of network effect as "indirect" or "cross-side." What is especially interesting here is that different market sides offer the potential for a platform business to generate revenue without directly building products or delivering services themselves. Furthermore, platforms can access different market sides to substitute for contracting with traditional suppliers, investing in internal firm capabilities, or directly owning critical assets. For example, Apple, Google, Microsoft, and Facebook did not have to build their own engineering teams or write contracts and pay third-party suppliers to create all of the millions of software applications that work on their platforms, even though they built some applications themselves. Similarly, Uber, Lyft, Didi Chuxing, and Airbnb did not have to own any of the cars and homes that their users accessed when they got rides or rented rooms, even though they may someday decide to own or lease vehicles and buildings.

SOLVE A CHICKEN-OR-EGG PROBLEM

Third, in order to link multiple market players and get the network effects started, industry platforms all must solve a *chicken-or-egg problem*. This means that one market side usually needs to come on board first and provide something that attracts another side. The dynamics vary with the type of platform and the specific business. Sometimes two sides need to come on board at almost the same time and grow together in a kind of zigzag fashion like credit card users and merchants.[20] Nonetheless, the business challenge always remains the same: where and how to start, as well as how to get enough momentum and then scale. Solving the chicken-or-egg problem and then generating *strong* network effects can be very difficult if one side of the market realizes value only when another side is fully engaged. This is usually the case. As a result, platform companies must decide which market side to line up first: drivers or potential ride-sharing passengers, people with extra rooms to rent or potential renters, or smartphone handset makers or software app developers.

Traditional companies generally have more direct influence over how customers perceive their stand-alone products and services. The companies may depend heavily on suppliers but not so much on third-party firms to voluntarily make complementary investments. Many new platforms also fail to grow because they misjudge which side of the market is most important. This is one reason why the Apple Macintosh never achieved more than a modest share of the global personal computer market. Other new platforms never get beyond the initial stage because they require too much money to subsidize one side of the market and run out of cash or venture funding before generating large enough scale economies and strong enough network effects to be profitable and survive.

PLATFORM BUSINESS MODELS: TWO BASIC TYPES

Platforms in the digital economy can do many things, and we might construct a complex typology based on the huge variety of applications. However, to make things simple, we divided digital platforms that emerged with the personal computer, Internet, and smartphones into two basic types, depending on their primary function. (See Figure 1-2.) Chapter 3 discusses this typology and the different strategic and operational challenges in more detail, but here we offer a brief overview.

The first type we call *innovation platforms*.[21] These platforms usually consist of common technological building blocks that the owner and ecosystem partners can share in order to create new complementary products and services, such as smartphone apps

Transactions ←   *Innovations* →

The platform serves as an intermediary for direct exchange or transactions, subject to network effects

The platform serves as a technological foundation upon which other firms develop complementary innovations

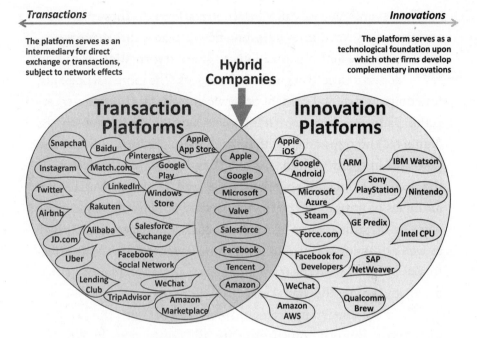

FIGURE 1-2: **TWO BASIC PLATFORM TYPES***

or digital content such as from Apple iTunes or Netflix. By "complementary," we mean that these innovations add functionality or access to assets that make the platform increasingly useful. The network effects come from the increasing number or utility of the complements: The more there are or the higher quality they are, the more attractive the platform becomes to users and complementors, as well as other potential market actors such as advertisers (and investors). Microsoft Windows, Google Android, Apple iOS, and Amazon Web Services are commonly used operating systems and cloud computing services that serve as innovation platforms for computer and smartphone ecosystems.

---

* An earlier version of this graph was developed by Annabelle Gawer in collaboration with Carmelo Cennamo and Michael Jacobides.

The second type we call *transaction platforms*.[22] These platforms are largely intermediaries or online marketplaces that make it possible for people and organizations to share information or to buy, sell, or access a variety of goods and services. The more participants, functions, and digital content or services available through a transaction platform, the more useful it becomes. Again, it is mostly the digital technology and scale that make these platforms unique and powerful in today's world. Google Search, Amazon Marketplace, the Facebook Social Network, Twitter, and Tencent's WeChat are examples of transaction platforms used by billions of people every day. Credit cards such as Mastercard, Visa, and American Express, as well as catalogues such as the Yellow Pages (think of this directory as bundled with the telephone), are transaction platforms that originated before the digital era.

There are important strategic differences between the two platform types. Innovation platforms usually create value by facilitating the development of new complementary products and services, sometimes built by the platform owner but mostly by third-party firms, usually without supplier contracts. Firms often capture and deliver value (monetize the platform) by directly selling or renting a product. In a few cases where the platform is free (e.g., Google Android), firms monetize the platform by selling advertising or other services. By contrast, transaction platforms usually create and deliver value by facilitating the buying and selling of goods and services or facilitating other interactions, such as enabling users to create and share content. The firms that own this type of platform primarily capture value by collecting transaction fees, charging for advertising, or both.

Some firms start with one type of platform and add the second type, or mix and link the two. We refer to companies that support both types of platforms as hybrids. Some people use the term "hybrid" to refer to companies like Apple, Oracle, SAP, or Salesforce that emphasize a combination of product and platform businesses.

In this book, however, as we discuss in Chapter 3, we use "hybrid" to refer to the combination of innovation and transaction platform strategies within the same company or within the same platform infrastructure.

WHAT THE DATA SAYS

Clearly, public and private capital markets have placed enormous value on platforms associated with personal computers, Internet services, and smartphones. Yet no one has done a systematic analysis of the performance of these relatively new companies over long periods of time and compared them to firms in the conventional economy. To fill this void, we analyzed two decades of company performance. We started in 2015, when we began writing this book, and then went back twenty years to 1995, when the mass-market Internet first exploded onto the scene with browsers from Netscape and Microsoft. Using the Forbes Global 2000 list, we identified forty-three companies in 2015 that laid the foundations for the new digital platforms—eighteen for innovations and twenty-five for transactions. (For the list of companies, see Appendix Table 1–1.) Our basic rule of thumb was that a company had to have at least 20 percent of its revenues from a business dependent on network effects to count as a platform. Note that we excluded older platform companies such as telephone and telecommunications operators as well as credit card companies, although they remain in the Forbes Global 2000 sample and continue to be important examples of platform businesses.

Our first finding was that publicly listed companies associated with personal computer, Internet, and smartphone platforms are relatively rare; we counted only forty-three out of approximately 2,000 firms. We also compared these firms to all the Forbes Global 2000 non-platform companies in the same industry categories. The companies in this industry control sample were similar in terms of revenues to the digital platforms, with median sales of about $4.8 billion compared to $4.3 billion, respectively. (See Table 1–1.) After using a variety of statistical controls, we found no meaningful differences in sales between platform companies and the non-platform control sample.[23]

What we did find is that, despite comparable revenues to other firms in the same industries, our sample of platform companies had about half the number of employees, much higher operating profits, and much higher market values as well as higher ratios of market value to sales. The platform companies spent significantly more on R&D and other expenses related to sales, marketing, and administration, but they also grew faster in revenues and market value. Similarly, the platform companies were more productive (in terms of sales per employee), much more profitable, and much more valuable than conventional public firms in the broader world economy, as represented by the Forbes Global 2000 list. To summarize, by almost any measure, the forty-three digital platforms in our sample performed extraordinarily well. We also checked our analysis by removing the largest companies (Apple, Amazon, Microsoft, and Google) and ended up with similar (and statistically significant) results.[24]

This data also allowed us to compare innovation and transaction platforms. The sample is small, but the two types of platforms clearly seemed different from each other, even though all relied on network effects to drive at least part of their businesses. We see in Table 1–1 that innovation platforms, compared to transaction platforms, were four to five times larger in terms of median sales and employees, and had median market values about three times higher. Innovation platforms also spent relatively more on R&D as a percentage of revenues and less on sales, marketing, and general administrative expenses. However, transaction platforms were growing faster in revenues and market capitalization, and traded at higher ratios of market value relative to sales. In other words,

TABLE 1-1: **MEDIAN VALUES FOR FORBES GLOBAL 2000, INDUSTRY CONTROL SAMPLE, AND PLATFORMS, 1995–2015**

VARIABLE	FORBES GLOBAL 2000	INDUSTRY CONTROL SAMPLE (MINUS THE 43 PLATFORMS)	INNOVATION & TRANSACTION PLATFORMS	INNOVATION PLATFORMS	TRANSACTION PLATFORMS
NUMBER OF FIRMS	1,939	100	43	18	25
SALES (MILLION$)	$5,586	$4,845	$4,335	$10,118	$2,119
EMPLOYEES	18,900	19,000	9,872***	26,600	6,349
OPERATING PROFIT %	13%	12%	21%***	21%	21%
MARKET VALUE (MILLION$)	$6,876	$8,243	$21,726***	$37,901	$13,277
MKT VALUE-SALES MULTIPLE	1.39	1.94	5.35***	4.19	7.07
R&D/SALES	4%	9%	13%***	13%	11%
S&M + G&A/SALES	16%	17%	24%***	22%	33%
SALES GROWTH	8%	9%	18%***	13%	29%
MARKET VALUE GROWTH	10%	8%	14%***	12%	21%
OBSERVATIONS	5,121	1,018	374	239	135

*** = p < 0.001 for Industry Control Sample vs. Innovation & Transaction Platforms comparison using two-sample Wilcoxon rank-sum (Mann-Whitney) test.

Mkt Value-Sales Multiple = ratio of market value compared to prior year sales.

S&M + G&A/Sales = Sales and Marketing Expenses + General and Administrative Expenses divided by Sales.

Growth numbers refer to prior year data.

Observations refer to the number of years of data for each firm, which depended on when the companies went public. We had on average 13 years of data for the 18 innovation platforms and 5 years of data for the 25 transaction platforms.

investors considered transaction platforms more valuable relative to revenues compared to innovation platforms.

We also analyzed the annual reports of the 43 publicly listed platform companies going back several years and counted 209 direct competitors (public and private) that were platforms and went out of business. In effect, the 43 companies in our sample were the survivors of this competition, and only 17 percent (43 out of 252) remained in 2015 as independent public companies. We discuss this data further in Chapter 4.

We can make one additional observation, looking at the financial performance of individual firms: It was often unclear if a company was successful primarily because of its *platform strategy* or its *product strategy*. Take Apple as an example. Is this company so profitable and valuable primarily because of strong network effects and the multisided market strategy surrounding the iPhone, which now accounts for about 60 percent of revenues? Or does a large part of Apple's market value come from its design skills, brand, and ability to charge premium prices for the iPhone and some other products and services? We can ask similar questions about other companies: How much of the success of Cisco, Oracle, SAP, or Salesforce came from platform strategy and network effects versus the excellence and brand value of their products and services? Amazon is even more complicated because of how it integrated and mixed platform and non-platform businesses. How much of its market value derives from scale and scope economies associated with the online store and its enormous physical warehousing system as compared to Amazon's "pure" platform businesses, Amazon Marketplace and Amazon Web Services (AWS)? In 2017, the online retail store accounted for about two-thirds of Amazon's revenues and Amazon Marketplace about 17 percent. AWS accounted for less than 10 percent of revenues but 60 percent of operating profits, and more in prior years.[25] Amazon did not always break out these numbers, which made it difficult to do historical analysis.

With these caveats, however, we can say that most platform businesses that survive to become public firms have been highly successful enterprises. This success was due at least in part to their platform strategies and business models, as well as to their strong product or service businesses.

OVERVIEW OF THE FOLLOWING CHAPTERS

We devote each of the following chapters to a specific theme and set of guidelines. Based on our experience and research, we believe the discussions will help managers and entrepreneurs understand how platform markets really function and how to build platform businesses viable for the long term.

Chapter 2 examines the fundamental drivers of platform markets and dynamics of a "winner-take-all" or "winner-take-most" outcome. In order to achieve a dominant market share, a company needs to master several dimensions of platform competition.[26] First and foremost, the company needs to encourage and take advantage of network effects. We use the historical example of the telephone and Yellow Pages to illustrate how both same-side and cross-side network effects work, even without the benefit of modern digital technologies. But we also show why network effects are not enough to dominate a market. For example, sometimes users participate on multiple platforms for the same purpose, a practice called "multi-homing." Dominant platforms usually make it difficult or unnecessary for users to multi-home. In addition, successful platform businesses reduce the impact of niche or differentiated competitors, which can further weaken market shares and network effects. And all companies need to build significant barriers to entry. We conclude this chapter with a discussion of how digital technology is impacting each of the four market drivers as well as platform competition more broadly.

Chapter 3 explains how strategies and business models differ for innovation platforms compared to transaction platforms. Both types follow the same steps to build their businesses, but they do so in different ways. Transaction and innovation platforms both need to identify key market participants and solve their distinctive chicken-or-egg problems (i.e., assess which side is more important in order to trigger interest and attract the other side). Both need to find business models that generate value and translate into revenues and profits. Both face similar governance challenges. However, the two platform types must engage different kinds of market participants, solve different launch and monetization problems, and preside over different types of ecosystems. We also discuss the trend toward hybrid strategies and the advantages they afford some of the leading platform companies. Innovation platforms can add transaction functions to help them distribute complementary products and services, as Apple, Google, Microsoft, and Salesforce have done with their app stores. And transaction platforms such as at Amazon, Facebook, Snapchat, Uber, and Airbnb can add innovation platform functions to help them add new features and services from third-party firms, with minimal in-house investment. Hybrid companies also differ in the degrees to which they connect or integrate the two types of platforms; some are highly integrated while others look more like modern-day "digital conglomerates."

Chapter 4 looks at the reality of starting a platform business and the mistakes that managers and entrepreneurs commonly make. Because of the importance of network effects, many people assume that first movers have the advantage in platform competition. Our data suggests the opposite. Being first can sometimes be an advantage in the conventional economy as well as the digital economy, but most first movers in platform markets have failed. More often, fast followers have come to dominate their markets. In all cases, though, timing and ongoing innovation are critical. Managers and entrepreneurs should hesitate to enter a market after it has already "tipped" toward one platform because network effects make it difficult to take away share from the platform leader. However, if the platform leader becomes complacent and stops innovating, or if other opportunities for differentiation and niche marketing appear, then it is possible to enter a platform business late and compete successfully.

Chapter 5 turns to the dilemma that conventional companies face. Has the digital revolution made old-economy firms the equivalent of dinosaurs, doomed to extinction? Or can traditional firms adapt to the new technology and new rules of digital competition? Clearly, the history of the personal computer and the Internet suggest that some traditional businesses that did not embrace a digital presence will be unable to adapt, such as bookstores, department stores, travel agencies, or brokerages. However, we have identified three strategies for "old dogs" who want to learn new tricks: Build, buy, or belong to an existing platform. Traditional companies can use these approaches to fend off new entrants and compete more effectively if platform challengers invade their space. To illustrate the opportunities and obstacles, we look at London's black cabs, Walmart's acquisition strategy, and General Electric's attempt to build a platform for the industrial Internet of things.

Chapter 6 explores platform governance and the legal, political, and social challenges that digital platforms often encounter. Many people believe platform companies and digital technologies are, in general, good for individuals as well as the world economy. They seem to represent technological progress and efficiency as well as facilitate the global flow of information, technology, and capital. Other people argue that platforms pose a threat to how markets and societies should function because they too often restrain competition, sometimes violate the law (e.g., with regard to taxation, labor, or sectoral regulation), and may invade our privacy and abuse the data we often unknowingly provide. Our view is in between these two extremes. We see platforms as "double-edged swords," with good and bad potential. We argue that platform companies must regulate themselves as well as build trust with users and ecosystem partners. Perhaps more importantly, we think it is possible for managers and entrepreneurs to anticipate and mitigate threats from antitrust, labor, and data privacy litigation.

Chapter 7 summarizes key points in the book and then looks to the future. How can we evaluate if an emerging technology might become an important platform over the next decade and beyond? Of course, no one has a crystal ball. Nonetheless, we can use the guidelines outlined in the previous chapters to identify platform potential and evaluate different future scenarios. We discuss several examples of ongoing platform battlegrounds, such as self-driving vehicles and how they are likely to affect ride-sharing platforms, and the "voice wars" competition around home digital assistants using artificial intelligence. Then we turn to examples of fundamental technologies that may evolve into new platform battlegrounds over the next decade or two, with their own technological, regulatory, and ethical challenges: the race to commercialize quantum computers and ongoing efforts to apply and build ecosystems around CRISPR technology for gene editing. We conclude that the age of unfettered, open platforms is largely over, and that platform businesses need to self-regulate or "curate" in order to remain socially, politically, and economically viable.

WINNER TAKE ALL OR MOST

MORE THAN NETWORK EFFECTS

NETWORK EFFECTS
Lessons from the Telephone and Yellow Pages

OTHER MARKET DRIVERS
Multi-homing, Differentiation/Niches, and Entry Barriers

DIGITAL TECHNOLOGIES
Impact on Platform Market Drivers

KEY TAKEAWAYS FOR MANAGERS AND ENTREPRENEURS

CHAPTER 2

The power of a platform is the potential for rapid, nonlinear growth, especially where a company wins all or most of a market. Indeed, over the last three decades, we have seen digital platforms attain market shares of approximately 70 percent or more in relatively short periods of time. Examples include Microsoft's Windows operating system and Office applications suite, Intel and ARM microprocessors for PCs and smartphones, Google's Internet search technology and Android mobile operating system, and Uber's American ride-sharing business. We also see very strong global positions at companies like Facebook in social networking, eBay in online auctions, Twitter in short social media postings (microblogs), and Airbnb in room sharing. In China, Alibaba accounts for the bulk of online shopping, and Tencent's WeChat has a billion users and dominates messaging as well as social networking. Sina Weibo is China's largest platform for microblogging, while Didi Chuxing has eliminated or absorbed most competitors in ride sharing.

These and many other platform companies, small and large, have benefited enormously from network effects. Yet network effects by themselves do not explain why a particular company ends up with all or most of the market or why other industries remain fragmented.[1] In this chapter, we focus on three critical issues impacting the dynamics of platform businesses: (1) the importance of different types of network effects; (2) the impact on company performance of other factors—multi-homing (use of another platform for the same purpose at the same time) as well as niche competition and supply-side barriers to entry; and (3) how digital technologies can influence network effects and other market drivers. We especially build on work

originally done on platform market dynamics by Thomas Eisenmann, Geoffrey Parker, and Marshall Van Alstyne.[2]

NETWORK EFFECTS: LESSONS FROM
THE TELEPHONE AND YELLOW PAGES

Most discussions of platform markets begin with network effects.
As a platform acquires more users or complementary innovations
like software apps or digital content stores, positive feedback loops
(i.e., network effects) emerge and can get stronger with the rising
number of users or complements. The network effects make the
platform increasingly valuable by attracting increasing numbers of
users and complementors. Yet many people do not understand how
network effects actually work. For example, even platforms with
relatively strong network effects may not dominate their markets or
generate much in the way of profits. Some historical examples help
illustrate how network effects impact market dynamics and company performance.

We have known for more than a century that some new products
and services, such as railroads and the telegraph and telephone, but
also electricity, radio, and television, benefited from strong positive
feedback loops with increasing returns to scale and usage. As the physical networks expanded, they attracted more users and more market
participants, and opened up various monetization opportunities. For
instance, American railroads in the mid-1800s started as closed systems, limited to one company and region, with incompatible track
gauges. However, after companies agreed to standardize their track
sizes (under U.S. government pressure), all the complying railroads
benefited from a direct network effect.[3] Thereafter, trains from one
company's network, such as in the Boston area, were physically able
to connect to networks owned by companies in other areas, such as
New York and Baltimore and, eventually, Chicago, San Francisco, and
Seattle. A railroad that could transport people and goods from Bos-

ton to San Francisco was far more valuable than just a local system. As railroads became more useful transportation systems, they also took advantage of government land grants to build complementary businesses as well as to attract third-party investments, such as for local transportation, real estate development, banking, construction, and other services. Similarly, electricity, radio, and television were not very useful technologies without complementary innovations such as electrical appliances and programming content. As more homes adopted electricity, demand rose for more electrical appliances. As more programming content appeared for radios and then televisions, more people wanted radios and televisions.

Today, with personal computers, the Internet, and smartphones, we live in a world of platform technologies and networks connected to other platforms and networks, both physical and virtual. Yet network effects that stimulate these markets do not occur by chance. Companies and governments have to make the right strategic and policy decisions in order to drive strong network effects and make a difference in the industry. Imagine what would have happened if railroads had not standardized their track gauges. Their physical platforms would have been restricted to single companies and would have been much less useful for transportation and economic development. Or think about a world where the inventors of electric power systems had tried to control production of all the devices that would use electric power. The number of innovative products using electricity would probably have been very small. In general, network effects emerge and benefit from specific strategic decisions, or they can languish and disappear if managers and policy makers make the "wrong" decisions.

THE TELEPHONE NETWORK

A familiar historical example that demonstrates the power of network effects among multiple market participants is the telephone network. In 1876, Alexander Graham Bell patented a simple telephone device that used analog technology to replicate sounds converted to electrical impulses and relay them over copper wires. Within a few years, Bell and his financial partners organized a holding company headquartered in Boston, Massachusetts, called American Bell Telephone (renamed American Telephone & Telegraph—AT&T—in 1899). The company eventually worked with some 4,000 local and regional firms formed by independent investors to commercialize Bell's telephone.[4]

Even today, the telephone system remains an essential communications platform, enabling billions of people to talk with each other as well as to communicate through other devices, such as fax machines. In the early years especially, the telephone benefited from powerful direct network effects. The more people who had telephones, the more other people wanted telephones. The network effects grew in strength as new telephone users inspired their friends, family, and business associates to acquire telephones. In our terminology, the initial telephone service was a *one-sided platform* because it targeted only individual telephone users, without making distinctions among them. Very quickly, though, the telephone business became a multisided market by identifying different segments—users who mostly made local calls versus those who needed long-distance services, and residential versus business users. Expanding usage among the different market segments became a major source of growth and profits.

AT&T in the early 1900s used the concept of network effects to justify to government regulators the decision to price the telephone service below marginal cost, which helped maintain its monopoly position. The details are more complicated than we present here, but company economists argued that universal coverage would benefit everyone on the network, and this was theoretically true.[5] Putting telephones in nearly every home and office would lead to a nonlinear expansion of possible network connections and, in turn, an extraordinary rise in the value proposition of the telephone as a communications platform. Note in Figure 2-1 that each additional user does not increase the potential value of the network by 1. Rather—and assuming that long-distance services would eventually connect all users with telephones to each other—each additional user multiplied the potential value of the network by *the number of other existing users (nodes) already connected.*

Today, we refer to the network dynamic described here as Metcalfe's law, after Robert Metcalfe, the primary inventor of the Ethernet local networking technology during the early 1970s. Metcalfe argued that the value of a communications network was the same as the number of links between its nodes. He described this relationship with a simple equation: For a network of n nodes, the value of the network is n(n – 1)/2. To illustrate, the number of potential connections for a network with two people (n = 2) is simply 1 or 2(2 – 1)/2. Five people in the network would have 10 connections. A network with 100 people would have 4,950 distinct potential connections. A network with a million users generates nearly 500 billion potential connections. What stands out is that the growth potential of a network business is not linear. (Some would say it is geometric or even exponential.) Explosive growth due to network effects enables platform businesses to expand (or decline) so quickly in scale, utility, and economic value.

The telephone business also had to solve the chicken-or-egg problem: how to get people to use the new technology at the beginning.

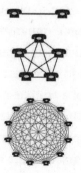

FIGURE 2-1: **CONNECTIONS OR NODES IN THE TELEPHONE NETWORK**
Created by Derrick Coetzee (2006), public domain.

As long as only a few people had telephones, the positive feedback loops were weak. But even without access to Metcalfe's law, the phone companies believed that network effects would grow in strength over time as each new user was able to connect to other users on the network. Perhaps most importantly, a subset of investors formed American Telephone & Telegraph (AT&T) in 1885 as a subsidiary of the Bell Telephone Company to enhance and monetize the network effects. The subsidiary provided lucrative "long-distance" services connecting the thousands of local telephone networks (including a few not owned by the Bell companies) to each other, especially between pairs of cities, then distant cities and rural areas, and eventually foreign countries.

In the United States, the Bell operating companies launched aggressive marketing campaigns to individuals and businesses, trying to persuade every household and organization to sign up for the new telephone service. Because telephones remained expensive, it still took twenty-five years for 10 percent of U.S. consumers and businesses to adopt them. It was another thirty-nine years before diffusion reached 40 percent of the U.S. market—much slower than the spread of television, the Internet, or smartphones.[6] But eventually nearly every person and organization in the United States (and ultimately around the world) ended up with telephones, first landline phones and then, in recent years, cell phones.

Bolstered by very strong direct network effects, AT&T and its subsidiaries achieved close to a 100 percent market share in the United States. They maintained this dominance for more than a century. One reason was that the parent company controlled long-distance services, which made the local networks much more useful and valuable. Other market drivers and agreements with government regulators also aligned in favor of a winner-take-all outcome. The U.S. government permitted only one telephone company to exist in any one local area, and the monopoly service remained tightly regulated. For almost one hundred years, barriers to entry were ex-

traordinarily high, and there were no differentiated or niche competitors and no true substitute technologies. Technological innovation
and regulatory change eventually allowed new competitors, such as
MCI (Microwave Communications Inc., founded in 1963), to use
microwaves (not phone lines) to offer telephone and data services
to large businesses. But there were still no mass-market alternative
telephone platforms until wireless companies like Sprint and then
cable TV companies and Internet-based services such as Skype
gradually got into the voice communications business, most notably during the 1990s and 2000s.

FROM THE WHITE PAGES TO THE YELLOW PAGES

American Bell Telephone introduced the White Pages in 1878
along with the first telephones in order to help people find each
other.[7] This was simply a catalogue, with names in alphabetical
order and divided by towns or local regions, of every individual
and organization with a publicly listed telephone number. The Bell
operating companies gave away the White Pages to customers for
free—or really "free but not free," because they bundled the directory cost with the telephone service.[8] The story goes that one of
the printers (R.H. Donnelley, now Dex One Corporation) realized
that some users might want a separate listing of businesses and that
companies might want to use the directory to advertise. In 1883 the
printer temporarily ran out of white paper and switched to yellow
paper for the new business listings. R.H. Donnelley formally took
over printing the business telephone directory in 1886 and continued to use yellow paper to distinguish it from the White Pages.[9]
For the most part, the Yellow Pages as a business remained under
the control of AT&T and its regional operating subsidiaries. The
telephone company also used profits from the Yellow Pages to subsidize universal coverage, which made AT&T's monopoly position
more palatable to regulators. (Update: The U.S. government forced

AT&T to divest the operating companies in 1982, after which control of the Yellow Pages business shifted to the now-independent Bell operating companies.[10] A reconstituted AT&T regained control later on and then sold a majority stake to Cerberus Capital Management in 2012.)[11]

Clearly, the emergence of the Yellow Pages was not a random event; it involved several strategic decisions, including segmenting out business from residential telephone users, and subsidizing what we would now call the "right" side of a platform market. If the regional Bell telephone companies had simply followed their own precedent with the White Pages, they would have given away the business directories for free to all telephone users and bundled the production cost with the telephone service. However, AT&T, R.H. Donnelley, and the regional operating companies all treated the Yellow Pages as a separate business opportunity. In our terminology today, we would say that they identified commercial telephone users as a distinct set of customers and believed that this "one side" of the market would probably be willing to pay in order to connect to the "other side."

To make this idea commercially viable, the Yellow Pages had to solve two challenges, which we now know are common to all platform businesses. (See Chapter 3.) One problem was how to encourage strong network effects between different market sides—in this case, residential and business telephone users. For example, the more businesses listed in the Yellow Pages, the more users would look to the Yellow Pages to find products and services, while the more usage there was of the Yellow Pages, the more businesses would want to be listed. A second problem was the business model: Managers had to determine which side of the market to charge and how much. It was possible that telephone customers would pay extra for a business directory, but probably they would not pay very much. Although companies were accustomed to paying for advertising, usually they wanted to know how many people would view their ads. For a new offering like the Yellow Pages, viewership was a complete unknown.

How did the Yellow Pages solve these two challenges? Management decided to give away the Yellow Pages to residential customers for free and to charge companies that wanted to be listed. This decision made the Yellow Pages the primary way telephone users would search for products and services.[12] No one could guarantee how many people would actually read a particular company's advertisement. Nonetheless, by delivering the directory to residential phone users for free, the Yellow Pages could guarantee to every advertiser that 100 percent of the telephone customers in its locale would have a copy of the ad in their homes, *whether they wanted it or not*. To this day, the former Bell operating companies in the United States maintain this guarantee by continuing to deliver the Yellow Pages once per year to every customer with a landline telephone.

In our terminology, the Yellow Pages became a *two-sided transaction platform*. The phone companies subsidized residential customers in their search for business listings and made sure there was a wide audience for the business ads. Financially, this business model led the Yellow Pages to a spectacular run for nearly 130 years! Estimates are that the Yellow Pages franchises in the United States were "wildly profitable," with profit margins up to 50 percent. It remained a growing business in the United States as late as 2007, worth at least $14 billion a year in sales.[13]

Of course, no business lasts forever, not even a winner-take-all platform. Today the printed Yellow Pages still exists but is mainly consulted by older people. This demographic is declining, along with the number of homes with landline telephones. Not surprisingly, R.H. Donnelley and several other companies that relied on the Yellow Pages filed for bankruptcy and reorganized or, like AT&T, sold their interest in the business.[14] The Yellow Pages has survived as an online digital service and as a paper directory. Although this is not likely to continue for too many more years, nearly

70 percent of U.S. households continue to receive the Yellow Pages. Most local businesses also continue to pay hundreds and even tens of thousands of dollars per year (New York City rates were the highest) to advertise in the Yellow Pages.[15]

THE YELLOW PAGES COMPARED TO DIGITAL PLATFORMS

If the Yellow Pages story sounds familiar to a modern reader, well, it should. We have seen similar business models many times and in different forms: A company gives away part of a product or service for free or at low cost to stimulate adoption, and then charges for another essential part of the product or charges another market side. People and organizations paid for the telephone service and received the directories for free, and companies paid for advertisements in the Yellow Pages. As for more modern examples, we know that Microsoft licensed DOS and Windows at low prices to PC makers and attracted applications producers with free software development kits. Adobe made its Acrobat Reader free for individual users and then built up a multibillion-dollar business around enterprise server software and editing tools. Google, Facebook, and Twitter built up their user numbers through free access and then sold advertising. Alibaba built its online marketplaces by making listings free but charged for preferential placements as well as transaction fees on sales in some of its marketplaces (such as Tmall).

Over the past two decades, Google Search and other search engines have gradually replaced the printed Yellow Pages, but we can still compare the business models. Both the Yellow Pages and Google Search provided free-of-charge "windows" into information networks (one on paper and the other digital) and made it possible for two market sides to find each other. Both sold advertising to the one side that most wanted to reach the other side. The Yellow Pages was really a complement to the once tightly regulated telephone system in the United States. Google Search was really a complement to the global Internet. It took the dismantling of regulation to undermine AT&T's telephone monopoly as well as digital competition to undermine the 100 percent market share of the Yellow Pages business in the United States. AT&T and the operating companies controlled this business, sanctioned by government regulators. The comparison is not exact, but Google Search attained a 90 percent market share in most parts of the world without government support. In fact, in some countries, such as China and Russia, the governments limited Google's operations. In these markets, Google Search had dramatically lower shares compared to local firms, which illustrates the power of government regulation.

OTHER MARKET DRIVERS: MULTI-HOMING, DIFFERENTIATION/NICHES, AND ENTRY BARRIERS

Strong network effects are a powerful driver toward a winner-take-all or winner-take-most market outcome. But we have pointed out that network effects alone are not enough because other factors, in addition to government regulation, also contribute to the market shares gained by particular firms. With instant messaging, for example, there are very strong same-side network effects—just like the telephone. Yet most messaging platforms, ranging from ICQ and Yahoo on personal computers to WhatsApp and BlackBerry Messenger on smartphones, never made money. One exception seems to be WeChat in China, which has expanded from a messaging (transaction) platform into an innovation platform such as for video games and payment services, with several ways to make money, albeit with protection against global competition from the government. (We will say more about WeChat later.) But why, in general, was it so hard to tip and monetize the market for instant messaging? Because a market is unlikely to coalesce around a particular platform if users can easily use *multiple platforms* at the same time for the same purpose; if competitors have *differentiated or niche platforms* that divert users with unique features; or if new firms can *easily enter* the same market and compete with better services or lower prices. All these conditions generally apply in the instant messaging market, as well as many other industries, conventional and digital. So let's examine in more detail three other market drivers that can reduce or enhance the power of network effects.

MULTI-HOMING

No company in a conventional or platform business likes to see its customers use products and services from competitors. In Michael Porter's framework, the more competitors there are, the more intensive the rivalries.[16] Intense rivalries often lead to price competition that can reduce profits for everyone. Platform owners want their customers to stick to one platform, whether it is for computing, cell phone devices and services, online shopping, room renting, or ride sharing.

In contrast to conventional businesses, many platforms (e.g., the Yellow Pages, Google Search, Bing Search, the Android operating system, Facebook, or WeChat) did not charge users directly. For these types of platform businesses, there was no immediate reduction in sales if users multi-homed because the platforms did not directly sell a product or service. Instead, multi-homing weakened network effects, which these platforms depended on to attract other market sides, such as advertisers or producers of complementary innovations.[17] So we can see that *multi-homing by users can inhibit a platform even with strong same-side (direct) network effects from fully monetizing cross-side (indirect) network effects.*

Think about Twitter, a classic example of strong direct network effects. Popular tweeters attracted followers and encouraged more tweeters and more followers. Similar to Google, Twitter monetized its free services by selling advertisements. However, until very recently, Twitter made little or no profit because of high operating costs, the expense of new customer acquisition, and relatively low advertising revenue. Part of Twitter's problem was that many tweeters multi-homed. Twitter users spent time (usually more time) on Facebook, Instagram, Snapchat, or WhatsApp to communicate about personal or detailed matters, such as vacation plans and tastes in music or movies. Consequently, the time and attention as well as the personal details of Twitter users, along with their purchasing power for third-party advertisements, were divided among multiple platforms—despite Twitter's strong direct network effects.

The key point is that multi-homing impacts network effects and, indirectly, impacts a platform's potential revenues and profits. Therefore, how to limit multi-homing is an important goal for all platform companies. The solutions are not always obvious. Some innovation platforms build proprietary standards (e.g., Microsoft Windows or Apple iOS), while others tie complementary services to the platform (e.g., Google Android and the Google Play Store for smartphone apps). Some transaction platforms create loyalty programs (e.g., Expedia), following the lead of airlines and credit cards. But some platform companies also make mistakes or find themselves making choices they would have preferred to avoid. In particular, whereas low prices on the "right" side of the market can attract users, low prices on the "wrong" side can encourage multi-homing and weaken cross-side network effects.

Video games are a good example illustrating the risks of competing with an aggressive subsidy to one side of the market without overcoming potentially negative consequences from multi-homing.[18] In the early and mid-2000s, Microsoft and Nintendo decided to sell their new game consoles (Xbox and Wii, respectively) at near cost, that is, for a few hundred dollars. Sony responded by keeping prices relatively low on its PlayStation, though generally still higher than the other consoles. All three companies decided to subsidize the user base and make most or all of their profits by charging game developers high license fees and royalties to write games for their platforms. The console makers hoped that a large and growing base of users, attracted by low console prices, would exert a strong pull on the complementor side of the market, the game software producers, and eventually produce a steady stream of revenues and profits. Microsoft, Nintendo, and Sony developed some games themselves and invested in studios to seed the market, but they also saw the need to foster a vibrant independent ecosystem of game developers. In the video game market, each console was technologically incompatible, so Sony, Microsoft, and Nintendo were able to line up some exclusive content for their platforms. Only the biggest developers had the resources to write software for more than one platform.

But the strategy adopted by the platform leaders resulted in an unintended consequence: *Low console prices encouraged multihoming.* Serious video gamers (mostly teenagers and young male adults) generally bought more than one console, especially those that had compelling games. These "hit" software products also varied with each new generation of the hardware. As a result, we have not seen one company take all or most of the video game market and sustain that lead over multiple product generations, as Microsoft has done with Windows for personal computers or like Google has done with Android for smartphones. Market shares have varied from console generation to generation, depending on which company had the most compelling new video games or differentiated hardware features.

DIFFERENTIATION AND NICHE COMPETITION

All companies worry about competitors that make their products and services stand out through better quality or serving the special needs of particular types of customers. Even platforms that do not directly sell a product or service need to worry about differentiated and niche competitors. Similar to the challenges created by multihoming, a fragmented market with niche players reduces network effects and the likelihood of a winner-take-all outcome. The more homogeneous the market, the higher the likelihood that strong network effects will attract the vast majority of users, which could drive the market to tip toward one platform. Think about smartphones: On the surface, one might have expected the market to tip to the player with the early lead in market share, much like the PC market tipped to computers running DOS in the 1980s and then Windows in the 1990s. Apple was the early leader in the modern, touch screen smartphone market after introducing the iPhone in June 2007. However, devices running Google's Android eventually dominated the market.

One particularly important decision Google made to help tip the market dates back to November 2007. This is when Google mobilized handset makers that wanted to compete with Apple by forming the Open Handset Alliance. Network operators and software developers also joined the coalition and agreed to promote "open standards" (i.e., technologies that multiple companies could freely license and use). Most importantly, members (i.e., Android licensees) could freely use the software as long as they agreed not to create incompatible or "forked" versions.[19] Google wanted to maintain control over the operating system and make sure that handset makers and software developers continued to use Google services, such as its search, browser, and mapping-location technology, which Google used to sell advertisements. Some forked versions of Android still appeared. However, in general, Google's strategy worked because Apple would not license its technology to anyone for any price. Android provided a compelling alternative (free, good enough, and open to improvement). Apple failed to keep a majority of the smartphone market, which it briefly achieved after introducing the iPhone. Nonetheless, Apple's highly differentiated product and growing ecosystem of app developers allowed it to keep high-end customers. Several analysts even estimated that Apple earned over 90 percent of handset industry profits with less than 18 percent market share during 2015–2017.[20] Apple's ability to differentiate the iPhone as a product and a platform enabled it to charge premium prices (although this may change in the future) and prevented Google from taking more than 80 percent of the total smartphone market.

Another illuminating example is the market for freelance labor, dominated in 2018 by Upwork, a classic transaction platform created by the merger of Elance and oDesk. Similar to many transaction platforms, Upwork experienced powerful cross-side network effects: The more freelancers who joined the platform, the more value companies realized from using Upwork; and the more corporations looking for freelance labor, the more value seen by freelancers around the world that seek employment on Upwork. Indeed, by early 2018, Upwork announced that $4 billion of cumulative work had been completed through the platform and its annual run rate of gross services volume had reached $1.5 billion.[21] Upwork reported that 28 percent of Fortune 500 companies posted jobs on the platform in 2017, and the company's platform had 5 million corporate clients and 12 million freelancers.

However, CEO Stephane Kasriel summarized the challenge for Upwork, estimating that there were at least "500 competitors in our space, most of them focusing on small niches."[22] Despite the obvious power of network effects and Upwork's strong brand and growing platform, niche companies thrived by focusing on specific industries, specific job types, and specific geographies (local as well as global). Upwork's horizontally designed platform was competing against vertically specialized players who had more local expertise and could siphon off both corporate clients and specialized freelancers. Despite two decades of operations and strong growth, continued fragmentation prevented Upwork from tipping the market or even making money. When the company filed its S-1 in late 2018, it was still not making an annual profit.[23] (Nonetheless, the company went public on October 3, 2018, with a 40 percent surge in the stock price on the first day.)

BARRIERS TO ENTRY

All companies share a desire to limit new competitors from entering their markets. In general, if switching costs are low and entry is easy, then markets are unlikely to be highly profitable. Low entry barriers encourage more competition, which generally leads to lower prices and lower profits for everyone. In the platform world, most companies focus strategically on the demand side of the market: how to get more users (customers). But when traditional barriers to entry are low, even in markets where companies feel protected because of their strong network effects, new entrants can still enter the business on the supply side and fragment the user base, preventing a market from tipping toward one big winner.

The unique dilemma for many platform businesses is that the initial cost of market entry can be very low because of advances in digital technology, which we will discuss in more detail below. In the world of lean start-ups, the amount of capital required to develop, produce, and distribute a new product or service, or even a new platform, is a fraction of what it cost ten or twenty years ago. In the gig economy, it has been especially easy to start new transaction platforms like handyman services (e.g., Handy or TaskRabbit). In Chapter 4, we discuss how twenty-nine companies entered on-demand services, even though few survived. Similarly, dozens of companies have entered the market for online communities, web portals, and B2B marketplaces, mostly because the entry costs were relatively low.

In markets where barriers to entry are high, we see a different pattern: much more industry concentration, with a higher probability of the market tipping toward one or a small number of firms.

In capital-intensive businesses, like developing new cloud services and related innovation platforms, there are a relatively small number of dominant firms (e.g., mainly Amazon, Microsoft, and Google, followed by IBM and Alibaba). Similarly, costs can be very high for subsidy-intensive businesses like automobile ride sharing (e.g., Uber). In addition, when companies such as Qualcomm have been able to protect their market positions with patents, unique technical know-how, government regulations, and other barriers to entry, markets have had a higher likelihood of tipping toward one platform.

There are also unique barriers to entry in platform markets that we rarely see in the conventional world. First, *network effects create barriers* in the form of an existing stock of complements around a particular platform. When a platform has millions of applications that run on—and only on—Android, iOS, Windows, Amazon Web Services, Facebook, or WeChat, they increase the barriers to switching to a new or competing platform. Second, and closely related, is that new entrants are often challenged by *the difficulty of replicating a platform ecosystem*. Successful platform companies have established virtual armies of complementors, such as the thousands of software developers who have already joined the Android, iPhone, Facebook, or WeChat developer networks, or the millions of people with rooms to rent or cars to drive who have already registered with Airbnb, Uber, Lyft, and Didi Chuxing. As the number of complementors grows, it becomes increasingly difficult for a new firm to enter late and build a competing ecosystem for the supply side of the platform. Third, *networks themselves create complex switching costs*. When the value of the platform depends on the number of complements and users who are directly connected, then it can be extremely difficult or expensive to switch. For example, if people want to stop using LinkedIn and move to a new professional network, they must convince their professional contacts to move with them, otherwise the new platform will have relatively little value.

DIGITAL TECHNOLOGIES: IMPACT ON PLATFORM MARKET DRIVERS

To summarize: At any given point in time, the likelihood of a winner-take-all-or-most outcome in a platform business will depend on the strength of network effects, the difficulty of multi-homing, lack of opportunities for competitor differentiation and niche competition, and the strength of entry barriers. At the same time, though, we live in a world where digital technologies are rapidly changing market dynamics. Moore's law drove the most fundamental market trans-formations, with a doubling of computer processing power every eighteen to twenty-four months from the 1960s until recent years. Once the personal computer emerged in the late 1970s and 1980s, a new generation of computing platforms appeared for basic software and applications. With essentially zero marginal costs for digital goods, the economics of platform businesses would change forever. And once the World Wide Web became a mass-market phenome-non after the mid-1990s, managers and entrepreneurs had their first opportunity to create truly ubiquitous global platforms. With new platforms came new opportunities to innovate and exercise differ-ent forms of economic, social, and political power, much of which we now associate with digital technologies.

During the last decade, the combination of mobile and cloud technologies, artificial intelligence and machine learning, as well as big data, has accelerated the diffusion and refinement of digital plat-forms. Advances in technology also have brought several formerly separate markets together. This "digital convergence" has been go-ing on since the mid-1990s, at least.[24] It helps explain why a single company—Apple—passed a trillion dollars in market value in Au-gust 2018, before falling back. The smartphone, which accounted for 60 percent to 70 percent or more of Apple's sales over the past decade, was at the same time a phone, a computer, a digital media player, a digital camera, a digital recorder, a personal digital assis-tant, a video game machine, and a handheld television, among other things. Apple's value reflected the integration of products and services in *all* these markets, including rapidly increasing revenues and profits from its digital content store (iTunes) and transaction platform (the App Store). Mastery of digital technology and a hybrid platform strategy also helps explain why Apple, Amazon, Google, Microsoft, Facebook, Alibaba, and Tencent were among the most valuable companies in the world.

In general, digital technologies can either help or hurt incumbent platform leaders, and they can either help or hurt new platform entrants. As a result, the impact on platform businesses is complex and requires a separate look at how technological innovation can affect the four fundamental drivers of platform market dynamics.

IMPACT ON NETWORK EFFECTS

What comes to mind first is that digital technologies should strengthen network effects. In fact, if one compares the potential for network effects in today's world with pre-digital times, the differences are stark. Think about how long it took to build out a railroad in the United States or to get broad adoption of the telephone and Yellow Pages or even credit cards. Numerous studies have shown that adoption rates have accelerated with new technologies, and digital platforms are no exception. Digital technology also enables platforms to connect faster and to link more people and organizations with each other than ever before.

For example, it was possible to use Facebook to connect with more than 2 million websites between 2008 and 2010, including 90 percent of the top 1,000 sites then on the Internet. At one point, that number was growing by about 10,000 websites a day. More importantly, about one-third of Facebook's users interacted with the social network through third-party sites every month.[25] As early as 2012, some 9 million applications and websites already operated within or were accessible through Facebook.[26] Since then, a growing portion of Internet activity has involved Facebook even without happening directly on the Facebook platform.

New software programs for analyzing massive amounts of data on user behavior can further enhance the power of network effects.[27] However, the general principle is that, as a digital platform collects more data and then applies machine learning and other artificial intelligence algorithms, the platform can become "smarter." For example, it can create more targeted advertisements or better search results and recommendations for additional purchases. Furthermore, as users contribute their own data in the form of content or ratings (as they do with Google, Amazon, eBay, Facebook, Twitter, Instagram, Snapchat, WeChat, Expedia, TripAdvisor, Uber, Airbnb, and many other platforms), data and analytics can also help improve the product or service. The big and the wealthy can get bigger and wealthier because they have more data and more money to invest in technology and marketing. This dynamic, driven by network effects, is surely part of why platform businesses have become so attractive to managers, entrepreneurs, and investors.

Clever firms also can use digital technologies to strengthen network effects in completely new arenas. Take Waze, the Israeli road navigation app created in 2008 that Google purchased in 2013.[28] Waze users not only *consumed* data but they also *generated* data, constantly and in real time. This app originated as a one-sided platform analyzing driver information. Later, it started to sell advertisements. Then it began to provide traffic information to TV and radio broadcasters as well as city traffic authorities for free, thereby increasing brand recognition and attracting more users and advertisers. Waze even added a social media element so that registered users in close proximity could contact each other and share information as they were driving. In addition, Google integrated information from Waze into Google Maps, to make its traffic information more accurate. As users drove with the Waze app open, they automatically generated data about their location and speed, while users added their own reports on accidents and other slow-downs. Waze computers captured and analyzed these data (initially with the help of volunteer map editors) and made suggestions for alternative routes in case of heavy traffic or accidents. The service continually improved, depending on how much users consumed and contributed to the service. (It is also true that Waze and similar navigation apps from Apple, Google, and other companies often directed drivers to the same alternative routes and sometimes created new traffic jams.)[29]

IMPACT ON MULTI-HOMING

While digital technologies have been creating more opportunities across the board for stronger network effects, those same technologies can *facilitate as well as reduce multi-homing.* How can this be? It depends on how well companies plan and execute their digital strategies. Especially with modern transaction platforms, the tangible costs to multi-homing seem trivial. In the old days, it was expensive and difficult for most users to own both a Windows PC and a Macintosh. Most users chose one platform and were restricted to applications available on that platform. Nowadays, applications are usually available on both types of personal computers and many more applications are available as web applications, accessible from different types of devices and platforms. For example, it costs nothing to do a general search on Google, compare airfares on Kayak, or seek travel advice on TripAdvisor or Expedia. There is no need to buy a particular computer or smartphone. All users need today is a device with access to the Internet.

In a purely digital world, we expect that consumers will have low cost or free alternatives widely available for nearly every activity and that they will be multi-homing as a matter of course. Google executives have made this argument, citing the ease of multi-homing to defray criticism of their dominant position in Internet search, since competitors are merely "one click away."[30] As we discussed earlier with the Facebook example, Mark Zuckerberg may have created the world's largest social network. However, it is easy for Facebook users to spend time on Twitter, LinkedIn, Snapchat, Pinterest, and other platforms, even if they may not take the trouble to adopt another social network for most of their activities. To control some of the revenues associated with multi-homing was at least one reason why Zuckerberg acquired Instagram in 2012 for $1 billion (considered a large sum at the time) and later used it to compete with Snapchat.[31] Zuckerberg's much more costly purchase of WhatsApp in 2014 for what amounted to $19 billion plus another $3 billion in Facebook stock was another defensive move against multi-homing for messaging as well as an offensive move to acquire more users and a potentially new revenue source.[32]

At the same time, clever use of data and sophisticated AI tools can discourage multi-homing because of better services. Waze and other digital platforms can analyze customer behavior and then refine platform functions down to the lowest technical levels, ranging from the design of user menus to the display of content and recommendations. Unlike the telephone or the Yellow Pages, sophisticated data analysis tools combined with the emergence of big data can help a digital platform provide more effective automated responses to user requests, more targeted searches and ads, better suggestions, or even more attractive prices—every time a customer uses the system to communicate or to look for something to buy. The result is that some digital platforms use their technological expertise and scale to offer such compelling services and prices that consumers often do not bother to multi-home. Almost 50 percent of American online shoppers simply start and end on Amazon; there is a similar pattern in China on Taobao. Or users do not bother to look at multiple search engines; they simply start and end on Google or, in China, on Baidu.

Digital technologies also discourage multi-homing as well as switching in the B2B world. Once a business integrates application stacks and platforms like SAP, Salesforce, Amazon Web Services, or Microsoft Azure into the fabric of their organizations, the cost of adopting a competing platform often goes up, even with new portability standards for cloud data and applications. Similar to the dynamics of enterprises adopting IBM mainframes in the 1960s or Windows personal computers in the 1990s, once an organization has committed to a particular technology, it generally spends significant resources to train its employees on that platform and builds specialized applications and interfaces or adds customized features.

IMPACT ON DIFFERENTIATION AND NICHE COMPETITION

There are many books and articles already written on how firms can use digital technology to make their products and services stand out or better serve niche customers. The challenge is that the digital revolution has made it easier to create new niches as well as easier for competitors to copy them. There are many variations in how platform companies have used their technological expertise to differentiate themselves or pursue markets. A few cases illustrate what is possible.

One well-known example is Snapchat, the widely used messaging app for millennials. Snapchat's cofounder, Evan Spiegel, had a simple idea: Young smartphone users hated the idea that their messages lasted forever. Whether it was a parent checking your phone, or your girlfriend or boyfriend seeing old messages, millennials wanted some privacy. Moreover, millennials liked their chat messages to tell a story. With digital technology, solving this problem was not technically complicated. Spiegel was able to quickly create a new messaging app in a crowded space with features that allowed messages to disappear after a specified time. As Spiegel wrote in his first company blog in 2012, "Snapchat isn't about capturing the traditional Kodak moment."[33] He wanted to let millennials avoid the stresses caused by the longevity of personal information on Face-book and other social media. The result was a high degree of differ-entiation from Facebook, Twitter, and other messaging platforms, and a viral explosion of users. By 2018, there were roughly 190 mil-lion daily active Snapchat users.

As for facilitating niche competition, we only need to look at the wide range of specialized online shopping sites to see how digital technology prevented the giant online stores and marketplaces at Amazon (globally), Alibaba (in China), and Rakuten (in Japan) from getting close to 100 percent of the Internet shopping business even in their home countries. In the United States, Walmart, Target, and every other major retailer created their own online sites and made acquisitions to compete with Amazon. (See Chapter 5.) In addition, Amazon had to contend with a growing number of niche market-places and digital stores.[34] For example, Star 360 (starthreesixty .com) sold shoes for men and women, representing nearly every ma-jor brand. Koovs (koovs.com), Lifestyle (lifestylestores.com), and PrettyLittleThing (prettylittlething.com) were online fashion por-tals representing major brands and offering large discounts as well as dozens of new fashion items every week. Bluemercury (bluemercury .com) specialized in beauty products. Horchow (horchow.com), owned by the Neiman Marcus Group, sold furniture. Etsy (etsy.com) dominated the marketplace for handmade items ranging from cloth-ing to arts and crafts. Winemonger (winemonger.com) sold wine, which users could search for by country and type. The list goes on and on for specialized retail platforms and digital stores.

The flip side of digital technology accelerating opportunities for differentiation and niche competition was that it could be equally easy for incumbents to copy. Mark Zuckerberg almost immedi-ately recognized Snapchat as a potential threat to Facebook. Given Facebook's size and scale, he logically tried to buy Snap for $3 bil-lion in cash before the company went public. When Spiegel turned him down, Zuckerberg ordered Instagram to copy Snapchat's most compelling features and turn Instagram into a Snapchat killer.[35] Especially after introducing Instagram Stories, Instagram zoomed past Snapchat, with over 700 million users. Although Snapchat was hardly dead (its market value had fallen dramatically but was still close to $6 billion in late 2018), Facebook's attack had taken a serious toll. By mid-2018, Snapchat's user base had begun shrinking for the first time in its history.[36]

Both new entrants and established firms can also utilize their expertise in digital technology to rapidly copy niche strategies and integrate acquisitions. When Amazon has observed (such as by analyzing transaction data on Amazon Marketplace) a new category that was growing fast, it frequently replicated its competitors' online platforms or just bought them outright.[37] Amazon followed this strategy when it bought the online shoe retailer Zappos in 2009 for $1.2 billion and the video game streaming company Twitch in 2014 for $970 million, as well as the Middle East's biggest online retailing site, Souq, in 2017 for $650 million. Amazon also combined Whole Foods, which it acquired in 2017 for $13.7 billion, with AmazonFresh and its online grocery business. Similarly, when eBay pioneered online auctions, many firms, including Yahoo and Amazon, entered the market with new features or targeted vertical markets. In a non-digital world, replicating those features and verticals might have been too expensive or taken too much time to be competitive. But eBay was able to quickly copy the best new features (e.g., insurance) and introduce its own vertical sites (e.g., eBay Motors).

IMPACT ON BARRIERS TO ENTRY

Digital technologies, especially when they strengthen or accelerate network effects, have both *lowered as well as raised entry barriers* into many industries. How can this be? With cloud computing and nearly ubiquitous Internet access, establishing new digital platforms has become easier than ever. Twenty years ago, firms had to build their own data centers and invest heavily in computing power to begin a digital business. With the advent of the cloud, new businesses can get started practically overnight. The cost of building a new software company or transaction platform focused on the mass market or particular segments, and launching it on Amazon Web Services, Microsoft Azure, or other cloud services platforms, has dropped dramatically. As more businesses are built in the cloud, it has become easier to connect more consumers to consumers, more businesses to other businesses, and more businesses to consumers. The rising number of new transaction platforms among the billion-dollar unicorns, especially those competing within the gig economy, may also help explain why so many new platforms have been unprofitable as businesses.

At the same time, digital innovations have enabled new scale and scope economies, or enabled entry for some and raised entry barriers for others, in ways unimaginable in the pre-digital era. Think about how Amazon, founded by Jeff Bezos in 1994, expanded from being an online store selling books to an online store selling nearly everything, from electronics products to groceries, and with same-day delivery for some products.[38] Even in the early days, Amazon used digital technology to promote online store sales, building a recommendation engine and collecting user evaluations. One estimate is that 40 percent of Amazon's sales today come through its recommendation engine.[39] Then, in the late 1990s, Bezos added the global Amazon Marketplace—what we have called a transaction platform—linking buyers and third-party sellers. Amazon combined the marketplace with its own online store and other fulfillment services, such as billing and shipping, in addition to a massive network of physical warehouses. Competing with Amazon has become a scale game, in which even Walmart, the largest company in the world by revenues, has struggled.

But "platformizing" a market with digital technology does not necessarily change the fundamentals of a business or make common sense and domain knowledge obsolete. For example, simply creating a digital platform to enter the grocery business with online ordering does not make groceries as profitable as selling digital goods or make irrelevant a deep understanding of how to handle perishable goods. An online vendor like Amazon must still deliver groceries in the real world and understand how different supply chains work. If groceries are going to be profitable for Amazon as an online business, then it will probably be because the company can link different businesses and assets in unique ways and achieve economies of scale and scope that other firms cannot. Or perhaps the secret will actually be the physical network of warehouses and delivery vehicles that Amazon invests in to complement its digital platforms.[40]

The leading Chinese platform companies also have used their digital expertise as well as knowledge of local markets and institutions to make it difficult for global platforms like Amazon to compete in China. Alibaba and Tencent started with "asset-light" platform business models: Their early operations were purely digital with modest capital requirements. But, similar to Amazon in the United States though at a somewhat lesser magnitude, Alibaba and Tencent have turned e-commerce in China into a scale game. In 2018, Taobao Marketplace controlled about 60 percent of China's B2C e-commerce. Alibaba also used its size and technological resources to enter cloud computing, payment services, and other related businesses, making it very expensive for Amazon or Walmart to compete effectively with Alibaba in its home market. The same was true of Tencent, which dominated Chinese messaging and social media with WeChat. Tencent exploited its size, customer base, and digital skills to add social media applications as well as expand into online payments, small-business credit and investment services, digital entertainment, and video games, among other areas.

KEY TAKEAWAYS FOR MANAGERS AND ENTREPRENEURS

In this chapter, we discussed the fundamental drivers of platform markets and the dynamics of a winner-take-all-or-most outcome. The most important factors are network effects among users and different market actors, such as between end users and advertisers or between end users and producers of complementary innovations. But we also pointed out how multi-homing and competition from differentiated or niche competitors can reduce network effects and monetization opportunities. Low entry barriers as well can lead to increases in the number of competitors and equally weaken network efforts and profitability. So when it comes to understanding the drivers and dynamics of platform markets, what are the key takeaways for managers and entrepreneurs?

First, it is important to understand what network effects really are, where they come from, and what impact they have on competitive advantage. We have defined them as self-reinforcing feedback loops that, ultimately, create platform value, directly or indirectly. The biggest business challenges for platforms are to nurture network effects and then translate the momentum and value created into a steady and growing stream of revenues and profits. More specifically, same-side network effects come directly from connecting users with other users. Cross-side network effects come from connecting different market actors to users. Platforms make money by facilitating these connections and associated innovations. In both cases, *network effects are not simply abstractions.* They derive from specific strategic decisions and investments, and avoidance of actions that can depress network effects, such as pricing too high on the "wrong" side of the market. Imagine what would have happened if Facebook had charged users to access the social network, like social clubs in the physical world? It would probably be a small, niche business today, or Facebook might have failed completely. It is also essential to realize that network effects can weaken or collapse as technology and market dynamics change, sometimes with little advance warning. This occurred when Apple introduced the hugely disruptive iPhone in 2007 and, in effect, destroyed the nascent smartphone businesses of Palm, Nokia, BlackBerry, Microsoft, and other companies.

Second, it is no accident that the world's most valuable public companies are platform businesses born after the emergence of the personal computer, the Internet, and the smartphone. But we also saw in this chapter that *enabling and sustaining platform dominance requires more than just network effects.* Successful platforms find ways to encourage users and third-party complementors to adopt their platforms and innovate on top of them. They make it difficult for users and complementors to use or switch to competing platforms. They may adopt other measures, such as forming coalitions or using subsidies to help tip a market toward their platform when multiple platforms compete. Remember, though, we learned from Apple that a platform does not have to get a majority of industry revenues to get a majority of industry profits as long as it focuses on the most profitable customers.

Third, *platforms enable "asset-light" business models* by connecting different market actors and leveraging network effects. As we discuss in Chapter 3, an innovation platform can facilitate and then take advantage of new products and services built by third-party firms that continuously make the core product or service—the platform—more valuable. A transaction platform can facilitate and then take advantage of interactions among market participants that would not otherwise occur, and get one market side to pay for access to another side or to supply critical assets. Think about how difficult and expensive it would have been if Microsoft, Apple, Google, Facebook, or WeChat had tried to hire all the engineers that built the millions of applications now available for their innovation platforms. Think about how expensive it would have been if Airbnb had tried to buy all the homes and apartment buildings its users accessed, or if Uber, Lyft, or Didi had tried to buy all the vehicles its drivers use.

In short, we learn from looking at market fundamentals that a platform business must compete in multiple dimensions. Some of these dimensions (like reducing the ability of other firms to exploit differentiation or niches and erecting entry barriers) are the same as competition in conventional markets. Other dimensions (like generating network effects or limiting multi-homing) are distinctive to platform businesses. Ultimately, however, platform companies must offer a compelling product or service that is superior to what the competition offers, whether the other firms are digital or conventional businesses. A successful platform company must be able to protect its competitive advantage in order to retain customers on the demand side as well as attract workers and asset providers on the supply side. If a platform cannot do these things better than the competition, then the company will lose money, like any other business.

Diving more deeply into the differences between innovation and transaction platforms, as well as the advantages of a hybrid strategy, is the subject of the next chapter.

STRATEGY AND BUSINESS MODELS

INNOVATION, TRANSACTION, OR HYBRID

THE FOUR STEPS TO BUILDING A PLATFORM
1. Choose the Market Sides of Your Platform
2. Launch: Solve the "Chicken-or-Egg" Problem
3. Design Your Business Model
4. Establish and Enforce Ecosystem Rules

HYBRIDS
Combining Transaction and
Innovation Platforms

**KEY TAKEAWAYS FOR MANAGERS
AND ENTREPRENEURS**

When Jack Ma was building Alibaba's Taobao in China in 2003, he had a simple problem to solve: He needed to match buyers with sellers and figure out how to make a profit. Ma could have copied eBay's internationally successful strategy where sellers paid eBay a fee. Instead, he decided to create a marketplace where neither sellers nor buyers would have to pay a fee for completing transactions. Although this strategy would evolve over time, in the early days active sellers on Taobao could choose to pay to rank higher on the site's internal search engine, generating advertising revenue for Alibaba.

Now compare Jack Ma's problem with Google's challenge of building an ecosystem around Android. At the time of Android's launch in 2008, Nokia, Apple, and BlackBerry dominated the smartphone business. Google needed to encourage software developers to create new games, applications, and content for its operating system, which was incompatible with its competitors. It needed to convince developers that this investment would be worth the risk. Google made the decision easier by giving the operating system away for free, licensing an open-source version, and providing software tools to allow external developers to develop new apps with less effort.

Both companies had to launch their platforms, but the specifics of how to launch and whom to attract required different decisions, strategies, and actions. These differences exist because all platforms are not the same; they do not all create value or operate in the same way. To select the right platform strategy and business model, managers and entrepreneurs should start with the value proposition they envision. If the value will come mainly from enabling third parties to build their own products or services that utilize and enhance the platform, then you should develop an *innovation platform*. If the value will come mainly from allowing different sides of a market to interact, then you should develop a *transaction platform*. Successful companies also have a natural tendency to grow and expand, which often leads platform businesses to adopt a *hybrid strategy*. For example, firms that start with a successful innovation platform tend to add a transaction side or a separate transaction platform (usually a marketplace). Firms that start with a successful transaction platform tend to add an innovation side or a separate innovation platform. Hybrids also differ to the extent that they integrate the two different types of platforms or keep them largely separate, much like a digital conglomerate.

In this chapter, we discuss the four strategic steps required to build an innovation platform or a transaction platform. The steps are the same, but we explain how execution and business models differ for each platform type. We also explain the different types of hybrid strategies and why hybrids are emerging as the most powerful and highly valued platform business model.

THE FOUR STEPS TO BUILDING A PLATFORM

All firms must go through the same four steps when they try to create and sustain a successful platform business. Figure 3-1 summarizes the steps.

The first step is to identify the various market sides you want for your platform, and how to create value through them: the role different actors play (buyers, sellers, or complementors) and who specifically will take on these roles. Second is to launch the platform, which requires solving the chicken-or-egg problem of how to get started and then how to attract increasing numbers of users or complementors in order to generate strong network effects. Third is to design a business model that will monetize those network

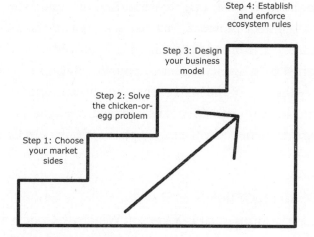

Step 4: Establish and enforce ecosystem rules

Step 3: Design your business model

Step 2: Solve the chicken-or-egg problem

Step 1: Choose your market sides

FIGURE 3-1: **THE FOUR STEPS TO BUILDING A PLATFORM BUSINESS**

effects without depressing them. This monetization challenge involves identifying where the cash flow and profits will come from, and choosing which sides, if any, will benefit most from subsidies. Fourth is to establish and enforce rules of conduct for ecosystem governance: In other words, managers and entrepreneurs need to decide what behaviors to encourage or discourage on the platform, and how to enforce the rules.[1] We will have more to say on platform and ecosystem governance in Chapter 6.

1. CHOOSE THE MARKET SIDES OF YOUR PLATFORM

Choosing who should and should not participate on a platform is a strategically crucial decision. While it might appear obvious in retrospect, the choice of which sides to serve requires creative thinking. Some firms are overly ambitious and try to connect too many sides too early in their development. The result is often an overly complicated platform, which does not scale. One such example was Brightcove, a media platform that serial entrepreneur Jeremy

Allaire founded in 2004. Brightcove started off with no fewer than four sides (content providers, advertisers, consumers, and syndicate affiliates). The broad platform quickly proved unworkable for many market participants. Other common mistakes include failing to identify the side of the market that will attract other sides, mispricing on the more attractive side, and entering a market too late. We discuss these and other causes of platform failure in Chapter 4.

INNOVATION PLATFORMS

Innovation platforms, such as Microsoft Windows, Google Android, Apple iOS, and Amazon Web Services, offer technological building blocks that *third-party innovators* use to develop new complementary products or services. The building blocks usually include tools and connectors that facilitate the creation of complements such as software applications for computers and smartphones. At least one side of an innovation platform always consists of complementors, and at least one other side always consists of end users.

The key for successful innovation platforms is to identify complementors that will stimulate demand for the platform by making new products and services that add significant value. Of course, we don't always know in advance which companies or individuals will create those innovations. Innovation platforms (especially digital ones) often try to solve this problem by broadly exposing their application programming interfaces or APIs (meaning they release information and allow access to the platform's internal instruction sets and communication protocols). They also actively encourage third parties to design complementary products or services, such as through sending out free software development kits and organizing developers forums, or creating incubators and venture funds that subsidize new developers of complementary innovations. Sometimes the platform company will build a few complements itself. Especially when a platform is new, delivering your own complements early in the process helps to stimulate demand for the platform's newest version.

Even with ample interest from third-party complementors, hurdles remain. Complementors often need technical and financial support from the platform owner. An important challenge for some platforms, especially new platforms, is the difficulty of identifying precisely which complementors to support. For example, Numenta—an artificial intelligence platform founded in 2005 by Jeff Hawkins and Donna Dubinsky—struggled for ten years trying to figure out who were the most promising complementors. Despite an abundance of inquiries, it was never clear what might become the "killer app" for this platform and who would build it.[2] Numenta licensed its technology to some organizations and the open-source software community, but it has remained small, with few active complementors and only around two dozen employees.[3]

TRANSACTION PLATFORMS

Transaction platforms, such as Amazon Marketplace, Google Search, Facebook, Alibaba's Taobao, Uber, Lyft, and Airbnb, are online marketplaces that enable the exchange of goods, services, and information. They can help people or organizations access and use assets such as cars or rooms, but also connect through social media, and attract advertisers. As our colleagues David S. Evans and Richard Schmalensee have emphasized, they act as matchmakers.[4]

For most transaction platforms, the choice of sides has been rather obvious. In the cases of eBay, Amazon Marketplace, and Etsy, the sides simply consisted of buyers and sellers of physical goods. For Upwork (formerly Elance-oDesk), the sides were buyers and sellers of freelance labor. For Airbnb, the sides consisted of individuals with accommodations to rent and people who want to rent accommodations.

While most transaction platforms start with just two sides, they often add other sides over time. The question of how many sides to add and when to add them is strategically important, and its answer may not be so obvious before the fact. For example, most of us take for granted that advertisers subsidize Internet search, but this was not always the case. Inktomi and AltaVista were first-generation search engines that did not rely on advertisers, nor did they monetize their search. Most of them failed as businesses. Google was initially no different: It provided search results for free and generated no revenue. Although Google developed a superior search technology, the management team's crucial decision was to turn its search engine into a transaction platform by bringing advertisers on board in a clever way. Identification of the appropriate market sides and how best to engage with each side was essential to Google's financial success.

Google positioned Internet searchers on one side and advertisers on the other. To users of the search function, Google's high-quality PageRank algorithm provided a valuable service. It had an ingenious design that crawled the web and reverse engineered the links connecting web pages to each other. But Google could have chosen not to have two sides and instead monetize search directly by charging users a flat subscription fee or a per-search usage fee. If it had done this, then Google Search would have emerged as an entirely different (and probably much smaller and less profitable) business. By adding advertisers to the other side, Google Search turned into a global mass-market transaction platform. By allowing advertisers to have their ads prominently located on the screen next to the search results, Google created obvious value to advertisers. It also connected them intelligently using its AdWords technology with the very users who were searching a topic close to the object of their ads.

Social networks such as Facebook, Twitter, LinkedIn, Snapchat, Instagram, and Tinder provide another set of examples. Like Google Search, we consider them transaction platforms because they facilitate exchanges of information among users who otherwise would have difficulty connecting. These platforms also generate and rely on network effects. But how many market sides do social networks really need? They are one-sided platforms if all users are similar, and multisided if they can distinguish different categories of users. But the criteria for identifying sides differ for each type of platform and application. Sides can be men and women on Tinder when individuals use the platform to look for people of the opposite gender. For men looking for men, or women looking for women, Tinder is more like a one-sided platform. Some social networks, like eHarmony, charge for access, like social clubs in the physical world or buyer clubs like Costco. They could sell services, such as enhanced mail, which LinkedIn provides as a premium service. Or they could bring in an advertising complement side, as Facebook and Twitter have done. Other transaction platforms such as eBay in its early years and WhatsApp (now owned by Facebook) chose not to add an advertising side.

When bringing new sides on board, timing matters a lot. Bringing in advertisers too early might damage the user experience and depress growth of the user base, whereas a small number of users may not provide enough value to attract advertisers. This was why Facebook did not start with advertising. Mark Zuckerberg's first task was to grow the number of users.

Sometimes firms experiment and change their strategy about adding sides. For instance, LinkedIn in 2007 envisioned a side of "experts" and planned to launch a research service in 2008. The aim was to provide access for a fee to institutions or individuals who were experts in specific areas. LinkedIn eventually dropped the plan because of limited interest.

2. LAUNCH: SOLVE THE "CHICKEN-OR-EGG" PROBLEM

Launching a platform and solving the chicken-or-egg problem is probably the most difficult challenge for platform strategists. When side A's volume depends on side B, and side B's volume depends on side A, how do you get started? Here again, innovation and transaction platforms need to approach this dilemma differently. Strategic choices generally fall into three categories: (1) Create stand-alone value for one side first, (2) subsidize one or both sides, and (3) sometimes bring two sides on board simultaneously.

INNOVATION PLATFORMS

Creating stand-alone value for one side—such as users—requires that the firm produce a strong product or service that does not initially need third-party complementary innovations. Third-party innovations may make the product even more valuable, and this is when a product can evolve into an innovation platform, provided that it has the right attributes. First, the product must be designed in such a way that it has "hooks" for outside firms to connect (like application programming interfaces for software platforms). Second, it must also be modular enough in design for outsiders to add significant innovations. Third, the company must facilitate easy access to the product's core functionality, such as through inexpensive or free licensing terms.

One strategy for launching an innovation platform in a market where no platforms exist yet is to identify an industry-wide problem. Then offer your product as a solution to that problem, or at least as a "core" or essential ingredient for the solution. In prior writings, we called this strategy "coring."[5] There are several examples. In order to solve the problem of how to build an IBM-compatible personal computer during the 1980s, which IBM tried to control as a proprietary product and platform technology, Microsoft and Intel broadly licensed or sold the core ingredients, the MS-DOS operating system (followed by Windows) and the x86 microprocessor. Similarly, in the late 2000s, Google offered the Android operating system as a solution for handset makers that wanted to build smartphones with capabilities similar to Apple's iPhone. ARM also made its microprocessor design the technology of choice for companies that wanted to build smartphones that used relatively little battery power.

When it comes to generating network effects, the chicken-or-egg problem for innovation platforms comes down to two questions: How can a platform owner make it attractive for potential customers to buy the platform even if there are few complementary applications? And how can a platform owner persuade complementors to invest in platform-specific innovations if there is uncertainty about the number of end users who are willing to buy the platform (and the complements)?

The general principle of "Get the engine running and build up some momentum" in order to launch applies to all platforms. What is unique about how complementors engage with innovation platforms is that complementors are not only adopting a platform: They also are acting as *technology suppliers* and *innovators* in their own right. When facing a decision to adopt an innovation platform and join the ecosystem, complementors must trust someone else's technology (the platform) to develop their own new product or service. At the same time, the owner of the innovation platform must entice complementors to *innovate on the platform* so that the platform becomes increasingly useful and valuable.

Innovation platforms can solve this chicken-or-egg problem by developing or buying some of their own complements. They can also provide free or inexpensive tools and technological assistance to help accelerate third-party innovations. Apple, for example, launched the iPhone and the iPad with a few bundled applications that it developed in-house, including a web browser (Safari), Mail, Photos, Video, iTunes, Notes, Contacts, and Calendar. It also obtained a few other apps from key external content providers, such as Google Maps and the *New York Times*, ensuring the provision of early complements.

By maintaining secrecy prior to launch and then staging mega-media events, Steve Jobs sought to stimulate maximum exposure for new products such as the iPhone and the iPad. This marketing strategy attracted interest not only from users, which constituted one side, but also from content providers and app developers, which constituted the other side.

TRANSACTION PLATFORMS

For most transaction platforms, solutions to the chicken-or-egg problem should be relatively straightforward: How can platform owners make certain there are enough buyers to attract sellers? And how can the platform deliver enough sellers to attract buyers?

When Brian Chesky and Joe Gebbia launched Airbnb in 2007, they decided that the first platform side to build up should be property owners with places to rent; in other words, build up the supply side. Their first challenge was to identify these property owners and rally them in large enough numbers to attract renters. Chesky and Gebbia had the clever idea to avoid starting from scratch, and instead used readily available information on property owners who wanted to rent out their properties. Where could they find this kind of information? A large number of owners had already posted their properties on a popular online classified website, Craigslist. Airbnb founders developed a piece of software that hacked Craigslist to extract the contact information.[6] They also took advantage of newspaper ads and other public postings.

Identifying members for their first side was just the beginning. The founders then had to encourage the property owners to post their listings on the new platform. Airbnb's value proposition was clear: While requiring no further investment from them, posting their property on Airbnb (in addition to Craigslist) would simply increase the *quantity* of the property owners' exposure to possible renters. In addition to increased exposure, Airbnb also helped the property owners increase the *quality* of their exposure by hiring professional photographers to take photos similar to what a person would see for hotel listings. This decision was not only a differentiating factor from Craigslist-type postings or newspaper advertisements; it also increased the renters' perception of the value they would get from the Airbnb platform. Renters began to see that they were getting hospitality services comparable to hotels, and usually for a significantly reduced price or in more convenient locations.

The way Airbnb attracted early members was ingenious and added value for both market sides, but this strategy also differed from how Airbnb expanded. For Airbnb to send photographers to each new member's residence was not easily scalable and financially unsustainable. More important, it was not necessary to continue subsidizing professional photo shoots. By initially subsidizing professional photos, Airbnb set a high bar for the quality of property photography on the Airbnb website. This practice soon became the new norm: Property renters would invest on their own in professional photography to differentiate themselves from other renters. In effect, Airbnb initially incurred a cost that raised expectations within the ecosystem and later simply took advantage of competition among the property owners.

There are three lessons we can learn from Airbnb. First, for many transaction platforms, there may be no need to start from scratch. Instead, platforms should try to make use of existing groups and information, such as by aggregating and analyzing publicly available data. Second, once the platform identifies its different sides, it can offer a service that helps attract members to the platform. And third, platforms may contradict the conventional wisdom for new ventures that says, "Start as you mean to go on." The launch phase can benefit from actions that just aim at getting started—even if they are not financially sustainable or practically scalable. In short, it is fine to start off in a direction that the platform cannot follow in the long term if it can ignite self-sustaining feedback loops along the way.

In order to launch, transaction platforms usually solve their chicken-or-egg problems in one of two ways: (1) Pick one side and build it up, and then, once that side is sufficiently populated, bring on another side; or (2) bring on both sides at once, little by little, in a zigzag fashion.[7]

Pick one side and build it up can work well because, once a single side is populated, it should attract the other side. Indeed, many platforms subsidize one side to get the ball rolling. The Yellow Pages, eBay, Etsy, Amazon Marketplace, Taobao, Facebook, Twitter, and Airbnb all subsidized one side of their platforms to get momentum started. The subsidy usually came in the form of no charge to be a user. A variation on this strategy consists of the platform subsidizing activities that help members become more attractive to another side, as Airbnb did at first when sending professional photographers to property renters.

Another tactic was offering stand-alone value to one side, much like the coring strategy we talked about for innovation platforms. If the platform could make a service valuable or even essential to one side's members, irrespective of the number of users on the other side, then it becomes easier to start the ball rolling. OpenTable (which Priceline purchased in 2014 for $2.6 billion) did this when it signed up its first restaurants by offering a very useful computerized table management system and charging only a small monthly fee for the technology. Once restaurants were on board with this solution to their table management problem, it was easier to attract them as users of the reservation platform.

Operating a one-sided platform and growing it (prior to bringing another side on board) can also succeed if members of the first side find value in communicating or interacting with each other, as they do with the telephone as well as social networks. Once that first side gets big enough, then it can attract other sides. This is what Facebook did when it launched the social network within the Harvard student community as a one-sided platform, and then gradually expanded to other universities and then to anyone over age thirteen who wanted to join. Only when the user side was very large, numbering in the millions, did Facebook focus on bringing in other sides such as advertisers, application developers, and digital content partners. This two-step strategy combined tapping first into the power of direct network effects, which helped develop and expand a single side of the network. Then, in a later stage, other sides joined the platform when it was more likely to generate cross-side network effects.

When platforms try to bring on both sides at once, they often have to subsidize both sides at the same time. But subsidizing both sides at once is a costly and risky strategy. It makes most sense only if three conditions prevail: (1) The platform has extremely deep pockets. (2) The platform has a realistic chance at a winner-take-all-or-most outcome. (3) Once all or most competitors have exited, there are barriers preventing new players from entering and then customers from switching or multi-homing.

Still, there are two problems with this approach. First, as we discussed in Chapter 2, winner-take-all-or-most outcomes are relatively rare. Second, the platform owner is betting that users and ecosystem partners will still want to remain affiliated with the platform, even if prices eventually go up. WhatsApp, for instance, offered a free service, in effect subsidizing all of its users. WhatsApp's owner, Facebook, hoped that, once it reached a billion users, it could charge its customers $1 per year. But despite the very modest fee, WhatsApp quickly discovered that even $1 could lead customers to switch, causing Facebook to abandon its plan.[8]

3. DESIGN YOUR BUSINESS MODEL

There is another problem with launch tactics that heavily subsidize one or two sides. Not only is this expensive, but some platforms get stuck in an "infinite launching loop." Platform owners keep burning money in order to gain adoption from multiple sides, heavily subsidizing participants for years. Uber has been the obvious poster child for this approach. Uber's management and its investors seem to be hoping for a winner-take-all-or-most outcome, where competitors eventually exit due to price competition and financial losses. Uber management also seems to believe that a large number of drivers and vehicles will provide new opportunities for related diversification (such as Uber Eats—delivering food) and eventually turn into high and stable streams of revenue and profit.

This optimistic scenario may well occur for Uber. After all, Uber has delivered a great value proposition for consumers: Conventional taxis are in short supply and relatively expensive in major cities and urban areas around the world. Uber's very low prices and convenient way to match driver supply with rider demand through a smartphone app has led to explosive growth for the ride-sharing service. But even if a platform has enough funding to overcome the chicken-or-egg problem, it does not guarantee that the business will produce more revenues than its expenses. This is especially true if the company has high employee turnover (the downside of "contract workers") and repeatedly incurs start-up costs as it expands into new geographic areas or new business ventures, some of which it may not understand well. As a result, even with a clear identification of market sides and very strong direct and indirect network effects, platform companies can still find it difficult to identify a profitable business model. WhatsApp in 2018 had 1.5 billion active users who loved the service, but WhatsApp has not yet made a dime. All platform businesses need to find a way to extract significant value from at least one market side and eventually turn that value—fueled by network effects—into increasing revenues and, eventually, a profitable operation.

INNOVATION PLATFORMS

Most successful innovation platforms generate profit in one of two ways: (1) They increase their customers' willingness to pay for the platform itself, such as by adding new features and encouraging third parties to create complementary products and services that enhance the value of the platform. Or (2) they capture value as a portion of the sale of every complementary product or service sold for the platform, including complements they build themselves. In the PC world, Microsoft made it free and easy for developers to write new applications, and the price of DOS and then Windows rose accordingly. Microsoft also built Office and many other software applications that complemented Windows and made sure there was demand for each new generation of the operating system. In the video game world, Sony collected a licensing fee on every game sold for PlayStation. For smartphones and tablets, Google gave away the Android operating system based on the (correct) theory that the company could make money on mobile search.

The goal for every innovation platform is to create scale: Most digital platforms have relatively high fixed costs (the ongoing R&D requirements to create new features) and relatively low or zero variable costs (distributing software or data over an existing network). The key is to attract enough complementors to grow the ecosystem and help grow the number of users, which attracts more complementors, and then users, and so on. For a software platform, this dynamic can enable the platform to literally "print" money at scale. Microsoft, for example, spent $1 billion developing Windows XP, but it sold roughly 250 million copies at $60 per unit in its first year. Microsoft broke even in three weeks and "minted money" thereafter, or at least until it started to invest in the next operating system. Other innovation platforms, such as Nokia's Symbian, failed to attract enough complementary applications to its platform after the entry of Apple's iOS and then Google's Android. This situation led to a rapid loss in market share (negative network effects), a subscale business, and eventual failure (sale of the phone business to Microsoft). The lesson is that successful innovation platforms must continue to attract new complements, achieve and retain scale, and remain competitive in functionality lest they be overtaken.

TRANSACTION PLATFORMS

All transaction platforms generate revenue through fees for business deals, advertisements, or services. However, their business models vary in terms of who gets charged, what gets charged, and which services are free or subsidized. Since they may not be selling a product or service directly, transaction platforms must understand the willingness to pay of their various market sides, as well as the difference between how much each side wants the other side to engage. In theory, the demand characteristics from each side should be the main driver for the business model. In practice, it is very difficult for managers and entrepreneurs to assess the level of demand in advance. We don't know of any silver bullet to answer the question of how much one side should be willing to pay, but we can offer some principles and illustrate them with examples.

Transaction platforms tend to offer value to their various sides and ultimately generate profit in five ways: (1) matchmaking, (2) reducing friction in transactions, (3) complementary services, (4) complementary technology sales, and (5) advertising. We will discuss each of these approaches.

First, as matchmakers, transaction platforms help provide access to a large pool of users and identify suitable matches. These users can be buyers and sellers of goods or services as in online marketplaces such as Amazon Marketplace, Etsy, eBay, or Alibaba's Taobao and Tmall. They can be users who want to exchange information with each other, as in social networks, or exchange financial authorizations and authentication data, as in payment platforms. Much of the value that transaction platforms provide comes from increasing the size of the pool and then increasing the likelihood of a better match.

The extent to which side members are prepared to pay for being matched with another side varies from market to market. This difference explains variations in the pricing decisions of different platforms. Airbnb charges room renters and room providers but does not charge when they are simply room seekers or room listers. Tinder, the location-based meeting app, launched in 2013 as fully free but changed its pricing model in 2015 to operate a freemium model. Upwork experimented and changed its pricing model in 2015, charging less to companies that used its services for the largest jobs, hoping to stimulate more recurring business.[9] And as we shall see later, some platforms charge both sides but offer some degree of subsidy at least to one side.

One of the worst platform business models to date has been Uber, despite the obvious value it offers to users in terms of convenience and low prices. Uber lost some $4.5 billion in 2017 on gross revenues of $37 billion. It also has lost more than $11 billion cumulatively. We expect the company to finish 2018 with large (although diminishing) losses. The 2019 IPO will bring in more cash and help Uber expand, but it has to overcome several cost drivers before it can earn a profit.

To compete with taxis as well as other companies such as Lyft, Uber subsidized the cost of rides, keeping prices artificially low. Uber also paid many drivers a set fee in addition to per-ride compensation or had to pay other financial incentives to attract and keep drivers on the platform, including help with financing the cost of their drivers' vehicles. In addition, Uber advertised heavily to attract new riders. The largest cost came from driver turnover, called the "churn rate." This number was an estimated 12.5 percent per month, or 150 percent per year, which means that Uber had to replace all its drivers every eight months, on average. Assuming that Uber had 3 million drivers in 2018, it would need to find 375,000 new drivers each month *just to replace its existing workforce*, not to mention grow the business. With driver advertising and recruitment costs estimated at $650 per driver, in 2018 this expense alone could total over $240 million per month and nearly $3 billion for the full year! And there was more. Another big cost driver was high R&D expenses, such as more than $2 billion in 2017. These were mainly to develop self-driving vehicles—a big bet to reduce those enormous driver costs but not likely to have much impact in the next few years.[10]

Meanwhile, Uber was diversifying into related transportation services, hoping to leverage its existing drivers and logistics capabilities by delivering food (Uber Eats) and packages (UberRUSH). These activities still operated at a loss in 2018, though they may eventually be more profitable than ride sharing, which has become a commodity business with intense price competition.[11] Uber also plans to enter yet another transportation service. It will address the shortage of truck drivers by matching fully loaded trailers from big companies with drivers from small and medium-size carrier companies.[12]

In other words, Uber heavily subsidized both sides of its market, and had a potentially fatal flaw—very high driver turnover, the downside of using contract workers rather than potentially more stable regular employees. Consequently, the company was forced to spend billions of dollars in venture capital and operating cash flow simply to maintain the status quo. Rapid growth in existing as well as new markets then required additional expenses and investments. Overall, Uber has grown mostly because of generous capital providers (largely sovereign wealth funds and SoftBank's Vision Fund). Investors seem to be betting on a winner-take-all-or-most outcome where Uber outlasts both digital and conventional competitors, and then eventually raises prices or reduces costly subsidies.

Second, transaction platforms "reduce friction" to facilitate interactions among platform participants. Various books and articles have introduced this concept, including *Invisible Engines* (2006) by Evans, Hagiu, and Schmalensee, *Matchmakers* (2016) by Evans and

Schmalensee, and *Platform Revolution* (2016) by Parker, Van Alstyne, and Choudary.[13] This is a helpful concept, and we often see transaction platforms doing things like enabling the secure exchange of goods or money. Many transaction platforms also used the payment services of other transaction platforms, such as Google Checkout or PayPal, or provided a financial "escrow" service to sellers. Other friction-reducing or risk-reducing services included authentication (verifying users' identities), insurance, and, for cryptocurrencies such as Bitcoin, currency exchanges and virtual wallets.[14]

Third, transaction platforms often create additional value for their members by providing complementary services. Sometimes they offer these services for free, but most of the time they charge. For example, Taobao did not charge sellers and buyers to sign up, but it charged sellers for obtaining a better ranking in its internal search engine. Amazon offered, for a fee, ancillary services such as goods consignment (for sellers) and delivery for its Amazon Marketplace seller-users. The "Fulfillment by Amazon" (FBA) was a popular bundle of services that Amazon offered its marketplace users. Those who signed up for FBA outsourced to Amazon the consignment, packaging, and shipping of their products to customers. Another significant part of FBA's value for sellers is that it offered the possibility to have all their goods delivered with the Amazon Prime service, which provided expedited and free delivery. This valuable feature would often lead customers to choose certain products over other similar products.

Some platforms charge both sides for complementary services, although the services still need to be valuable, scalable, and difficult to copy in order for the companies to charge enough to make a profit. Consider Deliveroo, the online marketplace for British restaurants launched in London in 2013. As of 2018, this platform offered fast delivery (on average thirty-two minutes) of local restaurant-cooked food in over two hundred cities on three continents, avoiding the highly competitive United States. In a 2015 interview, Deliveroo's cofounder, William Shu, explained that a big misconception about his business was that people assumed his company was a pure online marketplace. If that were true, then perhaps Deliveroo could earn a profit by matching drivers with restaurants and keeping expenses very low. However, Shu noted that Deliveroo was really a logistics service.[15] The company worked with restaurants that did not have existing delivery services and provided them with drivers and access to a logistics platform built using machine learning algorithms to optimize routing. The business model charged both sides of the platform—the restaurants and the food consumers. Deliveroo took a commission from restaurants and charged a delivery fee to the customer. It relied on courier riders who most often rode their own bicycles to deliver the food. It did not consider the bicycle riders employees but as "independent contractors," similar to how Uber categorized its drivers. Deliveroo's couriers were not eligible for workers' benefits such as sick pay and the national living wage, nor were they covered by a company insurance policy in case they had an accident.

Deliveroo's employment practices (we discuss these further in Chapter 6) kept manpower costs low, but it had high expenses for technology as well as administrative staff and executives.[16] As of 2018, there were still not enough economies of scale, operational efficiencies, or value added for the company to make a profit. The company had raised just under $1 billion but lost $176 million in 2016, the last time Deliveroo reported financial data. Food delivery may be a $100 billion market, but delivery by itself was not a very sophisticated or high-value-added service. Deliveroo could not charge a lot or raise prices easily because there were different ways for restaurants to deliver food.[17]

Fourth, some transaction platforms sell technology or other goods and services apart from transaction fees. This approach seemed far superior to delivery services. We can see this with OpenTable, which matched people who want to make reservations with restaurants who accepted reservations online. It charged $1 for every reservation made through its system and 25 cents for reservations made directly on the restaurant's website, which amounted to a relatively large monthly fee for using the service. Some competitors, such as Yelp, also charged for the service and for specific reservations made through the system.[18]

Fifth, selling advertising is one of the most widely used business models for transaction platforms. It is particularly well suited to search engines like Google or social networks like Facebook or other types of transaction platforms with a social component. For example, TripAdvisor has user reviews of travel services and places, and these constitute an important part of the value that users obtain when searching on TripAdvisor. But to maximize value to the platform, advertising cannot be seen as an unwelcome "tax" on users that unilaterally degrades their experience. For advertising to play a positive role in the business model, it has to add value to both sides, even if not to the same extent. Google has mastered this approach with its AdWords auction, an effective and innovative method to best match the search user's interest with the relevance of the advertisements users see when they search.[19] The rise of ad blockers was also starting to threaten a number of advertising-based business models, inspiring those platforms to look for other means of generating revenue.

4. ESTABLISH AND ENFORCE ECOSYSTEM RULES

Ecosystem rules pose a basic question for anyone affiliated with a platform: Who should be allowed to do what? When Armin Heinrich posted his app called "I Am Rich" on Apple's App Store in 2008, and sold it for $999.99, the challenges of governing a platform became apparent to Apple. The app itself did nothing except show a glowing red stone with the text: "I am rich, I deserv [sic] it, I am good, healthy & successful." Eight people bought it, and Apple made

$2,400 in revenues (which was mostly profit). Obviously a scam of sorts, Apple had to decide how to govern its platform: Should it take the money and run, or establish and enforce standards for its end users? Apple chose to delete the app and create relatively strict standards that all app developers had to meet. As the following section suggests, Apple was not alone in struggling with the challenges of ecosystem governance.

INNOVATION PLATFORMS

Innovation platforms need to ensure the quality of complements and clarify who can connect to and innovate on top of the platform. Good ecosystem governance encouraged lots of innovation and allowed complementors as well as users to benefit in a sustainable manner. By "sustainable" we mean that platform companies and their complementors need to be able to compete effectively with rivals and make a profit. Some innovation ecosystems, such as in the software industry, revolved around de facto technical standards. These platforms also existed on a spectrum of technology openness. On one extreme, they were proprietary and tightly controlled or partially closed to third-party complementors (such as Apple's iOS). On the other extreme, they were "open source" and not owned by any one firm (such as with Linux and some versions of Android, itself a version of Linux).[20] Indeed, the primary governance issues for innovation platforms relate to key elements of their strategies: the degree of openness and the extent to which the platform company competes with its complementors.

In general, participants in many successful innovation platforms tend to view the platform owners as the legitimate custodians of the technical standards and the ecosystem more broadly. In particular, complementors feel they are part of a "collective," with a shared destiny. But legitimacy as a platform leader takes time to build and is easy to destroy. Innovation platform owners need to be careful not to hurt complementors' incentives to innovate by carelessly trampling over their businesses. This concern limits to some extent the freedom of platform owners to enter and compete directly in complementary markets.

Innovation platforms often competed with each other and sometimes with their complementors. It is well-known that Lotus, Word-Perfect, and Harvard Graphics dominated the markets for DOS and Windows versions of spreadsheet, word-processing, and presentation software during the 1980s, until Microsoft introduced Excel, Word, and PowerPoint, then bundled them in the Office suite from 1990. Accordingly, ecosystem rules tended to evolve over time along with changes in competition and cooperation between the platform leader and external complementors. We observed a similar pattern when Google bought Motorola Mobility in 2012. The acquisition generated anxiety and mistrust among mobile handset makers, which were using Android as an operating system. They were concerned that Google would favor Motorola handsets with the newest implementations of Android, putting Google's partners at a disadvantage. Despite Google's attempts to reassure its partners by making explicit statements that it would not play favorites, important Android licensees hedged their bets. Samsung started to push some phones with its own Tizen operating system, and LG introduced phones with webOS (initially developed by Palm).[21] In 2014, Google resolved the tensions by selling Motorola Mobility to Lenovo. However, Google reentered the space in 2018 when it bought part of the handset engineering group of HTC, the Taiwan manufacturer that had been producing Google-branded Pixel phones.[22]

Governance of innovation platforms becomes even more complicated when platform competitors are also platform complementors. Google, for example, was a leading provider of applications for the iPhone, with apps ranging from search to maps. On early models of the iPhone, Apple prominently displayed Google Maps on its home screen, providing prime "real estate" to Google. By 2012, however, Apple increasingly viewed Google as a competitor and not just a complementor. This led Apple to invest heavily in an internally developed competing product, Apple Maps. The Google Maps app was still accessible and downloadable from Apple's App Store, but Apple decided not to preload it onto the main iPhone screen. This decision reflected and reinforced a change in the relationship between Apple and Google, away from collaboration and toward more competition.

One of the specific ways innovation platforms govern their ecosystems is through the design of the technological interfaces between the platform and its complements, and in particular through the degree of openness of these interfaces. When platform leaders open up their interfaces (such as APIs), they send a clear signal to complementors that they are trying hard to improve complementors' businesses. When they close or restrict their interfaces, they send the opposite message. When platforms change the openness of their APIs without communicating effectively about the impact on the ecosystem, they weaken the shared sense of the collective, and this can create ripples of discontent throughout the ecosystem.

Twitter provides a good example of what can happen when the platform sends mixed messages. We think of Twitter as a social media transaction platform, but for several years it also operated as a hybrid, with a lively innovation platform side to the business. Yet Twitter greatly disappointed its community of complementors with its decision to restrict or shut down access to its APIs in 2012.[23] When Twitter first opened its APIs in 2006, the free and easy access stimulated a vibrant community of developers for Twitter-related apps, such as to enable users to view Twitter on their mobile devices (called Twitter "clients"). By 2010, Twitter was widely seen as a developer-friendly service and even launched a site for developers containing Twitter API documentation, platform status information, and forums. Some 75 percent of all traffic on the platform came through the Twitter API. But once Twitter developed its own mobile app, following its acquisition of Atebits, a start-up that had developed the popular Tweetie client application, it started to discourage external developers from creating different Twitter clients. Ryan Sarver, then director of the Twitter platform, announced that developers should not build new Twitter clients and existing clients needed to strictly adhere to Twitter's rules. The announcement also stated that "we need to move to a less fragmented world, where every user can experience Twitter in a consistent way," and mentioned changes to the terms of service related to Twitter APIs.

From 2012, Twitter also altered the rules of connectivity and in effect started closing off its public API. For example, in 2012, Twitter blocked Instagram's "Find Friends" feature, no longer allowing Instagram to access Twitter followers' graph data via an API. It also imposed a similar restriction on Tumblr and started to limit the number of users that outside services were allowed to access. But after poor market performance and growing disaffection among outside developers, from 2015 Twitter started to reverse its course. Cofounder Ev Williams even stated in July 2015 that the company had made a strategic error when it came to the Twitter API. In October 2015, cofounder and CEO Jack Dorsey stated at the 2015 mobile developer conference that Twitter wanted to "apologize" for the "confusing" and "complicated" relationship the company had created with developers, and claimed it wanted to "reboot" and have a great relationship in the future.[24] Consequently, after shutting down Twitter API access to Politwoops, an app that monitored the Twitter accounts of politicians by using the Twitter API to collect and display tweets, Twitter reversed its decision in January 2016 and reinstated Twitter API access. Twitter then started to look for other ways to increase user engagement on its platform in order to increase the number of hours per day users spend on Twitter. Higher levels of Twitter usage would enable the platform to monetize user activity further by selling more (or more expensive) advertisements.

Innovation platforms (including hybrids) that become dominant in the market face a unique challenge, akin to a winner's curse. As they become increasingly essential, the expectations of users and complementors grow. People come to expect innovation platforms to behave in responsible ways and pursue the overall good of the ecosystem, rather than simply maximize profits for the platform owner. This is why, not surprisingly, we sometimes treat powerful innovation platforms as if they were public utilities. We discuss this issue further in Chapter 6.

TRANSACTION PLATFORMS

The ecosystem rules for transaction platforms are similar to innovation platforms: Ultimately a transaction platform has to decide who can connect through the platform and what the various market sides can do on the platform. In addition, most transaction platforms have rules aimed at minimizing low-quality transactions, such as weeding out poor-quality goods and services, facilitating returns in case of unsatisfied customers, and fighting fraud.

Some transaction platforms impose and check credentials before members can perform an activity. We call this active limitation of who can engage on the platform "curation." For example, after a number of incidents, including the sexual assault of a passenger in India by the driver, Uber attempted to improve driver qualifications by checking licenses and performing background checks.[25] Didi Chuxing did the same thing in China after several sexual assaults and murders of passengers by drivers.[26] Platforms may also make their rules explicit in the form of "community guidelines." Uber's guidelines included general principles such as "Respect each other," "Give riders and drivers some personal space," and "No physical contact with the driver or fellow riders" (with the explicit mention of "As a reminder, Uber has a no sex rule"), as well as policies against "discrimination."[27] In a similar effort to fight (and to be perceived as fighting) discrimination, Airbnb required all members to approve the "Airbnb Community Commitment," agreeing "to treat everyone in the Airbnb community—regardless of their race, religion, national origin, ethnicity, disability, sex, gender identity, sexual orientation, or age—with respect, and without judgment or bias."[28]

In practice, though, platforms varied greatly in the extent to which they curated members and activities. Freelancer.com, the online workplace platform established in 2009, connected over 24 million employers and freelance workers globally. It did not restrict the number of types of freelancers. By contrast, rival Upwork, founded in 1999, performed algorithmic curation and used multiple means to verify that freelancers are who they say they are, including authenticating email addresses and providing results of online skills tests. It also allowed job advertisers to include custom screening questions in their job posts and provided chat and videoconference tools for interviewing finalists. However, Upwork did not take responsibility for the quality of the work performed, and explicitly stated that it was ultimately the responsibility of the job advertiser to choose the freelancer.[29] But the purpose of the curation was to improve the quality of work and build trust in its matchmaking functions.

Another way to increase the quality of engagement as well as users' trust was to increase the transparency of performance data on platform members. Reviews and evaluations are ubiquitous features of transaction platforms such as TripAdvisor, Expedia, Airbnb, Uber, Amazon Marketplace, Upwork, and many others. They usually offer a simple interface that allows users to review and grade the performance of those who perform the services accessible through the platform. The platforms then compute the results for an overall score and make the scores and individual reviews visible and searchable. In this way, transaction platforms generally allow complete strangers to assess quickly whether they want to engage or transact with each other.

Reviews and evaluations, computed automatically through algorithms, play the role of social vetting of platform members. They created a searchable repository of past transactions and reviews. Allowing members of various sides to build a reputation creates value for users and provides incentives for users to return to the platform, making it "sticky," instead of multi-homing with several platforms. Fake reviews and other undesirable postings continued to be a problem for many platforms, although they were investing in artificial intelligence tools to help identify fake or unauthorized reviews (such as those written by a restaurant or hotel owner, or by a product company to damage a competitor by submitting a negative review) as well as other inappropriate content. Authenticity of reviews was an especially critical part of the value that platforms provided to users. Some platforms, such as Facebook, Google's YouTube, and TripAdvisor, increasingly used people as well as AI tools to verify problematic reviews and content.[30] Upwork also displayed each freelancer's "Job Success Score" and feedback on past projects.

In some cases, platforms themselves monitored the work performed by one side. For example, Uber's rating system measured performance, and this had consequences: Drivers were "deactivated" or "taken off" the platform if their rating fell too low. Uber also encouraged drivers to work as much as possible and not turn down requests for rides; it even computed and posted a score for the drivers' acceptance rate. Freelancer work platforms such as Upwork also required time-tracking apps for hourly jobs, which monitored the work performed by taking (with the approval of the freelancer) screenshots of the freelancer's computer.

Although transaction platforms may provide tools for users to assess the quality or frequency of the service performed, they usually don't take responsibility for the activities themselves. There are exceptions. For example, some platforms offered a guarantee or insurance for the quality of the service to buyers, and some online marketplaces organized product returns. But platforms differed in the extent to which they provided these customer services. Amazon Marketplace had a guarantee and return service. It also offered to mediate between buyers and sellers to enforce sellers' rapid response to customer cancellation and return requests. Other online marketplaces such as the French Le Bon Coin did not.

Fraud prevention was another area where transaction platforms differed in how much responsibility they assumed. It remained a matter of debate to what extent firms such as eBay monitored and fought the sale of counterfeit goods; there were also differences across regions in how rigorously platforms applied their different rules. While eBay tended to be relatively strict (a policy we explore in Chapter 4), some of its competitors, such as Alibaba in China, historically took the opposite approach.

Many platforms take great care in limiting their liability. Airbnb stated in its June 2017 updated terms and conditions that, "as the provider of the Airbnb Platform, Airbnb does not own, create, sell, resell, provide, control, manage, offer, deliver, or supply any Listings or Host Services. Hosts alone are responsible for their Listings and Host Services. . . . Airbnb is not acting as an agent in any capacity for any Member." And with regard to its role within potential disputes, Airbnb stated that, "while we may help facilitate the resolution of disputes, Airbnb has no control over and does not guarantee (i) the existence, quality, safety, suitability, or legality of any Listings or Host Services, (ii) the truth or accuracy of any Listing descriptions, Ratings, Reviews, or other Member Content (as defined below), or (iii) the performance or conduct of any Member or third party." Finally, it stated that "Airbnb does not endorse any Member, Listing or Host Services."[31]

Ultimately, governance policies and skills could make or break a platform. Problems ranging from Russian interference in U.S. elections via Facebook to stolen content uploaded to YouTube can bring the very legitimacy of a platform's business into question.

HYBRIDS: COMBINING TRANSACTION
AND INNOVATION PLATFORMS

As we illustrated with Figure 1-2 in Chapter 1, some platform companies have adopted a hybrid strategy. They combine transaction
and innovation functions within the same platform infrastructure
or launch transaction and innovation platforms within the same
firm. The most valuable platform businesses (and these rank among
the most valuable companies in the world) are all hybrids: Microsoft, Apple, Amazon, Alphabet-Google, Facebook, Tencent, and
Alibaba, among a few others.

The hybrid approach seems popular and valuable because it
combines the best of both worlds: Transaction platform companies like Facebook or Tencent (with WeChat) can add an innovation platform function to access the innovative capabilities of
third-party firms. They can make their social media or messaging
activities more compelling with minimal in-house investment. Innovation platform companies like Apple or Google (with Android)
can establish a separate transaction platform or store to distribute
complementary innovations and digital content that make the platforms more valuable. As a side benefit, innovation platforms generate additional revenues from sales or transaction fees.

We also see two different types of hybrid strategies, although
they exist more along a spectrum rather than with sharp distinctions. On one extreme, we have platform companies that add the
second type of platform and connect the two in some meaningful
way. The connections can be through cross-marketing to a common
user base, relying heavily on digital technology, analytics, and uni-
fied customer databases. Or a firm might strengthen its innovation
platform by establishing a marketplace or digital store to distribute
applications and content. These investments make the innovation
platform more valuable and have the potential to generate cross-
side network effects, such as between end users and producers of

complementary innovations like smartphone apps. We refer to connecting the two different types of platforms within the same firm as an *integrated hybrid strategy*.

On the other extreme, a platform company might add the other type of platform but without connecting the two technically or operationally. This approach we refer to as a *conglomerate hybrid strategy*. These organizations tend to resemble conglomerates in the non-digital world that own several distinct businesses under one organizational umbrella or holding-company structure. There is no tight coupling of the businesses such as through technology, marketing, or customers, although there may be some flow of funds across the different business units and a central staff, such as for administration or research. In the conventional economy, General Electric was the largest and most successful conglomerate in the second half of the twentieth century. Even so, it struggled in recent years due to competition from more efficient, focused businesses. Most research in management suggests that conglomerates with unrelated businesses will underperform firms that expand through related diversification. Nonetheless, big platform businesses such as Alphabet-Google, Amazon, Alibaba, and Tencent, as well as Yahoo in prior years (it is now owned by Verizon), tend to have both integrated and conglomerate-like investments in their portfolios.

INNOVATION + TRANSACTION

The main reason why innovation platforms add transaction platform capabilities (in other words, a marketplace) is to facilitate and control the distribution channel of complements. Transaction features create value for the complementors by offering them a distribution infrastructure. At the same time, the companies can capture a larger part of the value created. Innovation platforms are relatively useless without applications and digital content, and the best and cheapest way to increase applications is to encourage third-party developers to innovate and then make distribution easy through integrated app stores.

Before the Internet, few companies combined innovation and transaction platforms. But in the last two decades, several innovation platforms added a transaction dimension soon after launching. Apple added its App Store about eight months after launching the iPhone. Google launched its app store (Google Play) about a year after it started licensing Android. Learning from these other examples, Amazon launched its app store for the Alexa home-speaker AI device along with introduction of the new platform. (See Chapter 7.) We should note that the Palm personal digital assistant (PDA), a precursor of the smartphone popular in the late 1990s, also launched an app store accessible through the web, so Apple was not first.[32]

App stores and digital content stores can generate significant additional revenue for innovation platforms and complementors. Apple and Google took a 30 percent cut from apps sold on their respective app stores. In 2017, Apple's App Store revenues reached $11.5 billion, while app developers received payments amounting to $26.5 billion.[33] Although Google also charged 30 percent in 2018, Google began its app store taking only a 20 percent cut in order to provide a bit more incentive for developers to write apps for Android.

TRANSACTION + INNOVATION

The main reason why transaction platforms add an innovation platform side to their business (in other words, they open their APIs and some customer data to outside firms) is to stimulate innovation by third parties. More apps or features generally make the transaction platforms a more compelling experience for users and create additional opportunities for monetization, such as to sell more advertisements or take different types of transaction fees. The data generated by the transaction platform on user behavior also becomes a valuable asset that the platform company and third parties such as advertisers can leverage to better understand user behavior and needs, or to design marketing strategies aimed at generating cross-side network effects among the platforms.

We mentioned before that Facebook made itself more compelling by enabling access to millions of applications and websites. This openness can also backfire, as we saw in the case of Cambridge Analytica as well as later revelations on how much data Facebook collected from users (often without explicit permission) and then provided to advertisers and app developers.[34] In general, though, as Microsoft and other companies discovered long ago, becoming a hybrid with an innovation platform function allows transaction platforms to add new capabilities or features without high internal R&D costs. Instead, they can access the external supply of creativity and software engineering skills available worldwide. But sometimes adding the second platform is more an act of desperation. Snapchat, for example, has struggled with competition from Facebook's Instagram. In 2018 it opened up its APIs to encourage third parties to build complementary innovations in the hope that some new apps would make Snapchat a more compelling experience for users and a better draw for advertisers.[35]

Besides Facebook and Snapchat, a less obvious transaction-to-innovation hybrid example was Expedia, the travel services platform. When Expedia established an affiliate program under the banner of "Your Business. Our Technology," it opened up a set of APIs. The APIs allowed outside companies to add hotel, flight, and car booking capabilities to their own applications. The Expedia APIs also made it possible for external developers to build applications that used Expedia's transaction capabilities, which supported over thirty currencies and ten different types of credit card payments. In addition to offering access to its transaction technology, the Expedia APIs made it possible for third parties to access the platform's "rich content," such as over 11 million images of property, 6.5 million room images, 100 characteristics per room, and 380,000 geography destinations, all supported in over thirty-five languages.[36]

INTEGRATED VS. CONGLOMERATE HYBRIDS

Some hybrid companies integrate their two types of platforms more closely than others. Apple, for example, tightly connected its main innovation platform (the iOS operating system for the iPhone and iPad) with its transaction platform (the App Store) and online store (iTunes), as well as other services (iCloud, iBooks, etc.). Icons for the App Store and iTunes come bundled on the iPhone boot-up screen, and product registration includes registration for apps and content, with some additional information requests, such as for a credit card. Tight integration has multiple benefits: The App Store provides a distribution channel allowing iPhone app developers to access the vast pool of iPhone and iPad users. The integration creates value for the app developers who want to sell their apps. Providing complementors and content providers with a global distribution channel increases their incentives to remain active within the Apple ecosystem and keep developing new apps and content for Apple. The existence of the App Store keeps end users interested in buying new iPhones and iPads, since a continuing stream of new apps and content makes the devices increasingly versatile and attractive. Benefits go in the other direction as well: The App Store generates increasingly large revenues and profits from the distribution of software, digital services, and digital content, which Apple hopes will one day encompass a very significant portion of the company's business.

Hybrid platform strategies provide other strategic benefits when they work well. They raise barriers to entry for innovation platform competition because it takes time for competitors to build a portfolio of apps and a developer ecosystem. Hybrid strategies also weaken competitors by giving the platform owner power to exclude rivals, although they need to be careful not to run afoul of antitrust regulation. (We return to this theme in Chapter 6.) For example, Android is open source and free to license, but Google imposed tight restrictions on smartphone makers who wanted to offer access to Google Play (the largest marketplace for Android apps). Smartphone makers needed to obtain a license for Google Mobile Services, which meant accepting a stringent (and ever-growing) list of device-centric requirements, with an obligation to continuously validate their devices against "Google's compatibility test suite."[37] Google Mobile Services included extremely popular apps such as YouTube, Gmail, Google Maps, and Google Docs. Smartphone makers who did not use the Google-approved version of Android had a hard time passing these compatibility tests and finding alternative services.

Google also has done more than simply tie Android apps to its Android operating system and services. In the early days of Android, vendors could introduce some variations into the free and open-source Android code and build their own apps. This led to some separate and incompatible ecosystems and allowed handset makers such as Samsung and Xiaomi to capture more value for themselves. However, Google wanted to prevent these "forks" in the Android software and their incompatible applications. No doubt Google also wanted to prevent other companies from drawing away advertisements or software sales. Consequently, Google moved the APIs for apps development from the Android operating system to the Google Play store itself. Since 2012, most developers now build their Android apps to be compatible with the "Google Play Services APIs." Google can also update this API layer independently of operating system updates (which smartphone manufacturers, not Google, control).

Making the Google Play Store into the applications platform was an elegant solution to the problem of Android fragmentation and potential loss of revenues for Google. Some of these tactics have run afoul of European antitrust regulators, however, and Google responded by changing some of its policies. Nonetheless, having both types of platforms and integrating them closely was a competitive advantage that Google had versus its rivals.[38]

Amazon is another case of a hybrid platform company with different levels of integration, albeit with economies of scale and scope even in seemingly unrelated businesses. The Amazon online store (new products that Amazon is selling or reselling) and Amazon Marketplace (which sells third-party goods, new and used) both offer the same types of goods. As users see only one interface screen, the network effects from the marketplace business directly reinforce the online store business. The two businesses also run on the same digital infrastructure, powered by Amazon Web Services (AWS), and collect and analyze customer transaction data. At the same time, AWS is a separate transaction and innovation platform for companies that want to rent cloud services and utilize bundled features and software engineering tools as an applications development environment. Then we have the Kindle and Alexa devices, which are separate transaction and innovation platforms, although both connect users to the Amazon online store and the Amazon marketplace to buy digital books and other goods.

The top hybrid companies in China also expanded from one platform type to the second type and operated their platforms and other businesses with different degrees of integration. Many Chinese users do not use personal computers or credit cards very frequently, so Chinese companies in some sense have leapfrogged these technologies. They have made the smartphone and applications like WeChat into a single platform for many activities and services. Tencent provides a good illustration. It started out in 1998 with a messaging platform (QQ) for Chinese users of personal computers, and generated income from advertising and a premium messaging service. From 2004, it expanded into developing and hosting online games for a fee. When mobile devices became popular, Tencent evolved QQ into WeChat, which added social media functions to the messaging app. WeChat today has over a billion subscribers. Tencent also evolved WeChat into a popular innovation platform. Tencent as well as third-party firms use WeChat APIs to build a wide variety of apps, offering services such as electronic payments as well as video games and ride sharing. (Tencent, as well as Alibaba, are investors in Didi Chuxing, which acquired Uber's Chinese ride-sharing operations.) Tencent also closely integrated WeChat with its game development and hosting platform. In terms of the business model, WeChat makes money by investing the cash that users deposit in their electronic payment accounts.[39] It also earns fees from video games and sending customers to its partners such as Didi Chuxing and JD.com, a major Chinese online shopping platform in which Tencent invested in 2014.

KEY TAKEAWAYS FOR MANAGERS AND ENTREPRENEURS

In this chapter, we discussed the differences between innovation and transaction platforms and how they followed the same steps in building their platforms: Identify platform market sides, solve the chicken-or-egg problem to launch and generate network effects, find a workable business model, and establish governance rules to determine who is allowed to do what through the platform. We also discussed hybrid platform strategies that combine innovation and transaction platforms or functions within the same firm. So, when it comes to selecting your platform strategy and business model, what are the key takeaways for managers and entrepreneurs?

First, and most obvious, is the need to *understand the strengths and weaknesses, as well as the potential costs and benefits, of the two*

different types of platforms. For example, successful innovation platforms are rare because they sit in the middle of enormous ecosystems with thousands, millions, and even billions of participating
firms and individual users. The world can support only so many
of these powerful innovation platforms, even though the platform
concept may be cheap to introduce (such as when a product firm
opens up its APIs to third-party firms). More often, innovation platforms are very expensive and risky to build from scratch (such as
to create a new mass-market operating system or cloud-computing
infrastructure). About 60 to 70 percent of start-up firms and billion-
dollar unicorns were transaction platforms. Why? It seems easier
and cheaper for entrepreneurs to create transaction platforms because they are relatively simple to build on a technical level and they
can provide value in many different markets, ranging from sharing
cars and rooms to sharing household tools and pets. Innovation
platforms, by contrast, require the creation of a core technology
that can serve as a foundation for other firms to build complementary products and services. This type of platform was most common
in markets for software and hardware system technologies. Consequently, we mainly hear about innovation platforms for computers,
smartphones, consumer electronics, video game development, and
cloud-based hosting and application development environments.
Nonetheless, the fact that transaction platforms like Amazon, Facebook, Tencent (WeChat), Uber, and Airbnb were adding innovation platform functions suggested that managers and entrepreneurs
should take a much broader view of where they can build useful innovation platforms.

Second, *innovation platforms can enable "open innovation" in a
variety of settings.* They can be an effective way for companies to enhance the value of their products and services with relatively small
in-house investments compared to the potential benefits from
thousands or even millions of third-party innovations. Not surprisingly, despite their relative rarity, we see new innovation platforms

emerging. IBM was trying to turn its Watson AI technology into a new consulting service as well as an innovation platform by building partnerships with application developers at companies and universities, especially for health care applications.[40] General Electric opened up its Predix operating system to other firms, encouraging them to build products and services for the Internet of things.[41] (We explore this case in Chapter 5.) We also have some open general-purpose technologies emerging as potentially new innovation platforms. Blockchain is a good example. This was once associated with Bitcoin, the cryptocurrency (also a kind of transaction platform technology). Various firms were starting to use blockchain software to track different types of transactions over the Internet, including shipments of food as well as transfers of money and confidential documents.[42]

Third, managers and entrepreneurs in many more industries probably need to give serious thought to *combining innovation and transaction functions—adopting a hybrid strategy.* It is clear to us that hybrids are the next phase in the evolution of platform thinking. They push even further the logic of what makes a platform such a powerful strategic weapon. Platforms are all about leveraging complementarities among existing assets and organizational capabilities. Sometimes the goal is to take advantage of user engagement to make customers more attractive to other market sides, such as advertisers or application developers. At other times, the goal is to leverage a shared asset by making it available to third parties for their own innovations.

But while both innovation and transaction platforms create value through increasing the use of existing assets, hybrids take leverage a step further. This is especially the case when hybrids use their expertise in digital technology to facilitate integration between various software-based services and allow the use or reuse of software modules and user data. Not surprisingly, hybrids seemed to work best when companies designed them so that the transaction and innovation platforms were integrated and took advantage of each other, technologically and strategically. Digital conglomerates with weakly connected or unrelated businesses should not have any particular advantages over traditional conglomerates. Yahoo comes to mind since it evolved from a web directory service into a hodge-podge of Internet properties (search, email, shopping, news, sports and financial information, etc.) selling mostly generic ads, with different user bases and minimal network effects.[43] However, as we have seen at Amazon, Google, Alibaba, and Tencent, hybrid firms can create new types of "relatedness." They can centralize customer data and analytics for cross-platform marketing and advertising. They can also take advantage of enormous scale and scope economies by using the same digital infrastructure to power and connect multiple platforms and other online businesses such as digital stores.

We also need to remember that strong network effects are difficult to generate and healthy business models tend to elude most platform ventures. The most common mistakes managers and entrepreneurs make when launching new platforms is the subject of the next chapter.

COMMON MISTAKES

MISPRICING, MISTRUST, MISTIMING—AND HUBRIS

PATTERNS IN PLATFORM FAILURES

MISPRICING, ON ONE
SIDE OF THE PLATFORM

MISTRUST, ESPECIALLY IN
TRANSACTION PLATFORMS

HUBRIS, OR DISMISSING THE COMPETITION

MISTIMING, OR FAILURE TO ACT
BEFORE THE MARKET TIPS

KEY TAKEAWAYS FOR MANAGERS
AND ENTREPRENEURS

CHAPTER 4

The inevitable result of pundits proclaiming a digital revolution has been a mad rush into the platform business. Similar to the first dot.com boom of the 1990s, there has been a predictable drive to become the first and the largest new platform in every space. It looks like a land grab, where companies feel they have to be the first mover to secure a new territory, exploit network effects, and raise barriers to entry for future players. Uber's frenetic efforts to conquer every city in the world at breakneck speeds and Airbnb's desire to create the platform for sharing rooms all over the world are the two most obvious recent examples.

The problem is that being the first mover has never been a guarantee of success in platforms or non-platform businesses. Some early movers, such as Amazon in e-commerce or Apple in a new generation of smartphones, have translated into powerful positions. However, the platform world has been littered by the failure of first movers in almost every category. Sidecar—not Uber—pioneered the ride-sharing market; VRBO and numerous vacation rental platforms—not Airbnb—pioneered the rental room market; Friendster and MySpace—not Facebook—pioneered and dramatically expanded social networking.

The power behind the myth of the first mover is FOMO: the fear of missing out. In markets where someone solves the chicken-or-egg problem and network effects kick in (like the Yellow Pages or Google Search), the consequences of failure can be devastating: Losers get locked out of markets indefinitely. But more often than not, first movers stumble. Friendster is a good example. It built a huge social network before Mark Zuckerberg, but Friendster made poor technology choices, which did not scale. Frustration with Friendster, which could take up to twelve seconds to load a single web page, left open the window for Facebook to explode onto the scene. eBay, which dominated e-commerce in the United States, was also the first mover in China. While eBay quickly grabbed a dominant share of the Chinese market, Alibaba overwhelmed it within a few years. Netscape captured 80 percent of the early browser market in the mid-1990s, yet it was crushed by Microsoft; then Microsoft had over 90 percent of the market, and ended up losing leadership in recent years to Firefox and then Google's Chrome.

PATTERNS IN PLATFORM FAILURES

To understand why and how platforms fail, we tried to identify as many failed American platforms as possible over the last twenty years. We reviewed the annual reports and proxy statements of the innovation and transaction platform companies that we analyzed in our database (see Chapter 1 and Data Appendix) and made a list of the competing platform companies they mentioned. The 209 failures that we found, while by no means exhaustive, allow us to make some general observations about why platforms struggle.

First, as shown in Appendix tables 4-1 and 4-2, the most obvious pattern is the predominance of failed transaction platforms, representing nearly 85 percent of the sample. Transaction platforms have a somewhat shorter life as well, averaging 4.6 years, compared to 7.4 and 5 years for the hybrid and innovation platforms we identified, respectively. Not surprisingly, many platforms, like Friendster, failed because they were weak platforms: Their technologies were outdated or their user interfaces were complicated and hard to use. Especially for transaction platforms, the barriers to entry for starting a marketplace have been low, and these platforms often failed because they could never get enough market participants on one or more sides of the platform to achieve positive network effects and take off. Many gig-economy platforms collapsed within two to three years because they did not have enough users and ran out of funding. One of the challenges for those firms in the local delivery and services space or in ride hailing was that the network effects were local, but the only way to rapidly get to scale and build brand recognition was to expand geographically. To do so required attracting more investment and having deep enough pockets to go potentially a long time before reaching profitability and positive cash flow.

Given the need for deep pockets, it should not be surprising that stand-alone firms tended to have shorter lives than those that were acquired or launched as part of a larger firm or consortium of firms. Overcoming chicken-or-egg problems was apparently much more challenging for stand-alone firms, which had an average duration of only 3.7 years. Acquired firms, which generally had stronger balance sheets, were capable of fighting longer (average 7.4 years), while firms that were part of larger entities averaged 4.9 years.

Consolidation was also a common pattern among platforms in the same space. Platforms frequently disappeared because they merged. This was especially true in certain categories. For example, a wave of acquisitions reduced the large number of web portals and search engines that emerged in the 1990s down to a few players by the mid-2000s. More recently, peer-to-peer car-sharing platforms saw consolidation as larger rivals acquired two major platforms. In addition, there was considerable consolidation among business-to-business marketplaces that emerged in the 1990s dedicated to specific verticals—such as exchanges for airplane parts, medical supplies, or chemicals.

In a relatively small number of platform spaces, failure was a function of a genuine winner-take-all or winner-take-most outcome for a competitor, even without an assist from government regulation. Mobile operating systems and social networking applications were prime examples, which we discuss later in this chapter. No third mobile operating system gained significant share since the market tipped to iOS and Android, despite the fact that competitors like BlackBerry, Windows, and Symbian entered the market first and had significant resources at their disposal. Similarly, in social networking, Facebook displaced earlier rivals like MySpace, Friendster, and GeoCities as the market tipped.

Social networking illustrated another pattern: Failing platforms sometimes sought out a niche in order to survive. The results, however, were mixed. For example, Ello pivoted from a general social network to a niche social network as a space for creative collaboration where artists could display their work and receive feedback from other artists. Though iVillage failed, it survived for a long time (eighteen years) with a focus on women, admittedly a very large niche. Disney's Club Penguin survived for twelve years until 2017 with a focus on kids, while Path tried a geographic focus on Asia. On the other hand, Kinly, a private social network for families, never took off and folded after two years.

Failure as a platform did not necessarily mean failure as a company. A number of online marketplaces (especially B2B) that failed to generate sufficient trading volume pivoted into adjacent businesses. One example is seafood.com, which launched in 1996 as a news service for the seafood industry. In 1999, it added both wholesale and retail marketplaces to the site, while continuing to provide industry news, including a subscription news service. In 2012, it dropped the marketplace and reverted to the news-only site, supported both by advertising and subscription revenue; as of 2018, it continued to operate as an industry news service. Another example was Exostar, launched in 2000 by Raytheon, Boeing, Lockheed Martin, and BAE Systems as an independent marketplace for the aerospace and defense industry. Over time, it pivoted away from its marketplace function and positioned itself to foster supply-chain collaboration in the industry, and later for a variety of industries. By 2018, Exostar had shifted its business model to one of "helping organizations in highly-regulated industries mitigate risk, solve identity and access challenges, and collaborate securely across their supply chain ecosystem."[1]

Other failed platforms faced challenges common to many businesses. A number of platforms emerged before the underlying infrastructure was available to sustain them. For instance, several broadcast streaming or online gaming platforms, including Mpath, broadcast.com, and globalmedia.com, launched around the turn of the century before broadband was widely available. More recently, two digital asset exchanges failed after a short time due to low trading volumes, as the number of people wishing to exchange Bitcoin for other currencies remained too small. Because platforms often brought a new model and structure to existing businesses, they often ran into problems with the legal and regulatory regimes. Uber and Airbnb have famously tangled with local regulators in various cities where they have done business. Other platform companies did not survive regulatory scrutiny. For example, AirPooler and Flytenow, aviation ride-sharing platforms that connected passengers with private pilots who had empty seats on their planes, both shut down in 2015 after the FAA ruled they were engaged in commercial aviation and would have to be regulated as such. In San Francisco, the on-demand valet service Vatler ran afoul of local permitting regulations and had to shut down after barely a year of existence.

As the aggregate data suggests, sources of failure are numerous. Firms fail all the time. Marshall Van Alstyne, Geoffrey Parker, and Sangeet Choudary, for example, offered six reasons that platforms can fail: failure to optimize "openness," engage developers, share the surplus, launch the right side, put critical mass ahead of money, and have the right imagination.[2] We agree that these are important reasons why platforms do not succeed, but we take a slightly different approach in this chapter that is less general. We focus on four common mistakes that lead platforms to fail as businesses: (1) mispricing on one side of the market, (2) failure to develop trust with users and partners, (3) prematurely dismissing the competition, and (4) entering too late—that is, after a market with very strong network effects and other conditions amenable to a winner-take-all-or-most outcome has tipped. We also explore the most important lessons to learn from companies that came close to winning but never crossed the finish line. What are the lessons of failed platforms that got off the ground, had big starts, but then were unable to tip or hold the market? We also examine the opposite challenge of entering the fray too late. While first movers frequently slip up, that doesn't mean a manager can sit back and wait. Once a firm overcomes the chicken-or-egg problems and network effects begin to kick in, delay can be deadly.

The bottom line for managers and entrepreneurs is that platforms have to avoid the most common, devastating mistakes, or even those that were early winners can quickly become losers.

MISPRICING, ON ONE SIDE OF THE PLATFORM

Pricing decisions have been extensively studied by platform researchers, yet managers still get them wrong. The key insight, which we explored in earlier chapters, is that a platform often requires underwriting one side of the market to encourage the other side to participate. Knowing which side gets charged and which side gets subsidized may be the single most important strategic decision for any platform. The challenges become even more acute when rival platforms face intense competition. Good, commonsense pricing may have to be thrown out the window when two or more platforms are racing to create a network effect.

A classic example of a first mover's failure to appreciate this pricing problem was Sidecar's missteps in the taxi market. In August 2015, San Francisco–based ride-sharing platform Sidecar announced it would "pivot" to begin focusing primarily on same-day deliveries. It had introduced this service earlier in the year to supplement its main peer-to-peer ride-sharing business. The company anticipated that the majority of revenues going forward would come from deliveries of food, flowers, and even medical marijuana rather than rides, a tacit admission that it had lost its battle to compete with the larger and more well-known ride-hailing platforms Uber and Lyft.[3] That pivot failed to pay off, and the company announced it would suspend operations entirely on December 31. The next month it announced that it had sold the bulk of its assets and licensed its intellectual property to General Motors, which was in the process of developing its own transportation service.[4]

Sidecar never became a household name. Its failure was nonetheless significant because Sidecar had pioneered the peer-to-peer ride-sharing model before Uber and Lyft transitioned their start-ups into the space. By 2015, ride-sharing platforms—where smartphone apps connected riders with nonprofessional drivers operating their personal vehicles—had become a pillar of the sharing, or gig, economy, despite the fact that such platforms had only existed for three years.

Sidecar's cofounder and CEO, Sunil Paul, claimed to have had the idea for such a service as far back as 1998 and received a patent for mobile ride hailing over a wireless network in 2002.[5] Paul developed the idea into Sidecar, which he founded in January 2012. The company began beta testing its ride-sharing service in San Francisco the next month and launched the service publicly that June. Riders requested a ride by entering their pickup and drop-off locations through the Sidecar app on their smartphones. A nearby driver would accept the request, and pick up and drop off the rider, who made payment through the app. No cash or other form of payment changed hands. In announcing the launch of the service, Sunil Paul claimed that "Sidecar is more than just the easiest way to get around the city. We have created a platform for the first crowd-sourced transportation network."[6] Over the next few years, Sidecar expanded slowly and was available in about a dozen cities across the United States by 2015, including Los Angeles, Seattle, Austin, Chicago, Charlotte, Washington, D.C., Brooklyn, and Boston.

On Sidecar's platform, payment was initially an optional "contri-bution" to the driver; the app provided information to riders about average donations to help them decide how much to contribute if they chose to do so. Sidecar (and competitor Lyft, which adopted the same payment model) claimed that since they only supplied the technology to connect riders and drivers, they were not a transpor-tation company and should not face the same regulatory require-ments as taxis and livery services. Defining payments as donations also allowed drivers to circumvent expanded insurance coverage requirements imposed on commercial vehicles like taxis and limos (although whether insurance companies would see things the same way was unclear).[7] The donation model proved unworkable, and in November 2013, in response to driver feedback, Sidecar dropped it in favor of set fares established when the passenger booked the ride. In announcing the change, Paul said that drivers had "told us loud and clear they would drive more frequently and take longer ride re-quests if they could reliably depend on fair payment every trip."[8]

Similar to any new platform, Sidecar had to figure out how to price their service to both sides of the market: providers and con-sumers. Pricing, in this case, meant more than who gets something for nothing and who pays. Ultimately, when platforms face intense competition from other platforms, successful platforms need to at-tract the critical resources to their platform—and keep them en-gaged. For livery services, that meant drivers. And as competing platforms emerged beyond the traditional taxi and car services, Sidecar failed to get the pricing right.

Just two months after Sidecar launched, a start-up called Zim-ride introduced a new peer-to-peer ride-sharing service named Lyft, also based in San Francisco. Zimride had been in business since 2007, operating a long-distance carpooling service that connected riders to drivers using Facebook. Initially marketed to college cam-puses and businesses as a way to facilitate carpooling for students and employees, Zimride had been largely unsuccessful in marketing its service to the general public. In 2010, Zimride hit upon the idea of local peer-to-peer ride sharing and developed it into Lyft, which launched in 2012. Lyft quickly eclipsed Zimride's existing long-distance carpooling business and became its main source of revenue and the company's major focus. Zimride reincorporated as Lyft in March 2013 and then, in July, sold its original Zimride business to car rental giant Enterprise.[9]

Meanwhile, things were getting worse for Sidecar: In 2013, Uber introduced its own peer-to-peer ride-sharing service. Uber, also based in San Francisco, had been in business since 2010, when it started as a way to request and pay for a traditional black town car using a smartphone app. By the time Sidecar launched in mid-2012, Uber had expanded to seventeen cities. Its model differed from Sidecar and Lyft in that Uber at that time partnered with existing taxi and car services, so its drivers were professional drivers, including the lower-cost UberX service introduced in July 2012. Recognizing the threat from Sidecar and Lyft, which could offer lower prices because of the reduced licensing and insurance costs faced by nonprofessional drivers, Uber responded. In September, Uber CEO Travis Kalanick told an interviewer, "If somebody's out there and has a competitive advantage in getting supply, that's a problem. I'm not going to just let that happen without doing something about it. . . . Uber started out at the high end originally, but the question is can you create a low-cost Uber? Uber has to become a low-cost Uber as well."[10] In April 2013, Uber announced it would begin offering ride-sharing services from nonprofessional drivers using their personal vehicles in cities where Sidecar and Lyft operated and began rolling out the platform under the UberX name that summer.

Despite its first-mover status, Sidecar expanded much more slowly than its rivals and was eventually squeezed out of the market. In the absence of competition, Sidecar's strategy might have worked. But the frenetic pace of growth, especially by Uber, eliminated Sidecar's first-mover advantage. By mid-2015, Uber had expanded to 300 cities around the world and had signed up its one-millionth driver, including over 150,000 active UberX drivers in the United States, and claimed to cover 75 percent of the U.S. population.[11] Lyft had expanded to 65 cities with 100,000 drivers, all in the United States, by March 2015.[12]

With Uber and Lyft in the market, competition for drivers and riders was fierce. Both Uber and Lyft aggressively recruited drivers, offering cash bonuses of up to $500 or even $1,000 for drivers who switched from another ride-sharing platform, including Sidecar. Current drivers also received bonuses by referring drivers from another platform. Riders received credits for their first ride and additional credits when they referred other riders. Uber and Lyft periodically cut fares to attract riders. Although the companies claimed that increased ridership would more than make up for the reduced fares in putting money in drivers' pockets, they took additional steps to avoid alienating drivers when they cut fares. When Uber cut its fares by 20 percent in January 2014, for instance, it reduced its commission on each ride from 20 percent to 5 percent until April, when it raised its commission back to 20 percent on the new, lower fares. Lyft followed suit, dropping its fares by 20 percent in April 2014, and reducing its commission to zero. On and off again subsidies for drivers increased the number available on both Uber and Lyft.

Uber and Lyft both lost money as they pursued aggressive growth strategies and incurred enormous costs just to find and replace drivers. For example, as we noted in Chapter 3, Uber in 2017 lost $4.5 billion despite gross booking revenues of $37 billion. Although Lyft and Uber were primarily targeting each other in their aggressive strategies, Sidecar was caught in the cross fire and attempted to match some of its rivals' tactics to induce more drivers to use its platform. In early 2015, it was giving $100 bonuses to new drivers, had dropped its commissions to zero in some markets, and offered guaranteed hourly minimums and bonuses for driving during peak Friday and Saturday night hours.[13] But it simply did not have the capital to compete at the scale of its rivals. Once Sidecar fell behind in recruiting drivers and riders, network effects made it extremely difficult to compete.

Lyft and Uber were able to sustain their aggressive growth strategies because they had raised billions of dollars in equity capital. By contrast, Sidecar had raised only $39 million by the end of 2015, creating what Sunil Paul called a "significant capital disadvantage" when announcing that Sidecar was suspending operations in December 2015.[14] He would later write that "the legacy of Sidecar is that we out-innovated Uber but still failed to win the market. We failed—for the most part—because Uber is willing to win at any cost and they have practically limitless capital to do it."[15] Earlier, when announcing Sidecar's decision to "pivot" from ride sharing to deliveries in August 2015, he cited the challenge of attracting drivers and riders with relatively little capital: "We were outraised. We have been outgunned in capital from the beginning. Customer acquisition and driver acquisition in this category are very expensive, and it does make a big difference when you offer promotions—$500 for a driver, or $20 credit—versus our more typical $5 offerings of credit."[16]

Sidecar's failure to keep up with Uber and Lyft in raising capital was a strategic blunder: Management misread the competition, misread the critical role of a supply side (drivers) for a platform market, and missed the logic of network effects. Sidecar deliberately pursued a conservative slow-growth strategy in its efforts to be fiscally responsible. As one early investor commented, "For most companies, the problem they have now is they raised too much money and the valuations are too high. . . . Sidecar was always very disciplined."[17] Perhaps Sidecar's fatal flaw was not recognizing the importance of attracting both sides of the platform—drivers *and* riders. Sidecar focused its energy on innovation—it was the first to introduce several new features such as inputting the destination when requesting a ride, shared rides, and a marketplace model where drivers set their own prices. But this meant that it spent less than its competitors on building a great platform by spending to attract drivers and market aggressively. As one analyst put it, "Sidecar was more of a technology company than it was a marketing company. Its feature set has been very exemplary, but I don't know that it used the same brainpower to create market share."[18]

Despite being crushed by Uber, Paul offered some grudging respect to his rival: "In some ways, I'm proud of Uber. They were able to take the ride-sharing innovation, rebrand it as UberX, and grow it and scale it like clearly no one else was able to—us or Lyft. It shows that our idea really does work. We're still proud of the authorship even if it ends up being executed by someone else."[19]

Of course, the jury was still out on Uber, as well as Lyft and other ride-sharing platforms that relied heavily on driver and rider subsidies. Beyond its enormous expenses and financial losses, Uber had to contend with new attempts to impose a minimum wage and regulate the number of drivers. In August 2018, for example, the New York City Council voted to put a hold on the number of licenses granted to ride-sharing firms for one year. In addition, the city imposed rules to assure that drivers were paid a minimum wage. Low compensation for taxi as well as ride-sharing drivers, along with a collapse in taxi medallion values, were causing severe financial hardships for both conventional taxi drivers (including six suicides) and ride-sharing drivers. Uber's strategy to counter the new regulations was to persuade drivers from Lyft and taxi companies to drive for Uber. It was not yet clear how this move would play out.[20]

In the long run, Uber seemed to be following a strategy similar to Amazon's initial strategy: Get as big as possible as fast as possible, continue to grow or diversify into related businesses that leveraged the same platform, and worry about profits later. In December 2018, Uber also filed documents in preparation for an initial public offering, tentatively scheduled for early 2019 to raise additional cash.[21] If conventional taxi companies and smaller platform competitors went bankrupt or closed down, and if Uber continued to shed its most unprofitable operations, such as in overseas markets, it might well be possible to earn a profit someday. At present, however, Uber lacks a truly profitable division like Amazon Web Services to compensate for its massive subsidies and operating expenses, making profitability harder for Uber to achieve.

MISTRUST, ESPECIALLY IN TRANSACTION PLATFORMS

Getting the pricing right is always important. But while getting the price right is necessary in any platform, it is not sufficient for success. Transaction platforms also require two or more parties, who may or may not know each other, to connect. In such a world, *building trust* is essential. Facebook and LinkedIn, for example, try to build trust by connecting you through friends or business associates; many e-commerce platforms attempt to build trust through rating systems, payment mechanisms, or insurance. In the absence of trust, the players on the platform have to make a leap of faith.

Sidecar was a start-up, and this helps explain why it missed an important platform dynamic. However, eBay had fewer excuses for mistakes that it made, especially in China. eBay was the quintessential e-commerce platform company of the new era: It was *the* leader in e-commerce platforms at the turn of the century. By 2002, it was the largest online auction site in the world and was the third-ranked website in terms of time spent on the site by users.[22] It generated $1.2 billion in revenue on gross merchandise sales (the total value of sales transacted on the site) of nearly $15 billion in 2002. At the end of the year, the company reported nearly 62 million users and over 638 million items listed for sale on its site. The market value stood at over $21 billion.[23]

Yet eBay's entry into China was another classic failure of a first mover. It is to the credit of Meg Whitman, then CEO of eBay, that she began expanding to international markets in 1999. By 2002, she had set her sights on China, buying a third of the Chinese consumer auction site EachNet for $30 million and then purchasing the rest for $150 million the following year. Whitman rebranded the company as eBay EachNet. Founded in 1999, EachNet more or less imitated eBay in style and content and, at the time of the acquisition, dominated China's online auction market with more than 80 percent share. (See Figure 4-1.)

Given eBay's success in tipping the market for auctions in the United States, eBay EachNet looked poised to do the same thing in China. It had a dominant share in a rapidly growing space. Moreover, Whitman identified China as a priority for the company's growth, stating in February 2005 that "market leadership in China will be a defining characteristic of leadership globally." She later told *Time* magazine that "China is unique. It is growing rapidly, and it has a tremendous amount of potential, which is why we have made it a priority for the company."[24] By the end of 2006, eBay had invested $300 million in its Chinese operations, yet it had essentially admitted defeat and yielded the Chinese online market to its major rival.

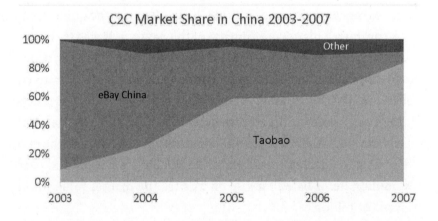

FIGURE 4-1: **CHINA'S ONLINE CONSUMER-TO-CONSUMER MARKET SHARES, 2003–2007**
Source: Compiled from iResearch data, various years, http://www.iresearch china.com/content/details8_19183.html, accessed August 1, 2018.

Why did eBay, the first mover, fail? As in the case of Sidecar, the story begins with competition and getting the pricing right. When eBay entered China, Alibaba was the largest player in the Chinese e-commerce world. Founded in 1999, Alibaba was, like eBay, an online marketplace. It did not own and sell inventory; rather, it facilitated transactions between third-party buyers and sellers, taking a commission on each sale. Alibaba differed from eBay in that it focused on business-to-business (B2B) transactions, providing a platform for small and medium-sized enterprises in China. eBay, on the other hand, focused primarily on the consumer-to-consumer (C2C) market. Despite the distinction, Alibaba's CEO Jack Ma saw eBay's entrance into China as a major threat to Alibaba's business. He recognized that the distinction between B2B and C2C commerce on the Internet was a blurry one. If eBay gained a foothold in the C2C market, it would be a short step for small businesses to list their wares on eBay to sell to both consumers and other small businesses and eat into Alibaba's business.

To respond to the challenge posed by eBay, Ma and Alibaba took on the American firm head-on, launching a rival C2C marketplace called Taobao ("hunting for treasure"). The two auction sites were initially identical in many ways. In fact, Taobao's first web pages were copied directly from eBay's design. But Alibaba quickly pivoted, recognizing that one cannot win a platform battle with a me-too product. Perhaps Jack Ma's first critical decision was to make Taobao's service free to buyers and sellers; unlike eBay, it did not charge listing fees or commissions. Ma was willing to lose money on Taobao, funding the site through cash generated by Alibaba's other businesses and concentrating on building market share. eBay, at least initially, followed its existing model of charging listing fees and commissions on each transaction. In addition, Taobao did not emphasize the auction model but rather direct sales: Only 10 percent of its listings were auctions, compared to 40 percent for eBay Each-Net.[25] Alibaba/Taobao recognized, in the words of one executive, that "what our customers really wanted, we realized, was simply a storefront for selling their products."[26] There was another difference: While eBay initially did not let buyers and sellers interact directly (perhaps fearing they would take their transaction off-line and avoid paying eBay's commission), Taobao encouraged buyers and sellers to communicate with each other and added instant messaging to the website, allowing buyers and sellers to build trust.

For any transaction platform to be successful, trust is essential. Online payments represented another important area of difference. In 2004, Alibaba launched its own online payment system called Alipay, similar to PayPal, which eBay had acquired shortly before entering the Chinese market. Alipay, unlike PayPal, used an escrow model. At the time of a transaction, funds would go into an escrow account and be released only after the buyer had received and inspected the item, which was important in a culture where trust and security were an issue. In addition, at a time when only a small fraction of Chinese consumers had credit cards, Alipay also formed partnerships with leading banks and the *China Post* so that customers without a debit or credit card could fund their Alipay accounts with cash at one of its 66,000 offices.[27] Alipay also exploited the fact that a Chinese-owned payment processing system faced far fewer regulatory restrictions from the Chinese government.[28]

Despite eBay's advantages, including its big balance sheet, global e-commerce platform, and the fact that EachNet was the leading online C2C auction site in China, Taobao had surpassed eBay on a variety of measures by 2005. By August 2005, Taobao was reaching 15,800 out of every 1 million Internet users in China, compared to under 10,000 for eBay.[29] User satisfaction was also higher for Taobao than for eBay—77 percent to 62 percent.[30] In the first quarter of 2005, Taobao's gross merchandise volume (GMV) surpassed eBay's for the first time—$120 million compared to $90 million for eBay, a remarkable feat considering that eBay's GMV was ten times that of Taobao at the beginning of 2004.[31]

eBay suffered a further blow in August 2005 when Yahoo invested $1 billion in Alibaba and handed over its China operations to Alibaba in return for a 40 percent stake in the company. The capital infusion obviously strengthened Alibaba in its fight with eBay, in part by enabling it to continue to offer Taobao's platform for free. At the time, eBay pledged to continue the fight, with Whitman calling China "a perfect market for eBay."[32] By March 2006, however, Taobao had become the market leader in China's online C2C market with a 67 percent market share, and Alibaba CEO Jack Ma declared that "the competition is over."[33] eBay admitted defeat a few months later when, in December 2006, it effectively withdrew from China, shutting down its Chinese website while forming a joint venture with Hong Kong–based Internet portal TOM Online, which had less than 10 percent share of the Chinese market by 2010.[34]

Why did eBay fail in China? In retrospect, it appears that eBay did many things wrong compared to Taobao. For example, eBay integrated EachNet into its global platform and global brand identity, reproducing the look and feel of eBay's website and eliminating localized features popular with Chinese consumers. Chinese consumers appeared to prefer Taobao's busier look and feel and found eBay's site too plain and minimalistic.[35] eBay also failed to give enough power to local executives, who complained that executives in California did not listen to them and directed operations from San Jose rather than trusting local leaders.[36] eBay also moved aggressively to sign exclusive partnership deals with China's largest Internet portals, effectively shutting out Taobao. But Jack Ma and Taobao relied on TV, print ads, billboards, SMS websites, and word of mouth, which proved to be more effective and less expensive strategies for bringing users to the site.[37] As Ma said in 2004, "The cost for eBay and international companies to come to China is so high. They spend $100 million dollars, we spend $10 million, but the effect is the same."[38]

Although many of these failures are symptomatic of any global expansion, the biggest lessons from eBay are common to many failed platforms. As the CEO of eBay China admitted to us in an interview, "eBay's single biggest problem in China was trust." Developing a new platform requires buyers and sellers to trust each other; and successful platforms build mechanisms to solve this problem. eBay relied on PayPal, which initially acted as it did in the United States: It was designed as a payment system, very much like a bank. For Chinese consumers, unfamiliar with e-commerce, that was not enough. Since Alipay used an escrow model (which did not release payment until the consumer was satisfied) and the existing financial system, Taobao neutralized eBay's early mover advantage.

Finally, eBay's failure to price "right," to offer its platform for free, was also crucial. As Jay Lee, eBay's managing director for Asia-Pacific, put it several years later, "It's very hard to compete with free."[39] In early 2006, eBay did begin offering free listings and integrated escrow services into PayPal, but by then it was too late. Alibaba had quickly become the default destination for consumers, which attracted more suppliers, which attracted more consumers. In other words, the network effects kicked in. In the end, eBay's experience in China seemed to validate one of Alibaba CEO Jack Ma's favorite aphorisms. Speaking of Western Internet powerhouses like eBay and Yahoo, he said that "they are the sharks in the ocean, we are the crocodiles in the Yangtze River. When they fight in the Yangtze River, they will be in trouble. The smell of the water is different."[40]

HUBRIS, OR DISMISSING THE COMPETITION

One common misconception among players in a platform market is that, once the market tips in your favor, you will be the long-run winner. Often this is true. But there is a better way to think about markets that have tipped: *It is the winner's opportunity to lose.* Hubris, along with overconfidence and arrogance, to name a few misdirected traits, can produce spectacular failures—even in markets that look like winner-take-all.

In 1998, we wrote a book called *Competing on Internet Time: Lessons from Netscape and Its Battle with Microsoft*. We explored how Netscape, a first mover with an early and overwhelming market-share lead, managed to lose the browser wars to Microsoft. Browsers were a classic innovation platform: Webmasters had to optimize their websites to exploit key features in a browser, while application developers took advantage of a browser's APIs. When Netscape dropped from 90 percent market share in 1996 to virtually zero, and Microsoft's Internet Explorer captured close to 95 percent by 2004, most pundits proclaimed the browser wars were over, the market had tipped, and Microsoft had won. It would require a monumental screwup for Microsoft to lose the market, but this is exactly what happened.

Perhaps the good news is that it took Microsoft almost a decade to lose its leading position. The failure came in two chapters: extremely poor product execution between 2004 and 2008; and then inferior product innovation between 2008 and 2015.

Internet Explorer and Firefox, 2004–2008: With its 95 percent share in 2004, Microsoft's competition primarily came from Firefox—the open-source Mozilla project. This browser originated when Netscape made the source code for Navigator available in early 1998 to any interested developer who wanted to download and modify it. While Netscape's decision to go open source was in some ways an admission of defeat, it also represented an effort to ensure a viable alternative to Internet Explorer. *Network World* put it this way when the project launched: "Netscape's source code give-away will create the market conditions necessary for sustaining a competing browser in a Microsoft-dominated world."[41]

Netscape reported more than 200,000 downloads of the source code within the first two weeks of making it available. Developers focused mostly on adapting the software for different operating systems, fixing bugs, and improving security, which could happen relatively quickly with a large number of developers working on the code.[42] Mozilla introduced its first browser in June 2002, with innovative features such as tabbed browsing, the ability to select a word or phrase and search the web for the selected text, and the ability to store common information for automatically filling in forms.[43]

The next round of the browser wars truly opened with Mozilla's release of Firefox in September 2004. Seeking to avoid software bloat and performance issues, two developers working for the Mozilla nonprofit foundation began what would become the Firefox browser in late 2002. Their goal was to produce a stand-alone browser that would be faster, simpler, and more secure. After its release, Firefox quickly began to eat into Internet Explorer's market share. One source reported that Firefox had 4.5 percent of the browser market by the end of November 2004, while Internet Explorer's share had dropped 5 percentage points to 89 percent.[44] By the end of 2007, Firefox had grabbed 17 percent of browser usage, compared to 76 percent for IE.[45] Why was Microsoft slipping so fast?

In late 2004, *Computerworld* wrote that "with no serious competitor, Microsoft stopped development of IE. New versions appear from time to time, but it has been years since IE offered groundbreaking new features. Meanwhile, development of other browsers has continued to the point where many consider them preferable to IE in performance, security, ease of use, added features and even help desk support." It went on to declare that all of its competitors—Firefox, Navigator, and Opera—had more features, were more secure, and were available on more different operating systems. In terms of speed loading pages, the article noted that all the other browsers "beat IE by a country mile."[46]

In effect, Microsoft took its dominant position for granted. Internet Explorer 6 was released in 2001 and Microsoft did not introduce a new version, other than for bug fixes and security patches, until 2006, opening the door to competitors. Security was a particular problem: Hackers and security experts continually found flaws, after which Microsoft would release a patch to fix the vulnerability, only to see new vulnerabilities uncovered. One issue was that Microsoft had integrated IE into the operating system, enabling the browser to execute Windows code. This integration made it possible to create web-based applications with richer features. The downside was that doing so created abundant opportunities for hackers to execute viruses and other forms of malware on users' machines, resulting in "a security nightmare for IT organizations."[47] Security became such a problem that the U.S. Computer Emergency Readiness Team, noting that important components of IE were "integrated into Windows to such an extent that vulnerabilities in IE frequently provide an attacker significant access to the operating system," recommended using a different web browser as a way to reduce vulnerabilities.[48] *PCWorld* declared in 2006 that IE 6 "might be the least secure software on the planet," and named it number eight on its list of the twenty-five worst tech products of all time.[49]

Microsoft admitted that it had failed to adequately shepherd its browser. The head of the Internet Explorer team noted in March 2006: "I want to be clear: We messed up. We messed up. As committed as we are to the browser, we just didn't do a good job demonstrating it." Bill Gates also acknowledged that Microsoft had left too long of a lag time between browser updates.[50] Microsoft responded by accelerating the timetable for IE 7. Despite its release in 2006, Firefox continued to gain ground, accounting for about 32 percent of web traffic by the end of 2009, while IE's share fell to 56 percent. Firefox's share remained flat for the next year or so, and then began a slow decline that left it with only 5 percent of the market by early 2018. Its losses were not IE's gain, however, as the browser wars entered a new phase with the emergence of a new competitor in late 2008, Google's Chrome.

Google Chrome, 2008–2016: Google launched Chrome in September 2008. It gradually gained traction in the market and soon began gaining ground on IE and Firefox, turning the browser contest into a three horse race. By one measure, total web traffic using Chrome passed Firefox at the end of 2011 and overtook IE in the middle of 2012. Other measures of users show Chrome passing Firefox in mid-2014 and reaching a near tie with IE by early 2016. (See Figure 4-2.)[51]

The trend was clear: Chrome rapidly took market share from both Firefox and IE in the years after its launch. When Google released the first version, it boasted that it had developed a new Java-Script engine that could execute JavaScript code ten times faster than competing browsers. *Wired* reported in September 2008 that the first version of Chrome ran some benchmark tests ten times faster than Firefox and Safari and fifty-six times faster than the current version of Internet Explorer, IE 7.[52] That's right: fifty-six times! Chrome was also developed with a multi-process architecture, when meant that each browser tab or plug-in ran as a separate process, so that if a web page or application crashed, it would not bring down the entire browser. In addition, Chrome was sandboxed, meaning that code executed in the browser could not access the underlying OS, reducing security threats of the kind that had so plagued Internet Explorer. Chrome was also the first to integrate

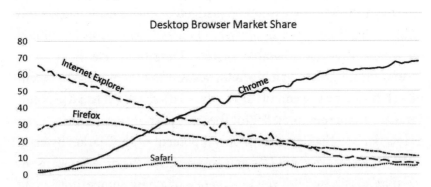

FIGURE 4-2: DESKTOP BROWSER MARKET SHARE, MEASURED BY TOTAL PAGE VIEWS, 2008–2016

Constructed from data in StatCounter Global Stats, http://gs.statcounter.com/, accessed April 19, 2016.

the search function into the main address bar and had a much more minimalistic and streamlined look and feel. Chrome's rapid development cycle—it released its seventeenth major version in early 2012, at which time IE was on version 9 and Firefox stood at version 10, despite their much longer life spans—meant that new features and fixes were available sooner. Chrome's automatic update process, which *Wired* called "reliable, consistent, and effective," worked to quickly move the vast majority of users to the current version. *PCWorld*, for instance, declared Chrome the best browser in February 2012, citing its speed in loading pages and executing JavaScript and HTML5 code, security, and availability of add-ons and extensions that expanded its functionality.[53]

What accounts for Chrome's rapid ascent, and IE's rapid demise? How can a market that supposedly tipped become unraveled? When Microsoft won the first browser war, it delivered the best product and then used its market power with Windows to create the best browser platform and drive competitors out of the market. By assuming it had won, by dismissing the threats from competitors, and by failing to innovate, Microsoft created an opening for Mozilla and then Google to exploit. While IE remained slow and buggy, with a reputation for poor security, Chrome offered speed, security, stability, and rapid development cycles (which enabled it to get fixes and new features to market quickly).[54] There is a critical lesson to be learned here: Although network effects are very powerful, they do not guarantee success forever. It took a long time for Microsoft to fail, but fail it did.

MISTIMING, OR FAILURE TO ACT BEFORE THE MARKET TIPS

Perhaps the most classic platform mistake is *mistiming* the market. In the browser wars, late movers were able to build strong platforms, but mostly because of the incumbent's letdowns. If Netscape had done some things differently, it might have survived the onslaught from Microsoft's Internet Explorer. Then, if Microsoft had kept Internet Explorer competitive, Firefox and Chrome probably would have failed to build credible competing platforms.

The smartphone market is a classic example of how great products plus all the resources in the world may still lead to failure in a platform market when *entry is too late*. Here again, Microsoft is the poster child for failure. In 2017, despite billions and billions of dollars of investments over a decade, Microsoft's Windows Phone was dead. It missed the platform window and never recovered.

When Apple released the iPhone in July 2007, it faced several entrenched players in the smartphone OS platform market, including Microsoft, Research in Motion's BlackBerry, and Nokia's Symbian. The last was the runaway market leader, accounting for over 63 percent of smartphones sold in 2007. Microsoft had 12 percent of the market that year, while BlackBerry had a 10 percent share. In ways that were not fully clear at the time, the iPhone revolutionized the smartphone category, leaving the entrenched players struggling to catch up. None did. By 2014, Symbian had disappeared and BlackBerry had all but vanished, its share measured in tenths of percentage points. Apple's iOS captured most of the handset industry's profits, but only about 15 percent of the unit volume in 2015.

The clear market-share winner in the global smartphone platform race was Android, the open-source mobile platform Google introduced in 2008. When Google announced Android in late 2007, existing smartphone platform leaders did not realize the implications. A spokesman for Nokia said, "We don't see this as a threat." Symbian's head of strategy told Reuters, "We have been going nine years and have probably seen a dozen new platforms come in and tell us we are under attack. We take it seriously, but we are the ones with real phones, real phone platforms and a wealth of volume built up over years." An executive for Microsoft's Windows Mobile project similarly dismissed the challenge: "It really sounds that they are getting a whole bunch of people together to build a phone and that's something we've been doing for five years. I don't understand the impact that they are going to have."[55] The impact turned out to be significant. With over 80 percent of the worldwide market in 2018, Android was clearly the dominant smartphone platform. The smartphone OS game became a two horse race, with other platforms—including Microsoft's—consigned to irrelevance.

The combined impact of the iPhone and the emergence of Android was to usher in a radically new phase in the evolution of mobile phones. Microsoft was caught flat-footed. Steve Ballmer famously gave an interview a few months after the release of the iPhone, saying, "There's no chance that the iPhone is going to get any significant market share. No chance."[56] Not perceiving a serious threat, Microsoft took three full years to release its rebooted Windows Phone 7, its first attempt to move into the post-iPhone world of touch-screen-centric user interfaces for smartphones. By the time the new Windows Phone was released in 2010, iOS and Android had nearly 40 percent of the global smartphone market between them and would reach a combined share of over 65 percent in 2011. Despite very positive reviews of Windows Phone 7 as well as Nokia's decision to abandon Symbian and join forces with Microsoft to create a third smartphone ecosystem, it was too late. The smartphone platform market had tipped into a stable duopoly, which made it difficult for a third viable platform to emerge.

Early reviews of Windows Phone 7 were very positive. *ArsTechnica* declared that Windows' new look made "iOS look dated, and Android cluttered and fussy."[57] *PC Magazine* declared Windows Phone 7 "a very impressive effort," with "a great-looking new design" and "powerful Office productivity and Zune [Microsoft's digital media platform] entertainment features." It predicted that, while it might take a few sales from the iPhone, "it was more of a threat to the chaotic Android consumer experience."[58] *Engadget* in its review concluded that, with "a fast and smart method of getting around the OS, great Office and email experiences, and a genuinely beautiful and useful user interface, Microsoft has definitely laid the foundation for the next several years of its mobile play."[59]

Reviews for subsequent versions of the Windows Phone OS continued to be positive, praising its smooth and fast performance, user interface, and Internet Explorer's web browsing capabilities. *Wired* gave Windows Phone 8, released in October 2012, a score of 8 out of 10, declaring that "the third mobile platform is finally, really here." The reviewer for the *Verge* wrote that "it's not a stretch to say that Windows Phone 8 has the best home screen—the perfect combination of flexibility, design, and simplicity—of any major platform right now."[60]

The positive reception afforded Windows Phone after its launch in 2010 gave observers cause for optimism. One reviewer pointed out that most mobile phone users were not yet smartphone users in 2010, so there was a large untapped market, not yet committed to iOS or Android, that Microsoft had a chance to win over with Windows. As one reviewer put it, "Yes, Microsoft is late to the game, but it's a game that's still in its early stages."[61]

The platform got another potential boost in 2011 when Nokia, at the time the world's largest handset maker, decided to abandon its own Symbian OS and adopt Windows Phone for its devices. Nokia CEO Stephen Elop predicted it would become a third—after iOS and Android—viable integrated ecosystem: "Today, developers, operators and consumers want compelling mobile products, which include not only the device, but the software, services, applications and customer support that make a great experience. Nokia and Microsoft will combine our strengths to deliver an ecosystem with unrivaled global reach and scale. It's now a three horse race."[62] Some suggested the partnership might revitalize Windows Phone's flagging fortunes: "Windows Phone 7 is no one's priority. But now Microsoft has a leading vendor committed to use the platform."[63] At a time when Windows Phone had about 2 percent of the smartphone OS market,[64] market research firm IDC predicted that Windows Phone would reach 20 percent market share in 2015, surpassing iOS for second place behind Android.[65] And another firm, Pyramid Research, believed that Windows would be the market-share winner![66]

Such predictions failed to materialize. In a desperate effort to keep sales of Windows Phone alive, Microsoft even acquired Nokia's devices business in 2013 for $7.2 billion. It was forced to write off the entire value of the acquisition two years later.[67] Although its partnership and acquisition of Nokia represented an attempt to integrate hardware and software along the model Apple pursued with the iPhone, Microsoft continued to license Windows Phone to other vendors. Not surprisingly, major players like Samsung, HTC, and LG put little effort into the platform. By the end of 2015, Windows Phone sales had fallen off a cliff, to under 3 percent of the market.

Why did an excellent product, backed by the largest cell phone manufacturer in the world, fail so miserably? The answer is that platform competition is fundamentally different from product competition. As we have said before, in a platform market, it is the *best platform*, and not the best product, that usually wins. Google Android had already lined up the majority of handset makers, application developers, and users. Apple also had a fiercely loyal following of users and application developers. The intense drive of the incumbents (Apple and Google), bolstered by the power of network effects driven by the number of users and high-quality complements, and the difficulty of catching up with users and application developers after a late start, probably doomed Microsoft's efforts from day one.

One persisting challenge was the relative dearth and lower quality of apps for Windows Phone compared to iOS and Android. As *PC Magazine* noted in 2010, "The battle is now shifting to apps. Windows Phone 7 has the basic features to make it in the marketplace. But Apple has a massive head start, and Android has huge market share which could make it appealing. If Windows Phone can draw third-party developers over from Android, it could sap some of that platform's energy."[68] Quality was also an issue. *Engadget*, despite its otherwise glowing review of Windows Phone 7, reported that for many apps "the results seemed second rate in comparison to the same applications on other platforms" and concluded that "the OS clearly needs time to mature, and developers will have to work a lot harder to get their apps up to spec with the competition." Windows, it concluded, "is a good year behind market leaders right now, and though it's clear the folks in Redmond are doing everything they can to get this platform up to snuff, it's also clear that they're not there yet."[69] Two years later, Windows was still struggling to catch up.

The simple fact was that developers could reach well over 90 percent of the smartphone market by building apps for iOS and Android. It was rarely worth the time and effort to develop for a platform with less than 3 percent market share. As one analyst put it in 2012, "Developers go where the money is, and the money is where people are."[70] In an effort to overcome that challenge, Microsoft at times paid app developers to write apps for Windows Phone, at a cost estimated at between $60,000 and $600,000 for each app in 2012. For example, Microsoft underwrote the cost of developing a Windows Phone version of the social networking app Foursquare in 2012, which the company would probably not have done otherwise. As Foursquare's head of business development put it, "We have very limited resources, and we have to put them toward the platforms with the biggest bang for our buck."[71]

In absolute terms, the number of Windows Phone apps available grew rapidly after its launch in 2010. From a base of only 1,000 apps available when Windows Phone 7 launched, the platform grew to 8,000 at the time of the Nokia agreement in 2011, to over 100,000 when Windows Phone 8 launched in 2012, and 320,000 by the end of 2014. Even with this growth, and despite creating a potentially potent hybrid platform, the Windows Phone ecosystem remained far smaller than competitors. Android and iOS respectively had 1.4 million and 1.2 million apps available by late 2014. While the sheer volume of apps was itself a major issue, the availability of popular apps was even more important. Instagram, for example, was not available on the Windows Phone despite the fact that, at the time, it had been available for iPhones for two years and on Android for six months. One reviewer concluded that "it's not like the store is empty—there are more than 120,000 apps available. They just aren't the apps you want."[72]

Many popular apps lagged far behind the launch date on iOS and Android. The music streaming service Pandora became available for Windows more than four years after it first launched on iOS. The ride-hailing app Uber came to Windows Phone over four years after its initial launch. The Windows Phone app for the social networking site Tumblr arrived nearly three years after it was first released, while the music streaming service Spotify was a little over two years behind the other platforms. The popular mobile messaging app Snapchat, which first launched in mid-2011, did not make an authorized version available for Windows Phone until early 2016.[73] And the list went on.

By 2017, Windows Phone was irrelevant. As one analyst described the situation: "Windows Phone is dead. Lumia can fade away. But Microsoft has already moved on" to new areas, such as the cloud.[74]

KEY TAKEAWAYS FOR MANAGERS AND ENTREPRENEURS

In this chapter, we discussed four of the most common mistakes that platform ventures make. These failures were driven by mispricing and inadequate subsidies to get network effects going, not building sufficient trust with platform users, not paying sufficient attention to competitors, and entering markets that have already tipped, without a viable strategy or understanding of why they tipped and what might overturn the status quo. So, when it comes to avoiding mistakes in platform businesses, what are the key takeaways for managers and entrepreneurs?

First, since many things can go wrong in a platform market, managers and entrepreneurs need to make concerted efforts to *learn from failures*. It is easy to say, "I would never do something stupid like that." Yet, with platform strategy, the challenges are more complicated to identify because there are so many moving parts. Firms not only have to coordinate internal operations, a supply chain, and novel methods of distribution. They also have to manage complements, overcome chicken-or-egg problems, and simultaneously stimulate multiple sides of a market. As we observed up front, platforms have high failure rates, like most start-up ventures. Despite the huge upside opportunities that platforms offer, pursuing a platform strategy does not necessarily improve the odds of success as a business.

Second, since platforms are ultimately driven by network effects, *getting the prices right and identifying which sides to subsidize remain the biggest challenges*. Uber's insight (and Sidecar's failure) was recognizing the power of network effects to drive volume by dramatically lowering prices and costs on *both* sides of the market. However, as we have noted, this strategy requires lots of venture capital or other sources of cash to sustain. In fact, most though not all of the most successful platforms we studied built their businesses on low-cost capital, which allowed the winners to aggressively acquire at least one side of a market. In addition to Uber, think YouTube (which was free for producers and content consumers for several years), or Facebook (which offered free access to its social network). Of course, outside funds are never free forever: Market-share winners still have to pay back investors eventually. Uber has struggled mightily to stem its losses, such as by selling money-losing operations overseas. It might have a successful IPO in 2019 because of its continuing rapid growth, though it may still be years away from making a profit, if it ever does. Nonetheless, other platforms, such as Google, Facebook, eBay, Amazon, Alibaba, and Tencent, successfully made the transition from losing money to making money as they gained scale and expanded until they found a business or a business model that made profits. Clearly, this is what investors expect of Uber.

Third, it is important to *put trust front and center.* Virtually all platforms require trust because they are intermediaries linking users and other market participants that generally have no personal interactions or relationships. Asking customers or suppliers to take a leap of faith, without history and without prior connections to the other side of a market, is usually asking too much of any platform business. eBay's failure to establish mechanisms for building trust in China, like Alibaba did with Taobao, is an error that platform managers can and should avoid.

Fourth, and this may sound obvious, but *timing is crucial.* Being early is preferable, but no guarantee of success; being late can be deadly, *unless your competitors screw up.* We have all sat in meetings with managers where they tell their boards and staff that they have the "best" product on the market, which is surely going to win. The problem is often timing: The best platform usually trumps the best product, but platforms and their ecosystems take time to build. This is especially true for innovation platforms, where you need armies of developers to innovate, and you need many consumers to attract those developers and then use those innovations. Come too late to that party, as Microsoft did with Windows Phone, and you are bound to fail, even with great products and virtually unlimited financial and engineering resources. It is essential that challengers carefully probe why a market has tipped and what strategies and investments might disrupt the platform leaders.

Finally, *hubris can lead to disaster.* Dismissing the competition, even when you have a formidable lead, is inexcusable. One of the greatest dangers in business is complacency. Andy Grove, former CEO of Intel, had a wonderful saying: "Success breeds complacency. Complacency breeds failure. Only the paranoid survive."[75] The dangers of success breeding complacency are perhaps no greater than in platform markets because of network effects. Once a market seems to have tipped, it is easy for managers to relax and believe that the tipping is permanent. Yet, in fact, it is extraordinarily hard in many tipped markets for competitors to build a viable platform business. Complacency, even among successful platform companies, can indeed breed failure—which Microsoft proved in the browser market during the 2000s, after it beat Netscape in the 1990s. If you cannot stay competitive, no market position is safe. A senior executive from Google even told us that he'd like to "erect a statue to Steve Ballmer" for performing so poorly in browsers and smartphones.

Traditional non-platform firms have an especially difficult challenge in the digital age. But even they should not simply give in to new platform competitors. How old dogs can learn new tricks—a challenge that is difficult but possible—is the subject of the next chapter.

OLD DOGS AND NEW TRICKS

BUILD, BUY, OR BELONG TO A PLATFORM

BELONG TO A COMPETING PLATFORM

BUY A PLATFORM (ESPECIALLY THE TECHNOLOGY AND THE TALENT)

BUILD A NEW PLATFORM YOURSELF

KEY TAKEAWAYS FOR MANAGERS AND ENTREPRENEURS

The question we ask in this chapter is simple: Can an old dog learn new tricks? While entrepreneurs are building new platforms every day from scratch, incumbent firms have struggled with adapting to the world of digital platforms. For many well-established firms, platforms challenge the core principles of their ongoing business. Many traditional enterprises have been accustomed to controlling all aspects of their destiny, from supply chain through distribution and direct control over customer relationships. But the dynamics of industry platforms and ecosystems challenge those assumptions. Platforms connect customers to customers (Facebook), customers to advertisers (Google), drivers to passengers (Uber), and software developers to buyers (now via app stores, such as from Apple and Google). Moreover, platforms often disrupt existing business models that focus on stand-alone products or services. How does a black cab in London compete with an unregulated Uber? How does a retailer such as Walmart compete with Amazon, eBay, or Alibaba? How should modern hotels respond to Airbnb? How should a firm like Nokia or even Microsoft respond to Google, which gives away the Android smartphone platform software for free?

Many established firms facing these challenges have actually found a way to adapt. Very few shrivel up and die. Mattel, for instance, introduced the Barbie doll in 1959.[1] Over the years, the company faced competition on many fronts, but it evolved the Barbie product into an innovation platform. Although Mattel had always made some accessories for the dolls, the company eventually realized that it would be more profitable if it licensed hundreds of partners to make clothes, fashion accessories, and a wide range of complementary products and services, including online Barbie doll chat rooms and videos, which would ultimately expand demand. Of course, Mattel still controls the Barbie doll experience, much the way Apple controls the iPhone experience throughout its ecosystem.

Traditional hotels also have discovered the potential magic of transaction platforms. When Airbnb got started, many hotels dismissed the platform as an irrelevant niche. But when Airbnb hit 2.5 million people staying on a single night in 2017, it was hard for hotels to ignore.[2] With 4 million listings, Airbnb was larger than the top five hotel brands combined. It was also far more valuable. It took a while, but several major hotel brands decided it was time to get into the home-sharing business. AccorHotels bought Onefinestay, a platform for renting upscale homes and apartments in London.[3] Hyatt invested and partnered with Oasis, a niche home-rental platform in twenty cities. And Marriott bought the Tribute Portfolio Hotels collection from Starwood Hotels, folded in an experiment on home sharing in London, and then bought Starwood outright to vastly expand its market share and base of loyalty program users.

There are numerous questions old dogs need to answer before they can compete successfully in a platform world. For example, what parts of your business would be better handled by using an existing transaction or innovation platform owned by some other company? Can access to an existing platform add value to your business by lowering your costs or increasing your customer reach? How can you prevent the platform owner from extracting all or most of the value? As platforms become more powerful and ubiquitous, should you become a platform yourself, build coalitions with other players, or focus on a niche, outside the reach of a mass-market platform?

Even modern product companies face the challenge of adapting to platforms. Consider the example of HTC Corporation of Taiwan, one of the pioneers of the smartphone industry. It delivered the first 3G phone, the first 4G phone, and the first Android phone. At its peak in 2011, HTC was the third largest smartphone company, behind Nokia and Apple. Annual revenues hit $16 billion and were growing close to 50 percent. Fast forward a half dozen years, and HTC's smartphone business was struggling: The big winners in the smartphone industry were the dominant platform players, Apple (iPhone) and Google (Android). Android, in particular, had commoditized the hardware industry, driving down margins for everyone but Apple.

Peter Chou, and later Cher Wang, HTC's CEOs, responded by moving aggressively into a new space: virtual reality. Wang knew that HTC had a high-end product, called Vive, which was better than its competitors, but HTC also had one of the best products on the market in the early days of the smartphone. HTC had a very close relationship with Google during the initial launch of Android, and, similarly, HTC had a close relationship with the leading platform for PC virtual reality gamers (Valve). In a world where platforms were likely to play an important role, how could a traditional hardware company adapt to a platform world driven by software and digital technologies? For more than a year, management and the board debated: How do we avoid a repeat of the smartphone experience?

The answer, repeated in several examples in this chapter, is that you have to be willing to play the platform game.[4] For HTC, it meant both "belonging" to existing platforms (Valve's Steam platform for PC games and Google's platform for Android phones) and "building" its own hybrid platform for educational, industrial, entertainment, and other virtual reality applications. HTC continued to work closely with Valve because virtual reality was a classic innovation platform: Virtual reality's initial success would depend on third parties building exciting applications, and the early adopters would be serious gamers. HTC also worked with Google because the high-volume, low-end virtual reality market would most likely emerge from the Android ecosystem. At the same time, Wang wanted HTC to have its own platform, called Viveport, which would seek to attract non-gaming applications. It was still too early to predict the success or failure of HTC's Vive and its Viveport platform, but the strategies of belonging to and building platforms have become increasingly common among traditional product firms.[5]

The key message of this chapter is that "old dogs" can learn to adapt to a platform world in at least three ways: They can belong to a competing platform, buy a platform, or build their own platform. The biggest nightmare for established firms is not being able to prevent a new platform from becoming the next winner-take-all or winner-take-most competitor in markets where they have competed effectively for years or decades. To analyze these options in more depth, we examine how black cabs in London have worked with competing transaction platforms to fend off Uber and how a creative retailer found ways to leverage the Amazon platform to its advantage. We also discuss how Walmart accelerated its progress in competing with Amazon by buying Jet.com, and how General Electric started down the road of building a new innovation or hybrid platform for the industrial Internet of things to leverage its product and service capabilities.

The path to success for old dogs is not a straight line. Setbacks are inevitable, as GE in particular has experienced. But these examples highlight the challenges and strategic options that many established firms can and should confront as "platformization" comes to their industries.

BELONG TO A COMPETING PLATFORM

In the early days of the Internet, some managers believed that the best way to defend your business against a new platform was to jump on the bandwagon. If Amazon or eBay made it easy to sell directly to consumers, why not become an Amazon or eBay seller and exploit a successful platform's hard work of connecting large numbers of customers? What many companies did not realize was that, once a platform had a large installed base, that platform could also gain significant market power and extract most of the value.

Recent research has shown that pattern has continued. Companies that realized material revenue growth selling their products on Amazon's platform ran a significant risk that Amazon would observe that success, enter the category, and take it over.[6] And for the brands that would use Amazon to sell their products directly, many found that the automated bots Amazon used to search the web and adjust prices to guarantee it had the lowest prices effectively put the traditional distributors at a competitive disadvantage. Moreover, Amazon's tactics had repercussions on the brands themselves, alienating them from their usual distribution network and further reinforcing Amazon's bargaining power.[7] This type of aggressive behavior is not unusual for a platform leader. In an earlier era, many software developers who worked on the Windows platform discovered that Microsoft would often copy and integrate third-party applications, effectively putting those players out of business.[8]

PHARMAPACKS ON AMAZON: LEVERAGE THE PLATFORM GIANT

In some cases, belonging to someone else's platform can be very profitable. A big successful platform such as Amazon can dramatically reduce search and transaction costs for customers. The challenge for firms using the platform is to learn how to exploit the advantages without being run over by the platform itself. The answer often exists in platform governance rules that allow participants to pick their spots.[9] Many creative businesses have found ways to belong to a platform, while mitigating that platform's inherent power.

A relatively unknown success case of belonging to a platform was a company called Pharmapacks, which got its start in brick-and-mortar retail in 2010. The founder, Andrew Vagenas, first ventured into online sales in 2011. At the time, Vagenas and a partner owned a retail pharmacy in the Bronx, which he described as a "pretty successful mom-and-pop shop." They raised money from friends and built their own website, with limited success.[10] Their sales only took off when they began selling on eBay and Amazon. By 2016, the vast majority of revenues came from online marketplaces—40 percent from Amazon alone.[11] And they emerged as one of the largest U.S. sellers on the Amazon marketplace.[12]

Some retailers had success by concentrating on a niche on the Amazon marketplace. By contrast, Pharmapacks made its money by selling lip balm, shampoo, razor blades, and other everyday items you might buy at a drugstore. Its business model was to offer high-volume and low-margin products, which it bought at a discount from a range of distributors and sold at a 3 percent to 6 percent profit margin.[13] Pharmapacks succeeded by capitalizing on the rules of the platform. Unlike a traditional retailer, as a marketplace seller they did not need to stock a full line of products all the time, but could adjust their inventory based on what products their suppliers discounted.

More importantly, Pharmapacks developed a pricing algorithm that would automatically adjust the price of a given item to ensure the price they were charging was low enough to show up at the top of the Amazon search page, but not so low that they lost money on the sale.[14] Vagenas told ABC in early 2016 that "every 45 minutes, our systems are changing prices. Whether it's increasing prices, decreasing prices, [based on] market demand or we're getting better deals or buying better. We always pass the profits straight to the customer whenever there's a discount given to us, so that's how we can drop prices."[15] As Pharmapacks refined their pricing formula, its products began to land the top spot and sales began to increase dramatically. Revenues grew to over $31 million in 2014, $70 million in 2015, and $121 million in 2016, a three-year growth rate of nearly 600 percent.[16] By mid-2016, Pharmapacks was shipping 20,000 packages a day.[17]

Amazon might compete directly with high-volume players in easily identified categories, but Pharmapack's strategy was probably less attractive and too much trouble for Amazon to replicate. The lesson for established companies is that if you can "manage" the platform, you can build an attractive business. Pharmapack managed the platform by offering the lowest prices and getting top billing. It leveraged Amazon's strength—reach and low-cost distribution—without worrying (at least in the short run) about Amazon moving into its territory. The bottom line: Pharmapack was a business that fit Amazon's strategy of offering great retail value, and it was not so large that Amazon felt compelled to copy it.

GM AND LYFT: SUPPORT A COMPETING PLATFORM

Sometimes belonging to the dominant platform can be a winning strategy when you can take advantage of the platform rules, but sometimes a new platform aims to put you out of business. In these circumstances, playing on the platform is usually not the answer. An alternative strategy is to support a competing platform. Especially early in the game, before a market has tipped or the new platform player has built significant scale, there may be opportunities to fragment the market and prevent a winner-take-all-or-most outcome. Every taxi company in the world, for example, has fretted over how to adapt to Uber. Suppliers to the taxi industry, such as General Motors, also have feared that the market could tip to Uber. When Uber starts building its own self-driving cars, GM could be frozen out of the loop. GM's response was to invest $500 million into Uber's competitor Lyft to improve the prospects of a competitive industry.

Within the taxi industry itself, firms across the world have been striving to fend off Uber's advances. The single most successful strategy has been political: In numerous cities and even countries, taxi organizations have lobbied local governments to put Uber into a compromised position. In Hong Kong, for instance, local authorities sent a message to Uber when the police arrested seven Uber drivers for carriage of passengers and operating without insurance against third-party risks.[18] The drivers were fined 7,000 Hong Kong dollars (about $900 U.S.) and lost their driver's licenses for twelve months. Suddenly, finding an Uber in Hong Kong was challenging. Similarly, in July 2016, Uber was forced to pull out of Hungary when the nation's legislature passed a law that made it impossible for Uber to operate its platform.[19] Even in our hometown of Boston, the taxi industry convinced our local airport (Logan) to ban UberX from picking up passengers for several years.[20] Forty other U.S. city airports did the same.[21]

In cities and countries unwilling to protect their local taxi industries, firms have had to make a choice: Join Uber or find competitive strategies to compete with Uber. In some cities, taxi companies opted to join Uber and operate on Uber's "fleet owners" platform. In other cities, such as London, the taxis have chosen to fight. Before the city of London declined to renew Uber's license in 2017 (a decision that was overturned with a temporary license in 2018), London's iconic black cabs provided an illuminating example of how an old dog can remain viable by supporting alternative platforms.

LONDON'S BLACK CABS: MAKING ALTERNATIVE PLATFORMS YOUR "HOME"

The London taxi business before the rise of ride sharing consisted of the city's traditional black cabs and thousands of private hire vehicle (PHV) operators, popularly known as minicabs. Black cab drivers were self-employed, determined their own hours, and functioned almost as a professional guild. Admission required rigorous training, including memorizing 25,000 streets and 20,000 landmarks in London. It typically took about four years of nearly full-time work to prepare for and pass the exam.[22] Once they passed the exam, drivers could buy a license, acquire a vehicle, and begin operating as a cabbie. The industry's regulator, Transport for London (TfL), mandated that vehicles had to meet strict standards (e.g., a specific turning radius, be wheelchair accessible) and pass safety inspections every six months.

London's black cabs had long faced competition from minicabs, which operated differently. Unlike taxis, minicabs could not be hailed on the street, nor were they allowed to use taxi stands. Instead, they had to be prebooked, either by phone or in person at an office or kiosk. Despite the hassle, demand for minicabs was high. By 2013, there were nearly 50,000 licensed PHVs in London, soaking up some of the demand left by the limited number of black cabs available, especially on nights and weekends.

Uber and other platforms: Uber launched in London in 2012, licensed as a PHV operator. Its impact on the black cab business was difficult to quantify, since there were no updated statistics on ridership. Anecdotally, cabbies said it had affected their business, and the number of licensed cabs in London declined slightly, falling from 22,600 to 22,500 between 2011 and 2015.[23] Despite cabbies' efforts to limit Uber's growth, in the second half of 2015 the number of Uber drivers passed the number of black cab drivers and reached 25,000 by early 2016.[24] Cabbies saw Uber as an existential threat. In the words of one black cab driver who also helped to run a driver training school, "I genuinely believe [Uber's] aim is to wipe us out. Starve black taxis into submission and then run riot with that marketplace."[25]

In response to Uber's challenge, many of London's cabbies turned to competing third-party ride-sharing platforms. By early 2016, the two major taxi-only ride-sharing platforms were Hailo and Gett, which together had signed up over 60 percent of London's black cab drivers. Hailo actually predated the arrival of Uber, launching in London in November 2011. The app was free to riders, who paid the same fare they would have if they hailed a cab on the street. Hailo's revenues came from taking a commission of 10 percent from the driver's fare for each trip it enabled. By August 2012, about 5,200 drivers had signed up for the service and some 200,000 Londoners had downloaded the Hailo's smartphone app. Drivers were attracted to the app primarily because it reduced their amount of idle time. One cabdriver who used the platform said, "I get about four more jobs a day than I did before. . . . The cut on each fare and paying the credit card fee isn't that big a deal. You lose more money driving around waiting to be hailed."[26] In September 2013, Hailo reported that 3 million taxi trips had been made in London over the previous two years using the app. This was a sizable number but a relative drop in the bucket compared to the number of black cab trips taken in London, which stood at 1.8 million per week in 2007 (the latest year for which statistics are available).[27] By November 2013, the number of drivers on the platform had risen to 16,000, or 60 percent of the licensed cabbies in the city, and Hailo had over 400,000 registered users.[28]

Joining Hailo to fight Uber was not problem-free, however. Hailo, like most platforms, had the power to change the rules. Originally, Hailo marketed itself as a platform exclusively for hailing London's black cabs. But, under increased pressure from Uber after its 2012 launch, Hailo opened the platform to private hire vehicles in May 2014. The decision provoked a backlash from drivers of black cabs. The head of the Licensed Taxi Drivers Association said: "There's a lot of resentment and anger out there . . . now the guys just feel betrayed."[29]

The good news for London black cabs was that the market had not tipped. There was yet another ride-hailing app in the city, Gett, which was based in Israel and operated in a number of cities around the world before coming to London. Its growth trailed Hailo's, but it profited from the backlash against Hailo's decision to open its platform, and signed up 10,000 cabbies in London by March 2016.[30]

By early 2016, London's black cab drivers, in addition to depending on their iconic status and legendary knowledge of the streets of the city, were committed to fighting Uber through a combination of direct action, political lobbying, and the adoption of rival taxi-only ride-hailing platforms. Of course, the battle for the London cab industry was not over. In early February 2016, Uber offered to open up its platform to London's iconic black cabs commission-free for twelve months, but cabdrivers rejected the offer.

While some might have predicted the death of the black cabs when Uber entered London, they have managed to adapt by choosing new platforms, which allow the old and the new way of doing things to coexist. London's black cab drivers also got some potential relief from city officials. On September 22, 2017, Transport for London announced it would not renew Uber's license to operate in the city when it expired on September 30, citing "a lack of corporate responsibility in relation to a number of issues which have potential public safety and security implications."[31] Uber appealed the decision, although Uber CEO Dara Khosrowshahi subsequently acknowledged that Uber had "gotten things wrong along the way" and apologized for its mistakes.[32] Uber also gained considerable support; by late October, some 700,000 Londoners had signed a petition calling for TfL to reverse its verdict. Uber, of course, appealed and was allowed to continue operations in London, pending the final decision.[33] In June 2018, Uber won its appeal to continue operating in London, and was given a probationary license requiring a review every fifteen months.[34]

CAVEAT: THE PITFALLS OF JOINING A DOMINANT PLATFORM

Smaller firms (or independent operators in the case of taxi drivers) often have few choices other than to join an existing platform. Larger firms may have more choices. Often, they can build or buy their own platform. Sometimes, incumbents simply lack the skills to build and operate a digital platform, and belonging to an existing platform may be the best answer. However, belonging to a powerful platform has many risks for traditional companies. Holdup problems are rampant. Platforms may pretend to be open and unbiased, but that has often been false. Once a platform achieves scale, it has the power to compete directly with one of its market sides.

A good example of this dilemma was the relationship between Toys "R" Us and Amazon. In the year 2000, Toys "R" Us signed a ten-year "exclusive" agreement with Amazon to participate on its platform. Realizing that its traditional brick-and-mortar retail strategy needed help and its online presence was not getting traction, Toys "R" Us joined Amazon's platform for both web presence and order fulfillment. Toys "R" Us paid $50 million per year, plus a percentage of its revenue. By 2004, however, the deal went south: With Toys "R" Us losing money and Amazon offering competing toy vendors on its site, Toys "R" Us sued for $200 million in damages. Amazon claimed it was offering toys which Toys "R" Us could not or would not provide. After a two-year legal battle, the courts ruled in favor of Toys "R" Us, allowing the toy company to sever its connection with Amazon, but awarded no damages. For the next decade, Toys "R" Us continued to struggle while Amazon sold an estimated $4 billion in toys. Toys "R" Us then declared bankruptcy in 2018 and closed all its stores.

Toys "R" Us made three mistakes. First, when it joined a powerful platform, the company should have extracted the maximum concessions up front. In this case, Toys "R" Us failed to adequately define the word "exclusive" in its contract. Second, Toys "R" Us might have built its own platform, not just for its own toys but for other toy companies as well. Three, Toys "R" Us might have bought a competing platform, which would have had the skills Toys "R" Us lacked. Especially when the threat of holdup problems are severe, bigger incumbent firms need to explore buying or building.

BUY A PLATFORM (ESPECIALLY THE TECHNOLOGY AND THE TALENT)

No one ever said that creating a platform business was easy. For many managers, particularly if they have strong balance sheets, the easy answer has been to buy a platform. But before heading down this path, it is important to recognize that buying your way into the platform world is fraught with danger. The skills to manage a platform can be antithetical to managing an old command-and-control organization. Notable disasters have included News Corporation's acquisition of MySpace and the AOL-Time-Warner merger.

Yet under the right conditions, buying a platform may be the right answer. In businesses where new, emerging platforms are likely to capture a significant share (e.g., taxis and retail), incumbent firms cannot sit on the sidelines indefinitely. In general, the biggest risk in acquiring a platform has been not retaining key talent, integrating technology into legacy systems, and cultural rejection from the parent. But, as we'll see in the Walmart example, there may be hope. Buying strong technology and empowering new, outside talent can sometimes overcome the natural obstacles to transforming an old dog into a new platform.

WALMART'S ACQUISITIONS

Few large incumbent companies have been more challenged by platform competition than Walmart, the biggest company in the world measured by sales and employees. "How did a peddler of cheap shirts and fishing rods become the mightiest corporation in America?" a *Fortune* columnist once asked. "The short version of Walmart's rise to glory goes something like this: In 1979 it racked up a billion dollars in sales. By 1993 it did that much business in a week; by 2001 it could do it in a day."[35] That same year, Walmart also topped *Fortune*'s Global 500 list, and it retained the top spot for most of the next fifteen years. In 2017, its revenues were close to

$500 billion, which outpaced the next largest company—China's State Grid—by more than $150 billion in revenue.[36] Walmart had become the dominant retailer on the planet by cutting costs ruthlessly in service to its everyday low-price model and steadily pushing competitors small and large out of business.

Walmart's biggest threat came from e-commerce. Though a small fraction of overall retail sales (about 14 percent in 2017), online retail was growing much faster (about 16 percent in 2017), compared to the 1.4 percent overall growth in retail. Online U.S. sales were predicted to grow from $390 billion in 2016 to $612 billion in 2020.[37] But, in the United States, Walmart faced head-on the new juggernaut of the retail world: Amazon. Although Amazon's revenue was much less than half of Walmart's in 2017, it was growing much faster: Amazon's retail sales had grown at an annualized rate of nearly 20 percent between 2011 and 2015, while Walmart's growth was in the low single digits. Amazon's dominance in e-commerce was nearly as complete as Walmart's dominance in brick-and-mortar retail. Amazon was also the world's most valuable retailer in 2018, more than three times the market cap of Walmart. As the CEO of Adidas put it, "Amazon is the best, without any comparison, transaction platform in the world."[38]

The Platform Challenge: The challenge from Amazon was not simply that it was a rival retailer and dominating e-commerce. Amazon had become an increasingly large platform for third-party retailers, ranging from individuals selling used books to retailers generating tens of millions of dollars in annual revenue on its marketplace.[39] Amazon originally launched its marketplace in 2000, and in 2007 introduced its Fulfillment by Amazon (FBA) service, which meant it would handle not only the online transaction but store, package, and ship items for third-party sellers who took advantage of the service. This feature distinguished Amazon from other marketplaces like eBay and allowed small retailers to reach a wide audience without having to build a fulfillment infrastructure.

The size of Amazon's marketplace was growing rapidly. Marketplace sales generated $9.2 billion in revenue for Amazon in the first quarter of 2018, about 18 percent of Amazon's total revenues in the quarter.[40] By 2018, roughly 65 percent of total unit sales on Amazon came from third-party sellers, and the number of sellers actively using the service stood at over 2 million. Through its Fulfillment by Amazon service, Amazon delivered over 2 billion items for other sellers in 2016, double the number for 2015.[41] The proliferation of third-party sellers vastly expanded the product selection available on Amazon.com; by one estimate between 80 percent to 90 percent of product variety was coming from third-party sellers, contributing the majority of the hundreds of millions of items available on Amazon.com.[42] The scale of the marketplace contributed to the site's attraction for consumers, who recognized they would be able to find whatever they were looking for at Amazon.

Amazon was the largest threat to Walmart's growth. However, other large retail platforms also gave them reason to worry. By giving small and medium-sized retailers an online presence with broad reach, marketplaces such as eBay and Alibaba in China left Walmart a smaller share of the online pie. While it might seem strange for the world's largest retailer, accustomed to driving other retailers out of business, to bring other retailers under its umbrella, it faced the same choice Amazon had dealt with fifteen years before: whether or not to allow those retailers to use its platform and at least get a percentage of those sales (and acquire greater selection that would bring customers to its site, where they might buy products sourced directly from Walmart) or risk losing a large swath of consumers altogether.

Walmart's Response: With dominant e-commerce platforms threatening its growth plans both at home and abroad, Walmart's leadership recognized the need to increase its online retail presence and poured billions into the effort. Walmart tried to build its own platform organically: It even sought to leverage Silicon Valley by creating a partnership with the venture capital firm Accel Partners to make Walmart.com into a viable competitor of Amazon. But after more than a decade of disappointing results, Walmart management concluded that it didn't have the right technology or the right team, and it needed to acquire those capabilities. Between 2011 and 2016, it made more than a dozen e-commerce acquisitions. The largest by far was the $3.3 billion acquisition of Jet.com in August 2016.[43] Walmart hoped Jet.com could bring e-commerce capabilities and technology that would jump-start Walmart's marketplace business. Walmart CEO Doug McMillon put Jet CEO Marc Lore and his team in charge of all of Walmart's e-commerce business. If Walmart was going to succeed in the new world of platform-based retail, the company needed a new approach, a new team, and a new leader.

Walmart had built its own marketplace into its website, but as of summer 2016 it had only about 550 third-party vendors, compared to over 2 million at Amazon.[44] Walmart's ability to grow its marketplace was hindered by the lengthy vetting process for adding vendors—which took an average of six weeks, compared to one day on Amazon and eBay.[45] When Walmart acquired Jet, a big hope was to quickly broaden its online selection.[46]

Jet.com had launched in June 2015. Part of its original strategy was to use revenue from annual $49.99 membership fees to maintain low prices by subsidizing money-losing transactions, but the company quickly abandoned it. Lore argued that membership was not central to the business model; he claimed that Jet could achieve 4 percent to 5 percent savings over competing sites (i.e., Amazon) without membership fees.[47] Jet's marketplace was distinctive in a number of ways. Rather than the user selecting the retailer for each item, Jet's algorithm selected what it called the "optimal retailer"—that is, the least expensive—for a given set of purchases based on various factors such as the shoppers' locations or the items in their carts. For instance, a small retailer that happened to be located close to the shopper might win out over a larger retailer with a lower-priced item because its lower shipping costs made the purchase cheaper. In addition, sellers could establish rules for how their goods were priced, giving customers discounts for buying in bulk, for accepting slower shipping times, for waiving their right to return items, or for opting in to receive marketing emails. All of these rules were factored into Jet's dynamic pricing algorithm and would help determine the cheapest option for a given basket of goods.[48]

From buyers' perspectives, the price of goods in their carts changed in real time as they added items or agreed to waive returns or opt in to receive emails. Behind the scenes, the retailer providing them might see changes as well, depending on the buyers' choices. This all depended on Jet's sophisticated pricing technology, which Lore saw as a crucial differentiator for the Jet platform that competitors would find difficult to imitate. As Lore noted in 2015, "Every product we look at, we've repriced relative to what's in your basket, looking at all the pools of inventory, applying all the rules retailers have set. There could be hundreds of retailers who set rules and you have to go through all of them to find out what the cheapest is and what the difference is. That's a lot of calculations." He went on to say that "the technology has been super, super hard. It's about getting it to the point where it can run these calculations at the speed we need it to run."[49]

It will take years to determine if Walmart's acquisitions will enable it to create a successful retail platform to rival those of Amazon and Alibaba, but early returns after the Jet acquisition were promising. The first year after the acquisition, Walmart appeared to turn a corner in its e-commerce efforts, generating significant growth and momentum. In the quarter ending January 31, 2017, the first full quarter after closing the acquisition, Walmart's domestic e-commerce sales and gross merchandise volume were up 29 percent and 31 percent respectively over the previous year. When Walmart announced its earnings for the third quarter in November

2017, its stock rose 11 percent to an all-time high. With e-commerce growth rates surpassing Amazon's, CNN declared that Walmart was "making Amazon sweat."[50] Part of the improvement could be attributed to increased selection: By February of 2018, the number of items for sale in its marketplace had risen to 75 million, up more than tenfold.[51]

Buying Jet.com clearly jump-started Walmart's e-commerce platform business. However, like many large acquisitions, it suffered from growing pains, execution problems, and integration issues. Growth decelerated sharply at the end of Walmart's 2018 fiscal year, with e-sales growth and GMV growth falling to 24 percent and 23 percent respectively. Walmart's leaders acknowledged the slowdown in online growth. CEO Doug McMillon said, "We are building a business. We are learning something new." McMillon went on to suggest that Jet would remain a smaller part of Walmart's overall business: "I think what you'll see is Jet will go through a period of adjustment and then it'll start to grow again in the future but focused on specific markets and opportunities, whereas Walmart will be the broad-based, big part of the business, and growing it will be a priority."[52] Specifically, Walmart's leadership was positioning Jet as a way to reach younger, more upscale urban consumers.[53]

Matters got worse in March 2018. Tri Huynh, a former employee in Walmart's e-commerce division, filed a whistle-blower suit. He apparently had been fired after repeatedly raising concerns—culminating in bringing them to Marc Lore—about Walmart's "overly aggressive push to show meteoric growth in its e-commerce business by any means possible"—even, illegitimate ones. Huynh claimed that Walmart had lowered its standards for third-party marketplace items, mislabeled items so vendors received lower commissions, and failed to process returns, resulting in inflated sales numbers.[54]

Walmart Invests in Flipkart: Undeterred by challenges at home, Walmart was moving at full speed to build out a global retail platform. In 2018, Walmart made its largest acquisition in history by investing $15 billion for a 75 percent stake in Flipkart, India's leading e-commerce player. As one of the world's largest and fastest-growing new markets for online commerce, India was an attractive target for Walmart.

Flipkart had been founded by two former Amazon employees in 2007 but was facing stiff competition from Amazon, which entered India in 2013. Jeff Bezos decided to pour $5 billion into the India operations, which in 2018 included fast delivery and Prime video streaming. Flipkart struggled to maintain its lead and needed additional financing. Meanwhile, Walmart was also struggling in India, operating only twenty-one wholesale stores, limited by rules that restricted foreign companies' ownership of local retail operations. The investment in Flipkart provided an opportunity for Walmart to sell directly to Indian consumers.[55] Although this decision was a much bigger financial gamble than the acquisition of Jet.com, it signaled Walmart's serious commitment to transition from brick-and-mortar competition to digital platform competition.

Failing in its retail platform business was not an option for Walmart management. Everyone understood that allowing Amazon to dominate the e-commerce segment would be the kiss of death for the world's largest retailer. Flipkart and Jet.com gave Walmart and its shareholders hope. At the same time, success would demand that Walmart learn, adapt, and fix its execution challenges—similar to any conventional acquisition.

BUILD A NEW PLATFORM YOURSELF

Building a new platform yourself is the most challenging option for incumbent firms, but potentially the most rewarding. Still, the inherent complexity of platform markets makes it difficult to predict how older industries will respond. Even if one market side accepts a new platform, the other sides must cooperate and engage. It is also difficult for a firm to overcome internal inertia and accept a new way of doing business. Even in the face of intense platform competition, internal factors will often limit the effectiveness of a build-your-own strategy.[56]

THE PROMISE OF A BUILD STRATEGY: GE'S PREDIX

While building a new platform from scratch remains extraordinarily hard, especially for "old dogs," it also held the promise of revolutionizing a business. At a minimum, the opportunity to take advantage of network effects could inject new growth into a mature market. To succeed, however, traditional firms needed to overcome the natural tendencies of command and control. Old dogs also needed to learn the lessons of this book: Identify the right type of platform, figure out how to solve the chicken-or-egg problem, build a business model that takes advantage of network effects, and learn how to govern a platform. The last challenge requires working with competitors and other sides of the platform, which for many established companies has been an unnatural act. There are no easy solutions. Ultimately, managers have to commit to new ways of doing business without being wed to the past. Our colleague Clay Christensen famously recommended that old dogs should establish separate organizations to handle new, disruptive business models such as digital platforms.[57] But there is very little evidence that this has worked for many established companies. Sometimes a platform needs to be integrated into a core business; other times it should be separated. The key is accepting a platform mind-set, with all of the techniques and tools we describe in this book.

Although General Electric has struggled mightily as a company as well as struggled with its digital platform, it is one of the bolder examples of a traditional firm trying to establish a new platform business. General Electric was one of the oldest companies in the United States and a member of the twelve original companies that made up the first Dow Jones Industrial Average. A mere decade ago, GE remained one of the largest companies in the world, with annual revenues peaking at over $180 billion in 2008. In 2018, after several changes in leadership and continued divestitures of businesses, GE was smaller, with revenues of about $120 billion, though still a leader in most of its remaining businesses.

The Industrial Internet: The core of GE's business was making products like locomotives, jet engines, and turbines for power generation. However, GE was also facing new competitive threats from the emergence of the "industrial Internet" or the "industrial Internet of things" (IIoT). The idea of the IIoT referred to the integration of sensors into machines to produce continuous streams of data. The key was how to link these data streams to the cloud and then analyze large pools of data through analytics and predictive algorithms. The promise of the IIoT was to generate real-time intelligence and valuable insights for users. For example, a wind farm could use data to optimize its production by allowing turbines to rotate in order to harness more wind power. Incorporating this type of data analytics, a 100-megawatt wind farm could increase energy production by 20 percent and produce an additional $100 million over the farm's lifetime, according to a GE report.[58] Another major application was predictive maintenance—using the analysis of sensor data to predict when a piece of equipment is about to break down and repair it before it malfunctions.

Former CEO Jeffrey Immelt believed that data and analytics could add a substantial layer of value to GE's businesses. If one of GE's existing competitors or a third-party software firm developed a winner-take-all platform that captured that analytics layer, GE could be forced to join the platform and cede a great deal of the value of its equipment, including maintenance services, to the owner of the platform.

GE's initial answer to this dilemma was to build a platform and go head-to-head with Amazon, Microsoft, Google, IBM, and other software giants that dominated cloud computing. But in the words of one analyst, "GE knows the machinery, the industrial side very well but Microsoft, IBM et al. understand software a lot more."[59] At the same time, start-ups backed by venture capital were racing to capture the value of the data and analytics generated by the Internet of things; the financial and technical resources being poured into the space "keeps me up at night," said one GE executive in late 2016.

On the positive side, the opportunity was huge. GE estimated that the market for an industrial Internet platform and applications could reach $225 billion by 2020. Other estimates put the figure as high as $500 billion. In the words of one GE executive, "I think the race is on from a competition perspective and everybody understands the size of the Industrial Internet prize."[60]

Predix—A Platform for the Industrial Internet: To win the prize, GE leaders realized that the company would have to become a software and data analytics firm, transforming GE into a "top 10 software company." However, capitalizing on the potential of the industrial Internet would mean transforming GE into a platform company. The key to this transformation was Predix, GE's "cloud-based operating system for the industrial Internet."[61] In our terminology, Predix's goal was to become an operating system, designed to serve as an *innovation* platform for applications development, providing the services that permit programmers to quickly build apps for the industrial Internet. The strategy was to enable big data analytics, monitor machines remotely, and facilitate massive machine-to-machine communications.[62] In this way, it was much like Microsoft's Windows or Google's Android. But instead of running on PCs and phones it would be an "edge-to-cloud" platform. This meant it would be deployed both on industrial machines (the "edge") and in centralized data centers (the "cloud").

Mid-course Corrections—Platforms on Top of Platforms: Rather than build its platform from scratch, GE based Predix on the Pivotal Cloud Foundry, a leading cloud platform. Cloud Foundry was originally developed as an open-source platform by VMware, and later transferred to a joint venture called Pivotal Software that VMware formed with EMC. GE invested $105 million to take a 10 percent equity stake in Pivotal in 2013. Built on top of Pivotal Cloud Foundry, Predix was a cloud-based platform-as-a-service (PaaS).

GE originally planned to build its own data centers. But the technological challenges to building an industrial cloud platform were significant: It had to be optimized for industrial applications where the stakes were much higher and mistakes much costlier. The platform needed to be scalable to handle the massive amounts of data being generated by IIoT machines and needed to be able to deliver that information under potentially adverse conditions. In addition, much of the computing functionality needed to be installed on the machine itself, rather than off-loaded entirely to the cloud, in order to reduce latency and speed up analysis.[63] At the same time, data had to be aggregated into a central place to permit analysis, which happened on the cloud platform.

The natural tendency for an established giant such as GE was to control everything in-house. Yet building a successful platform was about enabling others, and not control. GE initially fell into this trap. Outside observers appropriately questioned GE's argument that its experience with industrial equipment uniquely qualified it to develop an industrial cloud, arguing that the virtue of a public cloud was flexible enough to be adapted to a variety of uses.[64] Observers pointed out that government agencies were using public cloud providers, and their security needs were as high as GE's customers'.[65]

By late 2016, GE had reversed course: It abandoned its own cloud infrastructure in favor of running Predix on top of Amazon's AWS and Microsoft's Azure clouds. Bill Ruh acknowledged in 2017 that "we pivoted" and admitted that the massive investment made into data centers by the likes of Amazon, Microsoft, and Google was "not an investment we can compete with."[66]

Solving the Chicken-or-Egg Problem: GE initially deployed its emerging software analytics capabilities on its internal operations. Immelt mandated that all GE business units had to use it to manage their equipment. GE estimated that Predix and associated applications generated $500 million in productivity gains in 2015.

As it began to take Predix to market, GE addressed the chicken-or-egg problem by taking advantage of its existing customer base. After developing applications for its own industrial processes, GE released a commercial version to its channel and technology partners as well as customers able to build their own analytics on top of the platform.[67] GE began running a series of pilots with customers in a variety of industries to demonstrate the capabilities and promise of Predix. At this stage, however, Predix was not truly an innovation platform. Rather, it represented a complementary service to GE's products, a set of tools and services that could add to the value of a given industrial asset. In a classic solution to the chicken-or-egg problem, GE offered Predix as a product and service with stand-alone value, even before third-party applications emerged.

Attracting Complementors: Recognizing the value of a thriving ecosystem of third-party developers, GE began aggressively recruiting software developers to develop applications that could run on the Predix platform.[68] To cultivate a thriving developer community, GE released Predix developer kits in August 2016 to a limited group of programmers and partners before making them available to everyone by the end of the year.[69] Predix had all the resources provided by a typical innovation platform: documentation, guides, training, APIs, a virtual machine preconfigured for developing with Predix, and a machine data simulator.

In addition, GE established "Digital Foundries," incubators for local start-ups designed to spur both its customers and third-party developers to build innovative Predix applications. The goal of these foundries, located in cities such as Paris, Munich, Shanghai, Boston, and Singapore, was to cultivate an "innovation ecosystem" around the platform.[70] As a result of these efforts, by December 2017, GE had 22,000 developers building applications and there were some 150 distinct applications available.[71] To realize the goal of becoming the dominant platform for the industrial Internet, GE also needed to attract other equipment manufacturers to the platform, including its competitors. After initially embedding Predix only on GE machines, GE opened up Predix to hardware from other manufacturers.

Governance and Use of Data: The promise of the industrial Internet lay in the ability to gather, pool, and analyze large quantities of data in order to improve operating performance, predict and avoid defects, and eliminate unplanned downtime. In most contexts, GE's equipment was operating as a part of a larger industrial ecosystem made up of equipment from a variety of manufacturers. The platform and complementary applications could only realize their full value if data from all the equipment in a given plant—not just GE equipment—were combined into a single "data lake" for analysis. This raised governance concerns about the use and ownership of data. To be effective, data was required from a wide range of customers and a variety of manufacturers. But customers were reluctant to share their operational data for competitive reasons. In the words of one executive, "Maybe five or six years from now, we'll begin to see companies more willing to share data that could unlock new levels of collaboration," perhaps by sharing anonymized data.[72] To allay privacy concerns, GE enabled users to retain ownership of all their data processed on Predix, while GE would own the algorithms.[73]

Monetization—Subscription and Hybrid Business Models: Finally, to build a successful platform, GE needed a monetization strategy. Building Predix was costly: In 2015 alone, GE spent half a billion dollars. GE planned to monetize Predix using a subscription-based model, with either metered payments or predefined bundles for enterprise customers. In some cases, the price would be linked to outcomes, i.e., GE would get paid more if it did more to improve performance or reduce downtime. "We believe deeply in subscription models being the future, so we're trying to build subscriptions that are priced based on the value that they deliver," according to one GE executive.[74]

In addition to deriving income from customer subscriptions to its platform, GE hoped to generate revenue from taking a percentage on third-party application sales or subscription revenue. While Predix was primarily an innovation platform, GE wanted to position Predix as a hybrid platform by adding a marketplace. GE also developed several hundred application suites running on Predix that it offered as software-as-a-service offerings. However, the viability of this business model depended heavily on the broad and successful deployment of Predix. At best, it would take years to deliver a reasonable return.

As we finished this book, it was too soon to tell whether GE would be able to transform itself into a platform company. GE faced serious competition as well as significant execution hurdles. For example, Siemens, GE's biggest industrial competitor, offered its own platform, called MindSphere. Siemens described MindSphere as an "open operating system for the Internet of things."[75] MindSphere's architecture and technology were much like that of Predix: It was a cloud-based platform-as-a-service product, built on the SAP Cloud, which in turn was based on the Pivotal Cloud Foundry.[76]

IBM and Microsoft also planned to compete head-to-head with GE and Siemens. In 2015, IBM announced it was launching an Internet of things division that would bring the analytical capabilities of its Watson cognitive computing service to the analysis of data generated by billions of devices that make up the IoT. And Microsoft's Azure cloud platform, first launched in 2010, was both a competitor and a partner for GE. Even as GE and Microsoft announced that Predix would be available on Azure by 2018, Azure also offered many of the same features. In the meantime, other large firms such as Amazon, Cisco, and Hitachi were designing their own software platforms for the industrial Internet. In addition, there were over 125 start-ups trying to grab a slice of the IoT market. In the narrower category of IIoT platforms, there were at least a dozen start-ups, including C3 IoT, Flutura, and Uptake.[77]

Beyond intense competition, GE faced other problems rolling out Predix. Technical difficulties and delays dogged Predix's implementation. Porting legacy systems with old code onto the new platform proved to be difficult and time-consuming. As a result, some customers faced delays in installations or software that was buggy or lacked desired features. In the meantime, Predix failed to hit internal development goals. In the midst of these struggles, the head of Predix development, Harel Kodesh, left in 2017, and his successor called a two-month "time-out" to address the problems.[78]

After the time-out, GE adjusted its strategy. First, GE began to focus on applications, "which executives now saw as more useful for winning business and more profitable than the platform alone."[79] In September 2017, new CEO John Flannery, who replaced Jeff Immelt, insisted that "GE is all in on digital," but he stated that GE would target its platform to GE verticals—not the entire IIoT.[80] Second, along with the rest of GE's operations, Predix and GE's digital effort would need to reduce costs. Executives suggested that the $700 million invested in GE's digital efforts in 2017 would represent a "peak" in its investment in the space. In late 2017, GE leaders remained optimistic about Predix, but acknowledged that, in the words of one executive, "doing that right and at scale is a massive challenge."[81]

In 2018, GE also revealed dismal financial results: The company lost nearly $6 billion in 2017, the stock price was down over 50 percent for the year, and activist investors Trian Fund Management won a seat on the board. In response, Flannery was considering a wholesale reorientation of GE's strategy, including $20 billion in asset sales and possible restructuring of the business. Among the changes Flannery proposed was a continuing shift in strategy for GE digital that de-emphasized Predix as an innovation platform for the industrial Internet in favor of selling solutions to GE's existing customers. Flannery said the strategy would "focus on a handful of applications," including asset performance management and operations performance management. He went on to say, "We're going to focus our platform investments on the things that really differentiate in an industrial world . . . we're going to sell these focused platform and applications into our installed base." This more modest approach, Flannery claimed, would allow GE to cut its Predix-related spending by about $400 million, a reduction of about 25 percent.[82]

In his annual letter to shareholders in February 2018, Flannery also reported that "Predix-powered orders were up over 150% in 2017." At the same time, he said, GE expected "Predix product revenues will double in 2018, to approximately $1 billion," a modest figure in light of the $12 billion in digital revenue GE had projected to be generating by 2020. Nevertheless, Flannery insisted, "There is absolutely no change in our belief in the digital future—only some adjustments in our approach."[83]

But Flannery was in for another surprise, which shocked most of the business world. Due to missed financial targets, surprisingly dismal financial results, and ongoing losses in the turbine and power-generation business, the GE board of directors replaced Flannery as CEO in October 2018 after only fourteen months on the job. His successor was new GE board member Larry Culp, formerly CEO of Danaher Corporation.[84] Culp has successfully focused Danaher, another diversified industrial company, but GE was a much bigger challenge. It was unclear to what extent Culp would stay the course or shift direction on GE's Predix business.

What GE learned, and what we can learn from GE, is that building a new platform from scratch can be a Herculean effort. We believe that building a platform was the right strategy for GE. Nonetheless, getting the various market sides on board, solving chicken-or-egg problems, creating a sustainable business model, and designing acceptable governance rules was a massive, long-term task that seemed beyond the company's capabilities. Maybe even more important, few successful platforms have begun with such grandiose ambitions, and GE may have fallen into the trap of overreaching. GE leadership focused on the promise of platforms without truly understanding platform thinking and without internalizing the harsh realities of the digital revolution.

KEY TAKEAWAYS FOR MANAGERS AND ENTREPRENEURS

In this chapter, we discussed how established firms can enter the platform business, focusing on three options: partner with an existing platform to sell your own products and services, buy an existing platform, or build a new platform from scratch. Can old dogs learn new tricks? We think so, even though the challenges are many. We have four key takeaways for managers and entrepreneurs (including "intrapreneurs" attempting to launch new platform businesses within an established firm).

First, when firms become large enough to go it alone, *the choice with regard to how to enter the platform business is usually between building and buying.* Like many other strategic decisions to internalize a new activity, the choice of build versus buy starts with time-to-market. Platforms require a new set of skills, which many traditional businesses do not possess, especially facilitating partnerships and open innovation, and stimulating economic activity without exercising direct control. If those skills are available, and time-to-market is important, even the most sophisticated technology companies find that "buying" platforms is better than building from scratch. Remember that Apple did not build Siri; it bought it. Facebook did not build Instagram; it bought it. And Walmart recognized that building its e-commerce business would probably never reduce the gap with Amazon, which led to the purchases of Jet.com and Flipkart in India. As Walmart's challenges in integrating Jet.com into the company illustrated, buying doesn't "solve" the problem, but it can jump-start the process.

Second, *"belonging" to someone else's platform creates the opportunity to leverage platform economics*: greater reach and potentially lower costs. The key is to remember that your success on a third-party platform can lead to that platform becoming your biggest competitor. Amazon has been famous (or infamous) for entering product categories with aggressive prices when it sees a platform player building a successful business. Similarly, eBay bought Pay-Pal and became a competitor to many of its partners. In past years, it has also been common for Microsoft, Apple, and Google to duplicate third-party applications or services that once were complements of their innovation platforms and then to sell those products or services themselves.

Third, *small or new firms are generally better off building their platforms on top of existing platforms* rather than trying to go it alone. Building a platform can be a good strategic move, particularly when the field is relatively new and existing players or technologies are not readily for sale. The challenge with building any new platform from scratch, especially one as complicated as GE's Predix and the industrial Internet of things, is that it takes time and money, as well as cooperation from other companies. To succeed, firms generally need deep pockets and a long time horizon. Maybe even more challenging is that managers have to solve all the platform challenges we discussed in Chapter 3: Choose the right market sides (complementors, buyers, sellers, etc.); overcome chicken-or-egg problems and build an installed base; create a business model to monetize the platform; and develop governance rules, ranging from who will own the data and the algorithms, to what's acceptable and unacceptable behavior.

The fourth and most important lesson is that *managers in the tra-*

ditional economy should not give up. The transition from conventional command-and-control businesses to digital platforms is painful but not impossible with experimentation and frequent adjustments in strategy. Some failures and setbacks are inevitable, but these are better than doing nothing.

The governance challenges when building and managing your own platform is the subject of Chapter 6.

DOUBLE-EDGED SWORDS

HARNESS PLATFORM POWER, BUT DON'T ABUSE IT

THE MOOD CHANGE

DON'T BE A BULLY
Anticipate Antitrust and
Competition Concerns

BALANCE OPENNESS WITH TRUST
Privacy, Fairness, and Fraud

THE WORKFORCE
Not Everyone Should Be a Contractor

SELF-REGULATE
Work with Regulators Before They Pounce

**KEY TAKEAWAYS FOR MANAGERS
AND ENTREPRENEURS**

CHAPTER 6

Quotes from Mark Zuckerberg, cofounder and CEO of Facebook:

2009: "Move fast and break things."[1]

2018: "We did not take a broad enough view of our responsibility, and that was a big mistake."[2]

Successful platforms inevitably acquire power. Platform power, like corporate power more generally, can take on different forms—economic but also social and political. How platform companies exercise that power reflects their position toward another crucial aspect of the business: platform governance.

In the early stages, it may be desirable for start-ups to "move fast and break things," as Facebook's Mark Zuckerberg declared in 2009. However, once they have achieved strong market positions, firms that abuse their economic power or fail in other governance areas can end up losing big. This holds true for platforms as well as other businesses, and reflects the other side of the coin that Zuckerberg acknowledged with his comment in 2018. In particular, powerful platforms may disenfranchise their ecosystem members, driving up resentment and fear from business partners ("complementors") and customers alike. They may drive their beleaguered rivals into concerted action. They may also antagonize government regulators, who have demonstrated they will strike at platforms that do not keep their power or ambitions in check. To sustain the business long term, therefore, we argue that platform leaders must become aware of their potential for power and understand how to use it. The challenge is to compete aggressively while staying within the bounds of what most societies consider legal as well as fair and ethical.

THE MOOD CHANGE

Until recently, the dominant mood in the business press (and in many business books on platform companies) was unbridled enthusiasm for the efficiency of platforms and awe at the speed at which they introduced both innovation and disruption. We and other authors have shown that many platforms are indeed amazing: They can reduce search and transaction costs, and fundamentally restructure entire industries within a few short years. We have seen this dynamic in computers, online marketplaces, taxis, hotels, financial services, and many other fields. Nonetheless, the tide of public perception seems to have turned: Media coverage of platforms has become increasingly negative. Calls to break up Alphabet-Google have appeared in major newspapers. The "Delete Facebook" movement was gaining traction among the public. Uber nearly collapsed from internal chaos, failure to properly vet drivers, misuse of digital technology (e.g., "Greyball" software that helped drivers evade law enforcement in markets where Uber was prohibited), and opposition from local governments and taxi industry representatives.

Why now? After three decades of explosive growth around the world, why have competitors, users, and regulators started to raise serious questions about the use and abuse of platform power? Part of the answer is scale: The biggest platforms—Apple, Amazon, Google, Microsoft, and Facebook—have become so large and valuable that they appear to be more influential and wealthier than many governments. As a group, these top platform firms have garnered so much power that one *New York Times* columnist labeled them "the Frightful Five."[3]

These tech giants may have become too big to control. Google and Facebook dominate two-thirds of digital advertising. Apple has captured 90 percent of the world's profits in smartphones. Amazon presides over more than 40 percent of e-commerce in the United States. Microsoft still owns 90 percent of the world's PC operating systems. Intel still provides some 80 percent of the microprocessors for personal computers and more than 90 percent of the microprocessors for Internet servers. Facebook accounts for perhaps two-thirds of social media activity. The most powerful platform companies have started to look a bit like the big banks in the 2008–2009 financial crisis: too big to fail? Consider as well how platforms recently enabled the dissemination of fake news, Russian manipulation of social media, and electoral tampering, and clearly we have reached an inflection point. We now must view the most powerful platform companies as doubled-edged swords, capable of both good and evil.

Some threats reflect classical economic concerns, such as abuse of market power. In the non-digital world, governments traditionally addressed these problems via antitrust laws. Indeed, virtually every large platform company has faced American, European, or Chinese antitrust actions. Microsoft and Intel were targeted multiple times between 1994 and 2005; Google (and its holding-company parent since 2015, Alphabet) has been the big target in the last ten years, including high-profile cases brought by the European Commission against Google's practices with vertical search and the Android mobile operating system. Apple was found guilty of price fixing and conspiring with electronic book publishers to raise consumer prices. More recently, a Yale law student published a widely quoted treatise on why antitrust law must change to address the threats from Amazon and other platform businesses even if their shares in particular markets remain well below the usual thresholds for antitrust action.[4]

Still, antitrust concerns and signs of market power abuse are not the full story. The 2018 scandal involving Facebook and Cambridge Analytica, for example, revealed that 87 million Facebook users had their personal data accessed without their explicit consent. Cambridge Analytica exploited weak Facebook privacy controls and turned a list of 300,000 people who had voluntarily answered a personality quiz on Facebook into a weapon for manipulating voter perception on a national scale. Ultimately, the Cambridge Analytica debacle raised broader questions about who is responsible and liable for activities on a platform. Are the participants on the different "market sides" responsible for their specific actions? Or must the owner of the platform take responsibility? For example, is Alibaba responsible for counterfeit products sold on its consumer platform, Taobao? Is YouTube responsible for pirated content uploaded to its platform? Who is responsible for violent or extreme user-generated content posted to any number of platforms around the world?

At one end of the spectrum, some people argue that platforms are not at fault. They view platforms as passive conduits; their only role is to serve as intermediaries to facilitate innovations or transactions, including information exchanges and content creation. The line of reasoning goes like this: Should a telephone company be held responsible for illicit conversations that happen on its telephone lines? Probably not. But then we get into a grayer area: Should a railroad company be held liable for thefts or terrorist attacks on its rail network? Maybe not, but maybe—if the company did not make what society deems to be reasonable efforts to protect its users.

Some companies like to use the "technically impossible defense." They argue that it is impossible to monitor all the activities that might occur on their platforms. And clearly, with billions of users interacting every day, monitoring and controlling all platform activity is probably impossible, although it is becoming more feasible with advances in technology. Nonetheless, after a number of events involving Facebook and other platforms, broad swaths of society, as well as company executives and boards of directors, are now convinced that platforms do have a grave responsibility to police "bad actors" and illicit activities.

Not all the controversies over platforms have involved large and powerful American firms. In China, for example, there was a boom in small-scale lending platforms that arranged short-term loans between individuals and start-up companies or small businesses with weak credit ratings. These platforms claimed to be matchmakers and largely worked outside China's financial system, promising huge returns of as much as 50 percent to an estimated 4 million small investors. State-owned banks facilitated the money transfers and made the investments seem safer than they actually were. The government started to crack down in 2016–2017, jailing for life the founder of Ezubao, a $9 billion lending platform. In July 2018 alone, China closed down 168 of these dubious lending platforms, according to one industry source.[5] In retrospect, most of these platforms were little more than Ponzi schemes, operating under the cover of the "sharing economy."

The discussion of what governments should and should not permit is really about platform regulation. Some platforms have hidden behind their self-definition as "technology companies" to claim that sectoral regulation should not apply to them. Uber claimed it was not a transportation service and should not be regulated like a taxi company. Facebook claimed it was not a media company and that media regulation was irrelevant to its operations. Airbnb claimed it was not a hospitality or hotel company and merely connected renters and owners. The Chinese lending platforms presented themselves as matchmakers for peer-to-peer lenders and not as banks. These contested categorizations may seem like an arcane topic mainly of interest to regulators and corporate lawyers. However, they had real financial and logistical implications for the platform companies, individual users, and their investors.

In this chapter, we argue that managers and entrepreneurs should try to harness platform power but not abuse it. Platforms will try to exploit a dominant position, but they need to avoid or minimize the challenges posed by antitrust and broader societal concerns. We have organized our discussion around four guidelines: Don't be a bully, balance openness with trust, respect labor laws, and curate (self-regulate).

DON'T BE A BULLY: ANTICIPATE ANTITRUST AND COMPETITION CONCERNS

Given the many ways platforms can abuse their power, perhaps the most expensive consequences come with violations of antitrust laws. In a winner-take-all-or-most world where network effects drive industry concentration around a small number of dominant players, platform companies have many opportunities to exercise market power, harm consumer welfare, hurt local or global competitors, and extract monopoly or quasi-monopoly rents. Antitrust cases are costly and lengthy affairs that usually take many years to resolve. At a minimum, they represent a serious distraction for senior management. When governments determine that a firm has violated antitrust rules, the remedies can be painful. They range from huge fines (up to 10 percent of global revenues in the European Union) and behavioral restrictions (limitations on specific actions that may be core to a firm's competitive advantage) to structural solutions (such as breaking up a firm). Recall that the U.S. Justice Department in 2000 recommended breaking up Microsoft, but this remedy was overturned on appeal.

LESSONS FROM THE MICROSOFT ANTITRUST CASE

Microsoft's numerous antitrust cases in the U.S. and in Europe have been discussed extensively elsewhere, but let's review the key facts here to highlight the biggest risks and business lessons for current platform companies.[6] The Microsoft antitrust saga began with a

U.S. Federal Trade Commission investigation in 1990, followed by a consent decree signed in 1994 and a 1998 lawsuit from the U.S. Department of Justice and twenty U.S. states. One of the central issues hinged on whether Microsoft had used its monopoly in operating systems with Windows to force computer makers to exclude a browser made by Netscape. In 2000, a federal judge ruled that Microsoft had violated antitrust law, and ordered that the company be broken up, separating out the operating system business from the applications and Internet businesses. Microsoft appealed, which led to a new consent decree approved in 2002 that curbed some Microsoft practices. The U.S. consent decree officially expired in 2011.[7]

In parallel, the European Commission brought a different antitrust lawsuit against Microsoft for failing to provide interface information to allow rivals to connect into the Windows operating system.[8] The European Commission accusations were later expanded in 2001 to include anticompetitive tying of the Windows Media Player with the Windows operating system. In 2004, the European Commission concluded that Microsoft had broken European Union law by leveraging its near monopoly in the market for PC operating systems onto markets for group-server operating systems and for digital media players. It ordered Microsoft to pay a €497 million fine ($620 million) and to make interface information available through "reasonable and non-discriminatory terms." Other fines were added in 2006, 2008, and 2011, amounting to $2.1 billion for noncompliance.[9] When the U.S. consent decree expired in 2011, Microsoft released this statement: "Our experience has changed us and shaped how we view our responsibility to the industry."[10]

While the exact accusations differed across the lawsuits and between the U.S. and Europe, what they have in common is that regulators accused Microsoft (and found it guilty) of abusing the company's dominance in PC operating systems—the most widely used innovation platform before the smartphone. The first set of exclusionary practices involved *bullying* computer makers (usually referred to as original equipment manufacturers or OEMs). For example, Microsoft threatened to cancel their Windows licenses in order to discourage them from loading rival browsers such as Netscape Navigator onto computers bundled with Microsoft Windows. As we wrote in *Competing on Internet Time: Lessons from Netscape and Its Battle with Microsoft* (1998), Microsoft frequently resorted to these types of tactics and, in our view, clearly "stepped over the line," illegally using its monopoly power to reduce competition.[11]

The second set of exclusionary practices had to do with *tying*: Microsoft bundled complements such as the Media Player or the Internet Explorer browser with Windows at no extra cost to end users. By doing so, the platform owner effectively reduced or even eliminated the attractiveness to consumers of rival products.

A third set of practices deemed unlawful in Europe involved preventing third parties from having reasonable *access* to the platform in the form of interface information, making it impossible for them to become complementors. European antitrust authorities ultimately proclaimed that a platform company must provide access and create a "level-playing field" that was "reasonable and nondiscriminatory" for third-party complementors.[12]

The Microsoft case highlights an important lesson for today's platform companies: Very few of the actions that violated antitrust laws were necessary or critical to retaining a dominant market position. Platform businesses, once established, are difficult to dislodge. Microsoft most likely would have kept the vast majority of its share of PC operating systems and its dominant position in browsers and media players *without* illegally bullying PC manufacturers, competitors, or complementors. In many ways, Microsoft took unnecessary competitive shortcuts. Rather than relying on the merits of its products and technology, Microsoft tried to leverage its position with operating systems to put competitors at a disadvantage. Yet Microsoft had many natural advantages because of its huge market share with Windows and Office, deep pockets, and technical insights into how to best utilize its platform technologies. It was likely to win most battles without ending up in court. Nevertheless, one dominant platform firm after another has fallen into a similar trap of probably unnecessary paranoia followed by an abuse of power. Let's briefly consider one other example: Google with Android.

GOOGLE AND ANDROID

Alphabet-Google replaced Microsoft as the primary focus of antitrust actions, particularly in the European Union. In fact, the EU had three cases against the company. The first, launched in 2010, considered Google's behavior with its search engine. The EU accused Google of promoting its own "vertical search" results over general content search results. The second focused on how the company prevented websites that used its search bar and ads from showing competing ads. The third concentrated on Google's management of Android. The Google Android example highlighted how a dominant innovation platform could be vulnerable to antitrust complaints even if it was free (unlike Microsoft Windows).

We discussed in earlier chapters how Google licensed the Android mobile operating system for no charge to manufacturers of smartphones and tablets but made money from selling advertisements that came through its search engine. There is nothing illegal about this multisided platform strategy. However, the European Commission alleged in 2016 that Google imposed conditions on mobile phone manufacturers and mobile phone operators aimed at protecting Google's search engine monopoly.[13] The Commission complaint stated that Google breached EU antitrust rules in three areas: (1) requiring manufacturers to preinstall Google Search and Google's Chrome browser and requiring them to set Google Search as the default search service on their devices as a condition to license certain Google proprietary apps; (2) preventing manufacturers from selling smart mobile devices running on competing operating systems based on the Android open source code; and (3) giving financial incentives to manufacturers and mobile network operators on the condition that they exclusively preinstall Google Search on their devices. Commissioner Margrethe Vestager, in charge of competition policy, explained: "We believe that Google's behavior denies consumers a wider choice of mobile apps and services and stands in the way of innovation by other players, in breach of EU antitrust rules."[14]

In effect, the EU accused Google of the same kinds of tying, bullying, and exclusionary behavior of which Microsoft had been found guilty. Just as Microsoft was defending its 90-plus percent share of PC operating systems, Google was defending its approximately 90 percent share of global search and 80 percent share of smartphone operating systems. Although Android was ostensibly "free" and "open source," the Commission's investigation showed that it was commercially important for smartphone manufacturers using the Android operating system to preinstall the Play Store, Google's app store for Android. In its contracts with manufacturers, Google also made licensing the Play Store on Android devices conditional on Google Search being preinstalled and set as the default search service, tying these products and services to the Android platform. As a result, rival search engines were unable to become the default search service for most smartphones and tablets sold in Europe.

Similarly, Google's contracts with manufacturers required the preinstallation of its Chrome mobile browser in return for licensing the Play Store or Google Search. Google's defense was that it wanted to reduce fragmentation and make it easier for developers to write new applications that would work on all Android phones and make it easier for consumers to have a consistent experience. But the Commission argued that browsers were an important entry point for search queries on mobile devices, and Google's requirements reduced manufacturers' incentives to preinstall competing browser apps and consumers' incentives to download those apps.

The European Union fined Google's parent company Alphabet $2.7 billion in 2017 and $5.1 billion in 2018 for anticompetitive behavior. As this book was being published, Google was appealing. We contend that, before things got to this stage, Google should have learned from the Microsoft case: It should have been more attuned to European antitrust rules and used less aggressive contracts. In the early days, when Android was just getting started, it made sense for Google to push the limits of its power. It was a new entrant into the smartphone platform business. Fragmentation, with multiple versions of Android, multiple browsers, and multiple app stores, unquestionably caused confusion among consumers and reduced incentives for application developers to absorb the expense of supporting incompatible Android versions. But, similar to the Microsoft case, once Android "won" the mobile OS wars, the vast majority of smartphone manufacturers were likely to bundle Google Chrome and Google Search anyway, regardless of the contract conditions. (Remember, Apple does not license its platform technology to anyone, for any price.) Google might have lost a few smartphone models to another app store or browser, but they would have been unlikely to stem the tide behind Android. Given its dominant position, and the consumer benefits of having access to the Play Store, Google Search, and Chrome, being a bully was unnecessary for Google by 2015.

BALANCE OPENNESS WITH TRUST: PRIVACY, FAIRNESS, AND FRAUD

Antitrust is only one challenge for platform governance. Questions regarding responsibility and liability over activities conducted on a platform have become increasingly salient. All platforms require trust, which the dictionary defines as "reliance on the integrity, strength, ability, surety, etc., of a person or thing; confidence."[15]

Since most modern platforms connect market actors that would otherwise struggle to interact, trust is essential.

To maintain trust, platforms need to prevent "bad actors" from contaminating the platform, doing damage to other platform users, or hurting the platform's reputation in other ways. This proactive prevention process is often referred to as "curating" the platform. Curation can take several forms: restricting who can join; restricting what activities can happen; imposing transparency and authenticating members; providing controls to users such as who can contact them, who can see their content, how they can restrict access to information they provide (like Facebook or LinkedIn privacy settings); and monitoring activity on the platform (such as removing content deemed inappropriate or illegal).

But curation is no panacea, nor is it cost-free. Curation for a very large number of users and their content can be difficult to perform effectively and expensive to implement. Although artificial intelligence tools are making curation easier and cheaper, the technology today is not sufficiently advanced to replace human intervention. Companies need thousands or even tens of thousands of human curators to police a large platform. In addition, curating might be actually counterproductive: We discussed in Chapter 4 how eBay got rid of known counterfeiters on its China site and then lost 20 percent to 40 percent of its user base. Many consumers went to Alibaba because they *wanted* access to fake goods and bought them knowingly. Curation can even anger free speech advocates, who see taking down content as a step toward censorship.[16] Finally, curated platforms—by definition—restrict the number of users, which in turn can reduce the strength of network effects.

FACEBOOK'S GOVERNANCE CHALLENGES

Facebook is the poster child for examining the challenges of maintaining trust. Beginning in early 2016, Facebook faced a series of intertwined controversies that called into question its identity as an open platform, an identity Zuckerberg and other managers had strongly defended. We have already given some details of the controversy. The issues are complex, but they boil down to two major questions of platform governance: What is Facebook's responsibility to monitor and curate the content shared on its platform? And what steps should Facebook take to protect users' privacy and ensure that third-party developers and advertisers are not misusing user data?

Facebook has become increasingly important as a platform not just for sharing individual information but also as the major way people discover and consume news. Accordingly, it has come under increasing criticism for the nature and quality of content posted on its site. It had always policed content to some degree, such as removing content defined as violent, sexually explicit, expressing hate speech, or harassment. In its early years, though, Facebook primarily depended on users to flag objectionable content, which the company would review and remove if it violated platform policies.

Despite increasing influence over the news business, Facebook continued to insist it was an open and neutral platform, not a publisher or a media company. In fact, in early 2016, when Facebook came under criticism for allegedly suppressing conservative viewpoints, CEO Mark Zuckerberg was asked if Facebook "would be an open platform for the sharing of all ideas or a curator of content." He is reported to have replied firmly that "we are an open platform."[17] Events surrounding the 2016 election, however, called into question Facebook's commitment to neutrality in its treatment of news content. During the course of the campaign, the volume of fake stories on the platform proliferated and users often shared those fake stories. Most damning were revelations that Russian actors had used Facebook to mount a propaganda campaign to influence the 2016 presidential election by creating fake accounts to post fake news stories. Although the number of fake accounts was small relative to the overall size of Facebook, the viral nature of posts magnified their influence. One study of five hundred posts by merely six fake accounts showed that users had shared them 340 million times.[18]

All of this had the effect of increasing polarization and division within the United States, for which Facebook came under harsh criticism from both the public and politicians. The stakes were even higher in most developing nations (except China), where Facebook's mobile app had become the dominant way people consumed news. In recent years, false and misleading stories disseminated on Facebook have contributed to widespread ethnic and religious violence in countries such as Myanmar and Sri Lanka. As one observer put it, "The fact that Facebook is the Internet for many digital users, combined with low levels of digital literacy, makes fake news and online hate speech particularly dangerous in Myanmar."[19]

Critics charged that malicious actors using Facebook in this way were simply taking advantage of Facebook's platform model, which valued stories based on how often they were read, liked, and shared. It turned out that polarizing, simplistic, and false stories often generated more user engagement (and more advertising revenue) than sound news reporting! One Facebook executive acknowledged in late 2017, "If we just reward content based on raw clicks and engagement, we might actually see content that is increasingly sensationalistic, clickbait, polarizing, and divisive."[20] Ironically, that kind of content, while bad for the social fabric, was good for Facebook's bottom line. As *Wired* noted, Facebook "sold ads against the stories and sensational garbage was good at pulling people into the platform."[21]

The public backlash and scrutiny from politicians led Zuckerberg and Facebook to reexamine the way content on its platform is monitored and to do more to police content. In a significant step away from being a neutral platform, Zuckerberg announced in January 2018 that Facebook would alter its algorithm for selecting stories to show in the news feed. The new goal was to promote news sources that were "trustworthy" and "informative," with the trustworthiness of news sources based on surveys of Facebook users.[22]

Facebook also announced it would ramp up efforts to catch fake news, foreign interference, and fake accounts through human monitoring, the use of third-party fact-checkers, and improved algorithms. Guy Rosen, Facebook's vice president of product management, stated, "We are all responsible for making sure the same kind of attack on our democracy does not happen again."[23] Stepping up monitoring entailed compromises, however. As Zuckerberg noted, "When you think about issues like fake news or hate speech, right, it's a trade-off between free speech and free expression and safety and having an informed community."[24]

Until recently, social media platforms were adamant that they were not publishers but rather passive conduits of unedited and uncensored information that was generated by their users. In 2018, the big Internet platforms were not legally treated as publishers. This was due to the so-called safe harbor provision of the 1996 U.S. Communications Decency Act, a landmark in Internet regulation that stated that platforms were not responsible for what people published on their sites. But this law was originally intended to protect areas such as newspaper comment sections. The application of this law has become very broad, encompassing virtually all content on social media and sharing websites.[25]

One of the reasons why social media platforms do not want to be treated as publishers is because publishers are legally responsible for their editorial and publishing decisions. If a newspaper published a libelous or defamatory story, it could be sued. And if it infringed someone's copyright, it could be held liable for damages.[26] Another reason for platforms to resist curating or curtailing some content was simply a number's game: A Facebook executive, for example, argued that all content was good for platforms, as more content fed more users and fueled network effects. It has even been suggested that the more outrageous or shocking the content, the more traffic it actually drives.[27] But the backlash against the apparent neutrality, and what many have judged as callous behavior by Facebook and others, has made the "neutral" stance of social media platforms an increasingly untenable position.

In effect, by not only policing but selecting content, Facebook backed further away from its identity as a neutral platform and took a step closer to acting as a publisher. Facebook already employed some 15,000 content moderators in early 2018, and Zuckerberg promised the U.S. Congress that number would grow to 20,000 by the year's end.[28] The Cambridge Analytica scandal further exacerbated Facebook's legitimacy and trust problems. Cambridge Analytica collected its data by 2014, when Facebook's rules permitted apps to collect private information from users of the app as well as their Facebook friends. By 2015, Facebook had already changed its policy to remove the ability of third-party developers to collect detailed data about app users' friends, but for many of its users it was still unclear the extent to which third parties used personal data.

To address the obvious loophole in its privacy policies, in April 2018, Facebook put additional limits on the information third-party apps could access.[29] Imposing such limits, of course, generated more trade-offs. The ability of third-party apps to collect and analyze user data was critical to Facebook's business model as an open platform. High growth rates depended on both app developers and advertisers getting deep insights from user data, which enabled increasingly effective targeted advertising. As one observer put it, "Third-party developers [have] built millions of apps on top of Facebook's platform, giving Facebook users more reasons to spend time on the site and generating more ad revenue for the company. Restricting access to data would limit Facebook's usefulness to developers and could drive them to build on a rival platform instead."[30] Zuckerberg acknowledged the tension in a 2018 interview: "I do think early on on the platform we had this very idealistic vision around how data portability would allow all these different new experiences, and I think the feedback that we've gotten from our community and from the world is that privacy and having the data locked down is more important to people than maybe making it easier to bring more data and have different kinds of experiences."[31]

Similar to Facebook's problems with fake news, what Cambridge Analytica did pushed Facebook to engage in more robust oversight to enforce its rules around data sharing. When first informed of the data harvesting activity, Facebook asked for and received a legal certification from the developer that the data had been destroyed. Facebook also received assurances from Cambridge Analytica that they had not received raw Facebook data. Those assertions turned out to be false, and Zuckerberg would later acknowledge that accepting those assertions was a mistake.

Facebook provided numerous lessons for other platforms. Beyond the big hit to Facebook's stock price and market value, the potential loss of trust has provoked a more serious backlash and increased scrutiny. If movements such as #deletefacebook picked up steam, the long-run implications could be even more damaging for the company. Facebook's experience also foreshadowed the importance of preemptively curating, rather than waiting for the next crisis. At scale, powerful platforms cannot operate without enforcing rules of conduct on the platform and at least modest curation.

The trade-off between openness and curation creates a fundamental dilemma for platform governance: On the one hand, platforms should take some responsibility for how their platform is used. On the other hand, few people want platforms to become the new censors. For example, there was a raging debate in August 2018 when Facebook, Apple, Spotify, and YouTube moved to ban Alex Jones, the U.S. right-wing radio host and political commentator of InfoWars.[32] In effect, digital platforms were trying to have it both ways: Take advantage of the fact they were not publishers to escape responsibility and, at the same time, increasingly acting like publishers in deciding which views and people were permitted on their platforms.

THE WORKFORCE: NOT EVERYONE SHOULD BE A CONTRACTOR

One of the most attractive features of platforms for financial investors is that they can be asset-light. Uber does not own taxis. Airbnb does not own apartments or houses. OpenTable does not own restaurants. Instead, most platforms connect people or companies with valuable assets and skills to other people and companies who want access to those assets and skills. While asset-light platforms potentially provide highly leveraged returns to investors, they create another challenge for human capital: How should platforms manage a workforce largely composed of "independent contractors"? Unlike employees, independent contractors are due no benefits, guarantee of hours, or minimum wage, enabling the enterprises that employ them to keep labor costs low. There were 57 million freelancers in the U.S. in 2017; for one-third of these people, freelance activity was their main source of income.[33] Stephane Kasriel, CEO of Upwork, claimed that this class of workers is growing three times faster than the traditional workforce. One estimate suggests that, if the current trend were to continue, freelancers could represent 50 percent of all U.S. laborers by 2027.[34]

Platforms such as Uber, Grubhub, TaskRabbit, Upwork, Handy, and Deliveroo classify much of their workforce as independent contractors. The companies justify this practice because the workers tend to perform their jobs as a side activity, with significant flexibility in their hours. In reality, this classification is mostly about saving costs: Industry executives have estimated that classifying workers as employees tends to cost 20 to 30 percent more than classifying them as contractors.[35] The classification is therefore critical because many transaction platform start-ups rely on it to avoid high labor costs. Some even argue that the whole "gig economy" would collapse if start-ups were obliged by law to classify all their associated workers as employees.[36] But this widespread practice is becoming increasingly controversial. In the United States, the situation is particularly complex because laws that determine independent contractor and employee status vary from state to state, and even city by city, although many regulations focus on how much control workers have over their work.

The highest-profile debates over contractors involved Uber and ride-sharing platforms. Arguments could be made on both sides whether Uber drivers were employees or contractors.[37] On the contractor side, drivers supply the tools for their work (the cars), are paid by the job, and control their work hours, geographic area for pickups, and whether or not to accept a passenger's request for a ride. On the other hand, Uber sets the passenger pay rate, the method of pay, and which passengers the drivers must pick up, and the company immediately removes drivers who fall below a 4.6 rating from the app. By contrast, Uber's rival Lyft agreed in January 2016 to pay $12.3 million as part of a labor lawsuit settlement.[38] Lyft also agreed to change the terms of its service agreement with drivers so that it could only deactivate them for specific reasons, such as low ratings from passengers, and would give them an opportunity to address feedback before being deactivated. It also agreed to pay arbitration costs for drivers who wanted to challenge being deactivated or made other compensation complaints.

If an employer is mainly focused on the outcome of the work being performed, there is a good chance the workers are fairly being classified as independent contractors. But when their employer begins to control not only what work they do but how they do it, that classification gets murky, as several examples demonstrate.

HANDY

Handy was a start-up platform hatched out of Harvard University in 2012. It originally connected cleaners to people who wanted their homes cleaned and then expanded to other "handyman" services. As of 2018, the company operated in the U.S., Canada, and the U.K., and reportedly had raised over $110 million in venture capital. Handy offered an easy way to arrange help for cleaning and other tasks, with the person you hired vetted through customer ratings and a background check. As a transaction platform, it provided value to both service providers (workers) and users. Workers who used Handy had an easier time attracting new customers and ensuring they were adequately paid; with Handy, they made $15 to $22 an hour, based on their online rating. Users looking for help found it easier to identify people and benefited from them being vetted and knowing their review scores.

As with other platforms offering these types of services, Handy classified its unskilled workers as contractors, not employees. Handy CEO Oisin Hanrahan justified the classification by claiming the biggest benefit of the contractor system is that cleaners, who Handy dubbed "pros," were free to keep their own schedules. "Our pros value flexibility and getting to say where and when they want to work. Fifty percent work less than 10 hours a week and eighty percent work less than 20. Typically, they're folks who work another job, are in school, or caring for parents," Hanrahan said. He added that it was unreasonable to expect people who worked intermittently to be covered by the same system as someone who worked a forty-hour week with benefits.[39]

But opposition continued to grow toward the classification of such workers as contractors. California lawyer Shannon Liss-Riordan became notorious for leading worker class-action suits against transaction platform companies, having spearheaded lawsuits against Uber, Lyft, and nine other firms that provided on-demand services. In an interview with Fortune magazine, she scoffed at the comments made by Handy's CEO: "Those arguments ring hollow. The cleaners are not getting wage protection, and they're not getting workers' compensation or unemployment insurance," said Liss-Riordan. "Handy is not just Craigslist. It's an employer controlling a workforce." She added that Handy's use of training guides and the company's control over work rules and prices, as well as asking Handy workers to wear a Handy logo, proved that Handy cleaners were employees.[40]

In August 2017, the National Labor Relations Board issued a complaint against Handy, alleging that workers who provided its home cleaning services were employees, despite the company's claims to the contrary. It alleged that Handy "has misclassified its cleaners as 'independent contractors,' while they were in fact statutory employees" entitled to the protections of federal labor law.[41] The company Homejoy, another on-demand cleaning services company, was also sued in a class action over worker classification in 2015 and had to shut down. It is not yet clear how Handy will fare in the future or whether senior management will change its position.

DELIVEROO

The contractor versus employee classification dilemma is not just an American problem. We have seen similar complaints arise for Deliveroo in the United Kingdom, where its couriers are a familiar sight on London streets. Riding their bicycles, they delivered restaurant meals ordered on a mobile app. As self-employed contractors, Deliveroo couriers were not entitled to the rights available to regular workers, including sick pay and the national living wage.[42] The Independent Workers Union of Great Britain (IWGB) brought a test case in 2017 to fight for the right of union recognition at Deliveroo in Camden and Kentish Town, London. The hearing took place in front of the U.K. Central Arbitration Committee (CAC), an independent body that adjudicates on statutory recognition and de-recognition of trade unions in relation to collective bargaining. The CAC agreed with Deliveroo's argument that its riders were self-employed contractors, rather than workers.

The CAC decision rested on a specific practice called "unfettered right of substitutions," accepted by Deliveroo for their riders in Camden and Kentish Town. Deliveroo riders could nominate any individuals to perform deliveries in their place. This right was available without Deliveroo's prior approval, save only that substitutes could not have had their own supplier agreements with Deliveroo terminated, or could not have engaged in conduct that would have provided grounds for termination. There were no adverse consequences if a rider nominated a substitute. Equally, riders did not have to accept a certain proportion of jobs and were not penalized for turning down work. The ability of couriers to substitute or obtain a replacement for the job was central to the CAC's finding that they were not "workers."[43] Since the change in contracts happened only a couple of weeks before the adjudication, representatives of the IWGB claimed that Deliveroo "gamed the system."[44] The CAC decision impacted only a small geographic area in North London. In other places, Deliveroo had various forms of contracts with riders. The IWGB applied in 2018 to have the CAC decision reversed in a judicial review.

THE BIGGER PICTURE: A CHANGING LEGAL REGIME

The problem of how to classify workers is not specifically a platform problem. FedEx, for example, had long tried to classify its drivers as independent contractors. It faced challenges as well, including two class-action lawsuits brought by 2,000 drivers in California and another by over 12,000 in Indiana and eighteen other U.S. states. In these cases, drivers claimed they were undercompensated compared to full-time workers. FedEx settled the first case in June 2015 for $227 million[45] and settled the second case in 2017 for another $227 million.[46]

Workforce regulation will proceed amid a changing legal environment. It is going to become increasingly difficult for platforms or other firms to classify workers as independent contractors. In an April 2018 landmark ruling, the California Supreme Court narrowed significantly the circumstances under which California businesses may classify workers as independent contractors rather than employees.[47] The decision presumes that all workers are employees, sets out a new three-part "ABC" test that businesses must satisfy in order to classify workers as independent contractors, and places the burden on the business, not the worker, to prove that any particular worker is properly classified as an independent contractor. Under the ABC test, the business bears the burden of proving the worker satisfies all three of the following factors:

(A) The worker is free from control and direction of the hiring entity in connection with the performance of the work, both under the contract for performance of the work and in fact.

(B) The worker performs work that is outside the course of the hiring entity's business.

(C) The worker is customarily engaged in an independently established trade, occupation, or business.

This development marks a substantive change from previous regulation. For decades, the common law test in California of whether workers were employees or independent contractors involved the employer's "right to control" the manner and means by which workers performed their duties. In the new California ruling, a business's failure to prove any one part of the ABC test will result in the workers being classified as employees under the applicable California wage order. By shifting the burden to the business, the California Supreme Court created a presumption that workers are employees. Furthermore, the circumstances of the working relationship will decide the question; businesses may not avoid the ABC test by way of a contract in which the parties agree the workers are independent contractors.

This legal ruling has immediate ramifications for businesses throughout California, where many platforms operate. It is also likely to influence practices outside California. Shortly after the California Supreme Court ruling, San Francisco city attorney Dennis Herrera announced he was subpoenaing Lyft and Uber to see how they classified their drivers and to obtain data on pay and benefits. If those drivers should in fact be considered employees, the ride-for-hire firms would owe them minimum wages along with sick days, paid parental leave, and health benefits, according to Herrera. This would have drastic financial consequences for Uber and Lyft in California.

These issues were also part of a national debate in the United States about workers in the gig economy more broadly. We cannot predict with any certainty how this debate will end. Nonetheless, we believe that the days of large platforms treating everyone as a contractor are probably over, at least in the United States. Legal and reputational risks are rising dramatically for firms like Uber. For workers who perform tasks central to a business, the bigger, successful platforms will need to offer some benefits that are comparable to what regular employees receive. Start-ups can get away with using mostly contractors at first because they are still small and under the radar of regulators and competitors. As the companies grow in size, however, they need to grow up in terms of policies. Once platform companies get beyond the start-up phase, expectations of compliance and fairness, from workers as well as customers and regulators, will change. Platforms that get into the most legal trouble are likely to be those that do not recognize when they pass that threshold between start-up mode and established company.

As platforms move from cleaners and taxi drivers to highly paid white-collar contractors, workers in the gig economy will become more highly educated, with greater bargaining power. In order to be sustainable enterprises and to be accepted as beneficial contributors to society, platform companies need to adopt the same values as the societies in which they function. Given the growing sensitivity to issues of fairness, powerful platforms risk destroying their reputations. How platforms treat the people who contribute to their success will become an increasingly important part of building and maintaining their reputations. Reputations, in turn, will impact how well platforms compete long term with each other as well as with traditional businesses.

SELF-REGULATE: WORK WITH REGULATORS BEFORE THEY POUNCE

Platform start-ups often break rules. By finding new ways to do things, they often have skirted sectoral regulations and traditional tax collection. Some of the strongest critics, such as our colleague Ben Edelman, argue that platforms such as Uber have deliberately flouted regulations and that this systematic law evading is at the core of their business models.[48] Uber and Airbnb offer equivalent services to taxi and hotel companies, but by characterizing themselves as technology companies that are mainly "app providers," they escape regulations for safety, insurance, hygiene, and other regulatory requirements that apply to taxis and hotels.

On one level, the question is simple: Is Uber a transportation company? Is Facebook a media company? Is Airbnb a hotel company? Is Amazon a local retailer (subject to sales tax) and not an online catalogue company? If the answer is yes, then shouldn't these platform businesses be regulated like other firms in their sectors? At the heart of the issue is whether we can or should categorize a platform business as the same type of company that it competes against in the traditional economy. The answer has serious implications for operating costs and liability.

A number of national and international institutions (the European Commission, the OECD, the French Conseil National du Numérique, the German Competition Authority, the U.K. House of

Lords, and others) have engaged in vigorous debates as to whether platforms ought to be regulated with a new line of bespoke platform regulations. These debates are likely to continue for several years, although some countries have already changed their laws. The French Parliament, for example, adopted a law on "platform fairness" (*loyauté des plateformes*) in October 2016.[49] The broad direction for platform regulation in Europe can probably be predicted in the 2016 statement by the European Commission. This offered four fundamental principles to foster a "trusting, lawful, and innovation-driven ecosystem around online platforms in the EU": (1) a level playing field for comparable digital services, (2) ensuring that online platforms behave responsibly to protect core values, (3) fostering trust, transparency, and ensuring fairness, and (4) keeping markets open and nondiscriminatory to foster a data-driven economy.[50]

Managers and entrepreneurs at platform companies need to get ahead of this curve. Self-regulation tends to be less costly for firms than government-imposed regulation. Competitive advantage early in the life of a platform may come from exploiting regulation loopholes (e.g., Uber with drivers or Amazon not paying state and local taxes). But as platforms become more powerful, preemptive self-regulation is usually the better strategy, as Amazon did when it voluntarily decided to collect state and local sales taxes before being required to do so.

AMAZON SELF-REGULATES: SALES TAXES IN THE UNITED STATES

Amazon has drawn considerable attention because of its aggressive expansion strategy, leveraging its strong position as an online retailer, initially with books, to move into many other retail markets as well as related services. It also holds a dominant position in cloud computing. Yet most of Amazon's market shares are well below what we would normally consider monopolistic positions. For example, in 2018 it accounted for 43 percent of online retail but only 4 percent of total retail in the United States.[51] No government regulator to our knowledge has suggested that Amazon violated *existing* antitrust law. Nonetheless, some people have argued strenuously that we need *new* antitrust regulations to curb how Amazon and other platforms exploit their positions in one market to enter into others, such as by using customer data or platform transaction information to gain an advantage in pricing or market entry not available to competitors. The issue is particularly complex because platforms such as Amazon generally bring lower prices to consumers, at least in the short term. In the longer term, however, driving competitors out of business ends up restricting consumer choice, which tends to lead to higher prices. At least, that is the theoretical argument against the kind of customer tying (for example, marketing different products and services to Amazon Prime members) and vertical integration (such as using information gained on third-party sales through the Amazon Marketplace transaction platform to enter those product segments directly) that Amazon has pursued.[52]

Historically, Amazon took advantage of a 1992 U.S. Supreme Court ruling that a U.S. state can require retailers to collect a sales tax only if they have a physical presence in that state. This was originally designed to protect catalogue companies such as L.L.Bean, which shipped products nationwide from one or two locations. In its early days, Amazon exploited that law by keeping warehouses out of populous states like California. The research director of the Institute on Taxation and Economic Policy, Carl Davis, claimed that "there is no doubt that Amazon used its ability to not collect sales tax to gain a competitive advantage."[53] As recently as 2012, Amazon was collecting sales taxes in only five states and had "cut ties with in-state businesses to avoid collecting sales tax" in several states between 2009 and 2014.

But as the company grew and focused more on reducing delivery times, Amazon reached deals with many states to set up warehouses inside their borders. As part of those agreements, Amazon typically began collecting sales taxes within a few years. The company started to collect sales taxes on its own goods in 2012 in California, where it built warehouses, as well as in Texas, Pennsylvania, and a few other states. This activity steadily increased over the years. As of mid-2018, Amazon was collecting sales taxes in all forty-five U.S. states that have a sales tax. Joseph Bishop-Henchman, the executive vice president of the free-market-oriented Tax Foundation, said: "Other large e-retailers, most notably eBay, generally do not collect sales tax still." Amazon, on the other hand, "ultimately changed their position."[54]

There remains, however, an area of ongoing contention around sales tax at Amazon. On Amazon Marketplace, which accounts for more than half of all unit volume transactions performed on Amazon, sellers list their products for sale on the marketplace and determine their own prices. Many sellers take advantage of an additional program, called Fulfillment by Amazon, through which Amazon stores and ships their inventory. The sellers pay Amazon fees for those services, but the e-commerce giant leaves it up to them to collect sales tax where they are required to do so.

We applaud the decision to self-regulate on state and local taxes. Amazon was becoming a powerhouse in American e-commerce. Jeff Bezos and other managers must have understood that, like Walmart before it, powerful retailers are frequent targets of attack by local communities afraid of the loss of jobs and competition with local vendors. By taking sales taxes off the table, Amazon eliminated a potentially serious source of friction. At the same time, Amazon's competitive advantage no longer depended on offering lower prices by avoiding sales taxes. Recent research has suggested that paying state and local taxes was not even one of the top ten considerations for not buying from Amazon.[55]

YOUTUBE: HOW GOOGLE AVOIDED
REGULATORY INTERVENTION

The early days of YouTube under Google provide another example of the "Wild West" of platform media: Virtually all content went unsupervised from 2006 onwards. But in 2017 and 2018, YouTube faced heightened scrutiny in the wake of reports that it was allowing violent content to seep through past the YouTube Kids filter, which was supposed to block any content inappropriate for young users. Some parents discovered that YouTube Kids was allowing children to see videos with familiar characters in violent or lewd scenarios, along with nursery rhymes mixed with disturbing imagery. Other reports uncovered "verified" channels featuring child exploitation videos, including viral footage of screaming children being mock-tortured and webcams of young girls in revealing clothing.[56]

YouTube also repeatedly sparked outrage for its role in perpetuating misinformation and harassing videos in the wake of mass shootings and other national tragedies. Survivors and the relatives of victims of numerous shootings were reportedly subjected to online abuse and threats, often tied to popular conspiracy theory ideas featured prominently on YouTube. Parents of people killed in high-profile shootings tried to report abusive videos about their deceased children and repeatedly called on Google to hire more moderators and to better enforce its policies.[57]

In response to this increasing negative press and public sentiment, YouTube CEO Susan Wojcicki announced in December 2017 that Google was going to hire thousands of new "moderators," expanding its total workforce to more than 10,000 people responsible for reviewing content that could violate its policies.[58] In addition, YouTube announced it would continue to develop advanced machine learning technology to automatically flag problematic content for removal. The company said its new efforts to protect children from dangerous and abusive content and to block hate speech on the site would be modeled after ongoing work to fight violent extremist content. The goal of machine learning technology was to help human moderators find and shut down hundreds of accounts and hundreds of thousands of comments.

This application of technology seemed to be working. YouTube claimed that machine learning helped its human moderators remove nearly five times as many videos as they did previously, and that 98 percent of videos removed for violent extremism were now flagged by algorithms. Wojcicki claimed that advances in the technology allowed the site to take down nearly 70 percent of violent extremist content within eight hours of it being uploaded. "Human reviewers remain essential to both removing content and training machine learning systems because human judgment is critical to making contextualized decisions on content," Wojcicki wrote in a blog post.[59]

The various sides of the YouTube platform were affected by problematic content. Some advertisers pulled their ads because they were being placed alongside inappropriate videos with hate speech and extremist content. Then some high-profile brands suspended YouTube and Google advertising after reports revealed they were placed alongside videos filled with sexually explicit or exploitative content about children. YouTube announced in December 2017 that it was reforming its advertising policies, saying it would apply stricter criteria and conduct more manual curation as well as expand its team of ad reviewers.

In January 2018, YouTube announced that videos from its most popular channels would be subject to human review, preemptively checking large amounts of content to ensure it met "ad-friendly guidelines."[60] By doing so, YouTube raised the bar for video creators who wished to run ads on their content while hoping to allay advertiser unease about the video-sharing website. Advertisers were now able to choose ads on channels verified as "Google Preferred," which would be manually reviewed, and decide which ads would only run on verified videos. YouTube announced it would complete manual reviews of Google Preferred channels and videos by March 2018 in the U.S. and all other markets where it offered Google Preferred.

Facebook, Google, and other platforms could have avoided some current difficulties if they had pursued self-regulation measures earlier. Although they avoided punishing regulations in the United States, European governments have acted more aggressively. In May 2017, the European Council approved proposals that would require Facebook, Google (YouTube), Twitter, and other platforms to block videos containing hate speech and incitements to terrorism.[61] The regulations, which still need to be passed by the European Parliament before becoming law, would be the first EU-wide laws holding social media companies accountable for hate speech published on their platforms.

The good news for Google and other platforms is that self-regulation appears to be working, especially when the European Commission backed away from the plan to propose binding EU legislation that would force online platforms to remove posts containing hate speech. In a press conference in January 2018, EU justice commissioner Věra Jourová said she did not plan to regulate tech firms over hate speech.[62] Instead, she wanted to continue relying on a nonbinding agreement that she brokered in 2016 with Twitter, YouTube, Facebook, and Microsoft, which she said was now working. "Each of the four IT companies has shown more responsibility," Jourová told a news conference. "It is time to balance the power and responsibility of platforms and social media giants. This is what European citizens rightly expect," she added. Jourová praised Facebook's announcement in 2017 that it would hire 3,000 people to monitor its users' posts for hate speech. Facebook also said it planned to add five hundred staff members in Germany to review complaints about hate speech. According to the Commission's newest figures in January 2018, Twitter, YouTube, Facebook, and Microsoft reviewed about 82 percent of complaints about hate speech within twenty-four hours. This was a significant change from May 2017, when the firms reviewed only 39 percent. By January 2018, Facebook removed 79 percent of posts containing hate speech across the EU. YouTube took down 75 percent, and Twitter removed 45.7 percent.[63]

KEY TAKEAWAYS FOR MANAGERS AND ENTREPRENEURS

In this chapter, we discussed how digital platforms have morphed from beloved mavericks to feared tech giants. We showed how *the mood about platforms has changed*, especially with regulatory scrutiny on the rise. The most important minefields platforms face are running afoul of antitrust, pursuing growth and network effects at the expense of maintaining trust, and seeking labor cost reductions to the extent of possibly breaking labor laws and destroying workforce relationships. If we accept that managing platforms has become a "double-edged sword," capable of both good and evil, what are the key takeaways for managers and entrepreneurs?

The first and most important lesson from this chapter is that managers need to *find the right balance between pursuing growth without abusing their market power*. In the early days of Internet retail, social media, ride sharing, room sharing, and other gig-economy ventures, there were many areas of legal and regulatory ambiguity. The platforms that exploited these ambiguities gained an advantage over platform competitors as well as firms in the traditional economy. When the rules are black-and-white, platforms must take care not to cross the line into illegal behavior, whether it is antitrust, labor laws, tax issues, or industry regulation. But when the rules contain gray areas, platforms are likely to test the limits of the law and of social mores, such as classifying most workers as contractors rather than employees. It is fair to say that Uber and Airbnb probably would never have gotten off the ground if they had followed the letter and the spirit of the law. Nonetheless, two points need repeating: (1) The mood change means that platform behaviors which were tolerated in the past will be less tolerated in the future; and (2) as platforms grow in scale and power, they will come under closer scrutiny and must obey a different set of rules or adhere to existing rules more closely.

Second, emerging platforms can learn from the experiences of Microsoft and Google how to mitigate antitrust concerns. The natural tendency for many platforms has been to wait until the regulator acts, or to wait for a backlash from users and partners. Propelled by their entrepreneurial energy, and possibly cognitively constrained by it, sometimes it is difficult for founders to acknowledge their own "power." We say: Do not wait! To be more proactive, *platforms should build internal capabilities* (such as specialized teams) that keep abreast of regulations in different countries (and sometimes in different states) and learn what activities to avoid. Then they must educate managers, employees, contractors, and other business partners on what not to do. We know this is possible: After seeing how antitrust severely disrupted AT&T's business during the 1980s, Intel CEO Andy Grove introduced strict internal procedures to minimize Intel's exposure to antitrust scrutiny.[64] For close to twenty years, Intel under Grove largely avoided serious antitrust problems, despite its dominant market share in microprocessors.

Third, we believe that *platforms should preemptively self-regulate* and reduce the likelihood that governments will intervene and alter the playing field in ways that are not good for them, ecosystem partners, or consumers. As a start, platforms will have to invest much more in curation to provide the right balance between openness and trust. This will add costs, even as we make advances in artificial intelligence, machine learning, and other forms of algorithm-based surveillance. Similarly, platforms will need to evolve their workforce rules and benefits, and to adopt flexible work rules that will be consistent with local regulations, which will have to accommodate both full-time employees and independent contractors. We hope many countries will also adapt their labor regulations to accommodate the digital economy and more part-time "gig" workers. In any case, platform companies, like firms in the traditional economy, have to learn to value the benefits of a stable and capable workforce and figure out how to incorporate better working conditions into their strategies and business models. Contractors who work full-time for a platform should be full-time employees, regardless of the local, state, or national rules. The platform companies that only derive a competitive advantage because of flouting regulation or exploiting workers to the point that they cannot make a decent wage should not be allowed (either by the market or by regulators) to persist. We believe that a combination of market backlash and government regulation will make sure that they won't succeed in the long run.

Aggressive platform businesses will need to adapt to the current environment with greater self-regulation and curation. Curation is a tricky issue and is potentially counterintuitive, since the power of platform businesses relies on network effect–fueled growth. The logic of network effects is that platforms should naturally lean toward open membership, not curtailing members' behaviors, and not excluding members. In some cases, the paradox, as we have seen with Facebook, is that the most outrageous content often goes viral and attracts more users and more advertisers. But entrepreneurs, managers, and boards of directors need to be mindful of the potential abuse of platform power sooner rather than later, and before regulators pounce. We contend that the Wild West days of platform businesses in Western countries are coming to an end. (China is already an exception—it closely regulates digital platforms.) The global reach and power of platforms has become increasingly obvious. Consequently, we expect that the way platforms deliberately and strategically curate their content and memberships will define what they really stand for. How platforms govern their ecosystems will express the values of their leaders and entire organizations. Governance policies, in turn, will become an intrinsic part of their value propositions and either attract or repel users and ecosystem members.

What we expect from platform businesses in the future, at least in terms of new technologies and market opportunities, is the subject of the final chapter.

LOOKING FORWARD

PLATFORMS AND
THE FUTURE

THE BUSINESS OF PLATFORMS

PLATFORMS AND THE FUTURE

NEW PLATFORM BATTLEGROUNDS

EMERGING/FUTURE

FINAL THOUGHTS

CHAPTER·7

The dramatic testimony of Mark Zuckerberg in front of the U.S. Congress and European lawmakers in the spring of 2018 signaled a new age for the business of platforms. Complaints about fake news, privacy violations, unchecked expansion, and the growing specter of antitrust and labor regulation put the most valuable companies in the world on notice. Platforms were no longer neutral matchmakers or intermediaries for transactions and innovations. Allowing anyone on any side of a platform completely free rein could be potentially dangerous to democracy, social well-being, and global economic stability. Whether they liked it or not, companies such as Apple, Amazon, Microsoft, Alphabet-Google, Facebook, Alibaba, Tencent, and others would need to accept the new roles that their platforms played in the world economy and modern society as a whole.

Even as policy makers and thought leaders were criticizing platform businesses, it is worth remembering that successful platforms have long lives. With millions or billions of participants engaged and connected, platforms tend to be more enduring than standalone product or service businesses. Microsoft, for example, introduced DOS and then Windows in the 1980s. Since the mid-1990s, it has faced attacks from antitrust authorities, security problems, and growing competition from open-source software and cloud computing. Nevertheless, Microsoft has remained dominant in PC operating systems and key applications for nearly four decades and is still enormously profitable. As we have seen with other examples throughout this book, successful platforms are difficult to unseat.

However, nothing lasts forever. Platforms, ecosystems, and the technologies that drive them will continue to evolve and change.

Computing and communications platforms have faced continuous threats from new technologies over the past forty years. Some companies (ranging from Yahoo and MySpace to Nokia and Black-Berry) have seen their fortunes dramatically decline in short periods of time. Looking at the bigger picture, we can see that mainframes ultimately gave way to personal computers, the Internet, social media, mobile devices such as smartphones, and cloud computing. Old and new platforms coexist, though some have become more important than others. Looking forward from what we know today, artificial intelligence, machine learning, virtual and augmented reality, blockchain applications, and even quantum computing are likely to challenge currently dominant platforms, at least in some domains.

In this last chapter, we use the principles emphasized in this book to explore ongoing and future platform battlegrounds. We start by summarizing the book's key arguments. We then identify four trends likely to impact today's dominant players and the platform entrepreneurs and managers of tomorrow. We also explore how to evaluate emerging platforms and examine a few key competitions around next-generation technologies. In conclusion, we come back to the argument that large, successful platforms must increasingly engage in self-regulation and curation in order to adapt to a rapidly changing world. The end of truly open platforms seems to be upon us.

THE BUSINESS OF PLATFORMS

Table 7-1 summarizes the core principles we have explored in this book. Understanding the business of platforms begins with the drivers of platform markets in general and digital competition more specifically: the potential for generating strong network effects, limiting multi-homing, restricting differentiated and niche competition, and building high barriers to entry. We also pointed out that platform thinking is not new: More than one hundred years ago, platforms

TABLE 7–1: SUMMARY OF CORE PRINCIPLES BY CHAPTER

CHAPTER 2 WINNER TAKE ALL OR MOST	CHAPTER 3 STRATEGY AND BUSINESS MODELS	CHAPTER 4 COMMON MISTAKES	CHAPTER 5 OLD DOGS AND NEW TRICKS	CHAPTER 6 DOUBLE-EDGED SWORDS
Strong network effects	Choose the sides of your platform	Mispricing one side of the platform	Belong to a competing platform	Don't be a bully
Limited multi-homing	Solve chicken-or-egg problems	Failing to develop trust	Buy a platform	Balance openness with trust
Differentiation and niche competition	Design your business model	Dismissing the competition	Build a platform yourself	Not everyone should be a contractor
Barriers to entry	Enforce ecosystem rules	Missing the window		Self-regulate

like the telephone and the Yellow Pages, and those in several other industries, including railroads, electric power, radio, and television, depended heavily on network effects, low levels of multi-homing, and complementary innovations from ecosystem participants. But the platforms of today are largely digital, which is new. This technology, combined with the Internet, has enabled rapid, exponential growth on a global scale. It has also produced giant platform companies like Amazon, Alibaba, and Tencent with widely diversified businesses, often connected through user data. Some of these markets we can classify as winner-take-all, but most we cannot.

An important contribution of this book was highlighting the similarities and differences between two kinds of platforms. Most of the early platforms facilitated *innovations,* while the explosion of new platforms in the last decade or two has been driven by *transactions.* However, regardless of the platform type, managers had to deal with the same business challenges: Choose the key sides of the platform, solve the chicken-or-egg problem, design a business model (generate revenues and profit), and establish rules for using the platform as well as cultivating and governing the all-important ecosystem. As we discuss below, the commonalties or complementarities between transaction and innovation platforms have led to a growing number of hybrid companies, and this complex business model seems likely to become more common in the future.

Many industry commentators have positioned platforms as the Holy Grail of business strategy, as the one sure way to market dominance and enduring profits. This may be true if you end up as the "top dog" in your industry. But we also found that vast numbers of platform wannabes fail; in fact, there seemed to be far more losers than winners, just as the majority of start-up companies fail (some research indicates as many as 90 percent). Because of the complexity of platform businesses, it is especially easy to make mistakes. We found the biggest errors around mispricing on the most important market side, the failure to develop trust, mistiming entry, and simply ignoring the threat of competition. When firms get lulled into believing markets have tipped "permanently" in their favor, there is great danger in becoming complacent. Microsoft's failure in browsers was a classic example of overestimating market power when you are ahead and its failure in smartphones was a classic example of underestimating the power of network effects when you are behind.

One of the most daunting challenges is figuring out how established non-digital companies can adapt to platform competition. We argued that platforms are a serious threat to many traditional businesses, but there are alternatives. Old dogs can indeed learn new tricks, however difficult that may be. We suggested a simple framework for traditional businesses: Build, buy, or belong to a platform. When you are small, and when are you trying to prevent a market from tipping, established firms can leverage the power of platforms by joining an existing player. When you are large and time-to-market is essential, buying a platform can provide the skills and technology you may not have, and help traditional firms get over the hump and into the platform business. Building a platform from scratch is the hardest strategy and not for the faint of heart. But if you can pull it off, the rewards can be substantial.

Finally, we discussed how platforms have become double-edged swords: Platforms have enabled some firms to achieve great economic, social, and political power, which can be easily abused, sometimes unwittingly. With platforms increasingly coming under intense government and media scrutiny, it is critical to remind managers and entrepreneurs not to be a bully. There is nothing illegal or ethically wrong with following the logic of platforms and network effects into a dominant position. But once you become dominant, then different rules should apply. Platform companies need to anticipate the growing likelihood of antitrust intervention. In addition, platforms have enabled the sharing or gig economy, which has a logical extension: Every worker can become a temporary contractor. But, as we have seen in the backlash to Uber and other gig-economy platforms, that is not a viable labor strategy for the long term. Furthermore, fraud, violations of privacy, poor quality goods, and other platform "complications" have the potential to torpedo trust, which is fundamental to platform success. Most platforms are digital intermediaries or innovation facilitators; they do not have personal relationships with their users and complementors. Consequently, we believe that the largest, most powerful platforms will increasingly need to balance openness with economies of scale and scope, and self-regulate or curate to avoid potentially punishing conflicts with policy makers.

PLATFORMS AND THE FUTURE

The platforms we talked about in this book all started sometime in the past century or earlier. We know a lot about the histories of the company strategies and operations. But another question to explore is how emerging platforms are likely to evolve over the next decade and beyond. We see at least four major trends that could change the way we think about the business of platforms in the future.

First, digital competition will turn more and more platform firms into hybrids. In the old world (1980s and 1990s), innovation and transaction platforms were distinct businesses. Connecting buyers and sellers, advertisers and consumers, or users of the different social networks appeared to be fundamentally different from stimulating outside firms to create complementary innovations in the form of their own products and services that make the platforms increasingly valuable. But in the last decade a growing number of successful innovation platforms have integrated transaction platforms into their business models, and transaction platforms have sought to open APIs and encourage third parties to create their own complementary innovations. Rather than lose control over distribution, innovation platforms want to manage the customer experience (think Apple's App Store). And owners of transaction platforms recognize that not all innovation can or should be internal (think Facebook's platform). Prominent examples include Google's decision to buy and push Android, Amazon's decision to create multiple innovation platforms around AWS and Alexa, and the decisions of Uber and Airbnb to allow developers to build services on top of their transaction platforms. Another example is Snapchat, which allowed users to post messages or photos that quickly disappeared. It struggled to make a profit as a pure transaction platform, especially after Facebook's Instagram copied many of its most popular features. To inspire more innovation and user activity, Snapchat decided in June 2018 to open its platform and user database to application developers.[1] The underlying driver was digital competition. Unlike in the traditional economy, where companies require expensive physical investments to build out the business model, in the digital world, companies can grow rapidly with a clever use of data, software, and platform strategy.

Second, we see next-generation platforms driving innovation to a new level. Advances in artificial intelligence, machine learning, and big-data analytics enable organizations to do more things with less investment, including building businesses that were impossible in years past. Although AI is still in a nascent phase, Google, Amazon, Apple, IBM, and other firms are no longer treating their technology as proprietary. Instead, they have turned AI capabilities into platforms that third parties can access and build upon for their own applications.

Third, the logic of platform thinking, which is driven by network effects, multisided markets, and the potential for winner-take-all-or-most outcomes has led to growing market power concentrated in a small (but rising) number of firms. In the 1960s and 1970s, IBM represented the pinnacle of platform power. In the 1980s and 1990s, it was Intel and Microsoft. In the last two decades we are contending with the market power of Apple, Google, Amazon, Facebook, Alibaba, and Tencent, among others.

Lastly, we see virtually all large platform companies evolving from free markets to curated businesses. As we discussed in Chapter 6, many managers, entrepreneurs, and technical experts once believed that platforms would only bring "good" into the world: They would connect people, products, and services at ever-decreasing prices, and free the world from the frictions and imperfections of traditional marketplaces or modes of communication. But as we have suggested throughout this book, the new world and traditional worlds have to coexist. Not all actors in the digital world are do-gooders. Partisan politics, spies, terrorists, counterfeiters, money launderers, and drug dealers all have found ways to use platforms to their advantage. Platform companies are also profit-seeking enterprises, and this motive can sometimes lead to abuses of power and technology from the perspective of users and ecosystem partners. Once platforms get large enough to impact social, political, and economic systems, then they will increasingly need to reflect on the purpose of their operations as well as evolve from hands-off to more hands-on curation. Although it is a cliché, for the world's biggest platforms, growing power means growing responsibility.

NEW PLATFORM BATTLEGROUNDS

With all these issues in mind, we can look to several platform battlegrounds currently under way to help us think about what comes next and the increasing role platforms are likely to play in the future. Some early-stage platforms may evolve into proprietary products and services. And some current products and services or path-breaking technologies may turn into new types of platforms. In the remainder of this chapter, we discuss two relatively new platform battlegrounds and their possible evolution, if artificial intelligence impacts them the way we predict: voice wars and autonomous vehicle ride sharing. Then we will look at two emerging and future battlegrounds: quantum computing and gene editing.

CURRENT/ONGOING

Perhaps the most important new technology in the battle for platforms over the next decade is artificial intelligence and machine learning. For many industries, AI has disruptive potential. Two of the most obvious and powerful applications for AI are voice recognition and driverless cars. Both involve a dramatic change in platform ecosystems.

VOICE WARS: RAPID GROWTH BUT
CHAOTIC PLATFORM COMPETITION

Although artificial intelligence has been around for decades, one branch has made exceptional progress: *machine learning* (using special software algorithms to analyze and learn from data) and the subfield of *deep learning* (using hardware and software to build massively parallel processors called neural networks to mimic how the brain works). Applications of these technologies have led to dramatic improvements in certain forms of pattern recognition, especially for images and voice. Apple got the world excited about a voice interface when it introduced Siri in 2011. For the first time, consumers had access to a natural conversation technology that actually worked (at least some of the time). Despite its first-mover advantage, however, Apple's strategy for Siri was classic Apple: The company designed Siri as a *product* that complemented the iPhone, not as an innovation or transaction *platform* that could generate powerful network effects.

When Amazon introduced the Echo speaker device with Alexa software in late 2014, it set in motion a war for platform domination among Google, Apple, Microsoft, Alibaba, Tencent, and a host of start-ups. Amazon's strategy was to create a new platform powered by a combination of Amazon Web Services, speech recognition, and high-quality speech synthesis. CEO Jeff Bezos sought to bundle the technology with an affordable piece of dedicated hardware. Immediately identifying the potential for cross-side network effects, Amazon launched its Alexa Skills Kit (ASK)—a collection of self-service APIs and tools that made it easy for third-party developers to create new Alexa apps. This open-platform strategy accelerated the number of Alexa skills from roughly 5,000 in 2016 to over 50,000 in 2018.[2] Amazon offered a wide variety of skills, such as playing games like Jeopardy!, ordering an Uber ride, and asking about the weather and news. Our favorite app is that we can ask Alexa to remotely start a car, which will cool down the car in the summer and warm it in the winter. If you don't show up, the car shuts down after ten minutes.

The combination of very low prices (which were most likely below cost for Amazon and Google) and extraordinary ease of use led to an explosion in sales of these intelligent assistant devices. As an early mover, Amazon quickly captured the largest market share. But Amazon's success spurred Google, Apple, Samsung, and various Chinese companies into action. By late 2017, voice was morphing into a classic platform battle: Amazon and Google heavily discounted products to build their installed base, with each side racing to add applications and functions. The goal was to drive network effects. Amazon, for example, released its Echo Show, an Alexa speaker with a visual display. Amazon hoped that it would spread from family member to family member and to friends. Then, anyone with an Echo Show could make visual phone calls to each other, much like Apple's FaceTime. All the major players were also licensing their technologies to consumer electronics companies, car companies, and enterprise software companies, hoping they would incorporate their voice solutions, often for free.

The platform challenge was that multi-homing was easy: Any customer could own or use the Google, Amazon, Microsoft, *and* Apple voice interfaces. There were no significant switching costs (yet) for consumers. There were also many opportunities for differentiation and niche competition: Apple focused on the quality of music; Amazon on media and e-commerce; Google on search-related inquiries; and Microsoft on enterprise needs.

Each player also had a different business model. Amazon was building a hybrid platform, with third parties creating applications and customers doing transactions with their Echo devices. Indeed, the average Amazon household spent $1,000 annually on the site; Prime members spent $1,300; and households with an Echo spent $1,700.[3] Apple initially tried to make money on its hardware (which explained its high prices and low initial market penetration). No company in 2018 seemed to have a clear path to making a profit directly from this technology.

As we finished this book, it was too early to tell how the voice wars will play out. The market was still like the Wild West—more chaos than order. Between 2017 and 2018, improvements in machine learning and deep learning were creating better voice experiences across all competitors. Google appeared to be the technical leader in AI, with many applications in search, advertisements, and machine translation, among others. Apple, which lagged behind in early benchmarks, was improving quickly, as were the benchmarks for Microsoft's Cortana and Amazon's Alexa.[4]

In 2018, Google had the advantage of hundreds of millions of devices (Android smartphones) that have Google's voice capabilities embedded. Amazon had the advantage of the largest smart-speaker-installed base, with tens of millions of devices sitting in users' homes, especially in the United States. Ultimately, we expect voice to be a classic platform battle, where the winner(s) will depend on who can build up the largest installed base of users, who can create the best ecosystem for producing innovative applications, and who (if anyone) can lock in their customer base, limit multi-homing in the future, and create a sufficiently compelling solution to reduce competition from niche players and differentiation in the market.

RIDE SHARING AND SELF-DRIVING CARS: FROM PLATFORM TO SERVICE

While AI will spawn a range of new platforms, it will also enable new capabilities that may destroy existing platforms. One of the most exciting AI applications has been the emergence of self-driving cars. Ironically, this new technology may replace some of the most widely used platforms in the world: Uber, Lyft, Didi Chuxing, and other ride-sharing businesses. Despite the strong cross-side network effects, the ride-sharing platform revolution could actually disappear.

The business challenge for ride-sharing platforms is simple: They tend to lose money, and lots of it. The cost of attracting and paying drivers as well as keeping ride prices low has squeezed profit margins. In addition, many drivers multi-home (serve both

Uber and Lyft, or conventional taxi companies). Therefore, Uber, Lyft, Didi Chuxing, and other ride-sharing companies have announced that their long-term strategy is to move away from being a pure platform, matching riders with drivers, toward a model of "transportation as a service," in which they own or lease all their own vehicles, including both automobiles and bicycles or scooters. Tech companies like Google and most of the major automobile manufacturers like GM and Toyota were also investing aggressively in the same direction. Despite a long history of selling products, even the most conservative car companies see AI as the route toward becoming a service company. As Lyft CEO Logan Green said in 2018, "We are going to move the entire [car] industry from one based on ownership, to one based on subscription."[5]

The emergence of autonomous vehicle technology promises to remove human drivers, which could dramatically drive down the marginal cost of transportation services. Amortizing the R&D and fleet costs of self-driving cars is likely to be very high. But the economics could improve because there are no driver payments and cars will be utilized more intensively, dramatically reducing the cost per mile.[6] GM estimated that, when it launches its service in 2019, rides would initially cost $1.50 per mile, 40 percent less than current ride-hailing services.[7] Some estimates suggested that the cost per mile of a self-driving vehicle could fall as low as 35 cents per mile, down from an average of $2.86 per mile in 2018.[8]

Observers see the combination of new technology and better economics forcing Uber (and other ride-sharing platforms) to "either figure out a way to buy or at least manage an enormous fleet (possibly by going public to foot the bill), or face annihilation by others who will."[9] Facing this threat, Uber began investing in autonomous vehicle technology in 2014. Uber's cofounder and then CEO Travis Kalanick stressed the importance of winning the race: "The minute it was clear to us that our friends in Mountain View [i.e., Google] were going to be getting in the ride-sharing space, we needed to make sure there is an alternative [self-driving car]. Because if there is not, we're not going to have any business." Kalanick added that developing a self-driving car "is basically existential for us."[10] Uber announced in November 2017 that it would buy 24,000 self-driving vehicles from Volvo, giving it a fleet to test and later deploy in an autonomous ride-hailing service.

Lyft has taken a different approach. Rather than develop its own self-driving technology, it is trying to form partnerships through its "Open Platform Initiative," which resembled Google's Open Handset Alliance for Android smartphones. Lyft's platform initiative brings together several automakers, including GM, Land Rover, and Ford, to integrate their autonomous vehicle projects into one ride-hailing network.[11] Initially, the Open Platform Initiative is offering partners access to ride data for testing purposes, but ultimately plans to make their self-driving vehicles available on its ride-hailing platform. Lyft's chief strategy officer noted in late 2017 that "we're focused on partnering with the auto industry because frankly, we think we can't do this alone and need each other to be successful."[12] Lyft cofounder John Zimmer even predicted that "autonomous vehicle fleets will quickly become widespread and will account for the majority of Lyft rides within 5 years."[13]

Lyft's strategy may signal the emergence of a different type of transaction platform, where Lyft connects riders to self-driving vehicles from a variety of manufacturers. But many of its partners have also invested in ride-hailing technology and could launch self-driving taxi services of their own. In response, even Lyft invested in a self-driving research center to develop its own autonomous vehicle technology, indicating that it, too, might move away from the open-platform model.[14]

Who will win and who will lose remains uncertain. Moreover, self-driving car services may not come so quickly and may never be as profitable as high-volume transaction platforms like eBay, Priceline, and Expedia, and even Airbnb, which are asset-light and primarily match buyers and sellers or users and suppliers. Nonetheless, future consumers are very likely to benefit from more and cheaper ride-sharing services as long as these businesses have enough capital to survive until the businesses are profitable.

EMERGING/FUTURE

Now let's look at two other emerging platform battlegrounds: quantum computing and gene-editing technology. The nascent businesses and ecosystems are even more dependent on advances in science and technology, but the platforms should become more relevant in the future and remain so for many decades to come.

QUANTUM COMPUTERS: AN INNOVATION PLATFORM FOR NEXT-GENERATION COMPUTING

In 1981, Nobel laureate Richard Feynman challenged the physics and computing communities to build a computer mimicking how nature actually works—a quantum computer. Universities and then companies started research.[15] By 2015, McKinsey consultants estimated there were 7,000 researchers working on quantum computing, with a combined budget of $1.5 billion.[16] By 2018, dozens of universities, approximately thirty major companies, and more than a dozen start-ups had notable R&D efforts.[17]

The state of the technology today resembles conventional computing in the late 1940s and early 1950s. We have laboratory devices and some commercial products and services, but mostly from one company. We have incompatible computer technologies, mostly in the research stage and with different strengths and weaknesses. All the machines require specialized skills to build and program. Companies still work closely with universities and national laboratories. There is no consensus as to what is the best technology or design. Nonetheless, we believe quantum computers represent a revolutionary innovation platform for specialized applications, with the potential to generate new types of transaction platforms for "quantum computing as a service" and secure quantum communications.

Quantum computers are built around circuits called quantum bits, or "qubits." One qubit can represent not just 0 or 1 as in traditional digital computers, but both 0 and 1 simultaneously. Qubits give quantum computers the potential to perform astounding calculations, far beyond the reach of conventional digital computers. As few as 300 qubits can represent information equal to the estimated number of particles in the known universe.[18] To perform calculations, however, qubits need to exploit some unique properties described by quantum mechanics, and that makes building and using large quantum computers difficult.

There are several competing technologies, all with the potential to make quantum computers that are more stable, scalable, and flexible than current devices, most of which reside in research laboratories. The 2018 business and patents leader is D-Wave, a private company spun out of the University of British Columbia in 1999 to accumulate patent rights in exchange for research grants.[19] It has been funded mainly by venture capital, corporate investors such as Goldman Sachs, and, more recently, Jeff Bezos and the Central Intelligence Agency.[20] Google and IBM, as well as start-ups such as Quantum Circuits, are deploying a different approach, using electrons or nuclei.[21] Xanadu, a Toronto start-up, uses photons to build its quantum circuits.[22] Microsoft has yet another design, which it plans to build within five years and make commercially available via the cloud.[23]

There are potentially strong network effects associated with the number and quality of programming tools and applications for the competing quantum computers, but the ecosystems remain at a very early stage. The most important applications are likely to be mathematical problems such as in combinatorial optimization that require massively parallel computations. For example, in 2012,

Harvard researchers used a D-Wave computer to simulate protein molecule unfolding (which is useful in drug discovery).[24] More recently, Northrop Grumman has been using D-Wave to model software systems to detect errors.[25] And Volkswagen has been using D-Wave to optimize traffic routes for thousands of vehicles simultaneously, potentially useful for self-driving vehicles.[26]

Perhaps the "killer app" will be quantum encryption and secure communications. These applications utilize an algorithm discovered in 1994 by Peter Shor, formerly of Bell Labs and now at MIT. Shor demonstrated how to use a quantum computer to factor very large numbers, which makes it possible to create unbreakable cryptographic keys. Governments (the United States and China in particular) as well as companies (AT&T, Raytheon, Alibaba, Huawei, NEC, and Toshiba, among others) are pursuing these applications.[27] China is especially advanced.[28]

Will quantum computing become a successful new platform business? Network effects are weak so far because the application ecosystems are still nascent and divided among several platform contenders. As of this writing, D-Wave has the lead in applications and the largest patent portfolio, followed by IBM and Microsoft. IBM leads in recent annual patent filings. At universities, the patent application leaders are MIT, Harvard, Zhejiang (China), Yale, and Tsinghua (China). At the country level, the United States led with about eight hundred total patents, three to four times the numbers from Japan and China.[29] For the business to progress faster, however, quantum computers need more researchers able to apply these patents. They, in turn, need access to bigger quantum computers so they can build better programming tools and test real-world applications. IBM, D-Wave, Google, and Microsoft were aggressively moving in this direction and making their quantum computers available as a cloud service.

Quantum computers will probably never replace conventional computers. Nor do we see this as a winner-take-all-or-most market.

Quantum computers are likely to remain special-purpose devices that exploit quantum phenomena for certain types of massively parallel computations. They are not well suited to everyday computing tasks that require speed, precision, low cost, and ease of use. Multi-homing on different types of quantum computers is also likely to persist, keeping potential application ecosystems divided and weakening network effects. In particular, D-Wave computers cannot run Shor's algorithm and so are not useful for cryptography or quantum communications. IBM, Google, and Microsoft, as well as several start-ups, are designing more general-purpose devices, although these remain experimental or small-scale.

Quantum computing as a platform is also likely to face serious challenges in regulation because of cryptography applications. On the one hand, quantum computers may be able to break secure keys generated by the most powerful conventional computers, which now protect much of the world's information and financial assets. On the other hand, quantum computers themselves can potentially generate unbreakable quantum keys as well as facilitate secure quantum communications. Combined with hacker tools for entering computer systems and accessing cryptocurrencies, quantum computers clearly have the potential for social mischief as well as good. They can help solve currently impossible computation problems but also facilitate unbreakable data silos to hide illegal or unethical activities. The leading companies will have to figure out policies to regulate themselves as well as to work with governments, which are likely to play a major role in overseeing at least some quantum computer applications and services.

CRISPR: AN INNOVATION PLATFORM FOR GENE EDITING

Gene editing—altering DNA to modify the characteristics of plants, animals, and even people—was already a global market worth over $3 billion in 2017 and expected to double in the next five years. In

2018, there were also over 2,700 clinical trials under way for human gene therapies.[30] Much of the know-how remains in the research or pre-commercialization stages, though some technologies are spawning nascent innovation platforms and ecosystems, similar to what we have seen in quantum computers and other industries.[31]

One particularly promising technology is CRISPR, or "clustered regularly interspaced short palindromic repeats."[32] CRISPR refers to small pieces of DNA that bacteria use to recognize viruses. What scientists observed years ago is that specialized segments of RNA and associated enzymes in one organism can modify genes (DNA sequences) in other organisms. For example, this happens naturally when the immune system in bacteria fight against an invading virus. In 2012, several scientists discovered they could use CRISPR sequences of DNA as well as "guide RNA" to locate target DNA and then deploy CRISPR-associated enzymes as "molecular scissors" to cut, modify, or replace genetic material. The potential applications include diagnostic tools and treatments for genetic diseases as well as genetic reengineering more broadly.[33] An August 2016 article in *National Geographic* magazine described CRISPR's potential:

> CRISPR places an entirely new kind of power into human hands. For the first time, scientists can quickly and precisely alter, delete, and rearrange the DNA of nearly any living organism, including us. In the past three years, the technology has transformed biology. . . . No scientific discovery of the past century holds more promise—or raises more troubling ethical questions. Most provocatively, if CRISPR were used to edit a human embryo's germ line—cells that contain genetic material that can be inherited by the next generation—either to correct a genetic flaw or to enhance a desired trait, the change would then pass to that person's children, and their children, in perpetuity. The full implica-

tions of changes that profound are difficult, if not impossible, to foresee.[34]

Editing a human embryo's germ line is not simply a hypothetical possibility. In December 2018, reports surfaced that a "rogue" Chinese scientist already had used CRISPR to disable a gene in twin unborn babies that would make them resistant to HIV. The scientist reportedly couldn't disable both copies of the gene in one of the embryos but implanted it anyway. The babies were born normally, but the disabled genes could make them, and their offspring, susceptible to other diseases. This apparently secret experiment (the scientist has not yet published data to confirm what he did) would have been illegal in the United States and some other countries. It has also created considerable consternation among the scientific community because of the apparent lack of global controls on the use of a powerful technology.[35]

Nonetheless, gene editing will continue to evolve. The technology will provide opportunities for companies to pursue product solutions, such as to build stand-alone diagnostic tools or gene therapies for problematic diseases and conditions. This is possible because DNA resembles a programming language and data-storage technology that can be adapted to different contexts. Some institutions and companies have already created products, tools, and components that other firms are building upon. Like today's quantum computers, however, there are limitations. Each use of CRISPR requires specialized domain knowledge, such as the genome of a particular organism and disease, and then tailoring to the application, such as to design a diagnostic test or therapeutic product for a specific disease or to reengineer a plant to fight off insects. But, along with rising numbers of CRISPR researchers, platform-like network effects and multisided market dynamics are also appearing and helping the ecosystem grow. In particular, more research publications have led to improvements in tools and reusable component libraries, which have attracted more researchers and applications, which in turn have inspired more research, tool development, applications, venture capital investments, and so on.

An important player in the nascent CRISPR ecosystem is a nonprofit foundation called Addgene, founded in 2004 by MIT students. It funds itself by selling plasmids, small strands of DNA used in laboratories to manipulate genes. Since 2013, it has been collecting and distributing CRISPR technologies to help research-ers get started on their experiments.[36] The Addgene tools library consists of different enzymes and DNA or RNA sequences useful to identify, cut, edit, tag, and visualize particular genes.[37] There are also numerous start-ups, some of which have already gone pub-lic. CRISPR Therapeutics (founded in 2013) is trying to develop gene-based medicines to treat cancer and blood-related diseases, and is collaborating closely with Vertex and Bayer. Editas Medi-cine (2013) and Exonics Therapeutics (2017) are tackling diseases such as cancer, sickle cell anemia, muscular dystrophy, and cystic fibrosis.[38] Beam Therapeutics (2018) plans to use CRISPR to edit genes and correct mutations.[39] Mammoth Biosciences (2018) is fol-lowing more of a platform strategy and developing diagnostic tests that could be the basis for new therapies. The company is broadly licensing its patents and encouraging other firms to explore ther-apies based on its testing technology.[40] In fact, Mammoth's goal is to create "a CRISPR-enabled platform capable of detecting any biomarker or disease containing DNA or RNA." In a recent public statement, the company summarized its strategy to cultivate an ap-plications ecosystem:

> Imagine a world where you could test for the flu right from your living room and determine the exact strain you've been infected with, or rapidly screen for the early warning signs of cancer. That's what we're aiming to do at Mammoth—bring affordable testing to everyone. But even beyond healthcare,

we're aiming *to build the platform for CRISPR apps* [italics added] and offer the technology across many industries.[41]

Broad commercialization of CRISPR is still years away. The technology is also better at screening, cutting, and rewriting rather than inserting DNA.[42] And only recently have medical centers and companies applied to start CRISPR-related clinical trials. There are also alternative technologies with different strengths and weaknesses. In particular, TALEN (transcription activator-like effector nuclease), another gene-cutting enzyme tool, seems to be more precise than CRISPR and more scalable for some non-laboratory applications, though it can be more difficult to use.[43] In general, CRISPR is in the lead as a potential gene-editing technology platform, with several universities and research centers, start-up companies, and established firms actively publishing papers, licensing and applying for patents, and sharing their tools and depositories of genetic components. Most researchers are also focusing on CRISPR-Cas9, a specific protein that used RNA to edit DNA sequences.

One concern we have is that the business models of biotech start-ups and pharmaceutical companies depend on patent monopolies, making the industry ultra-competitive and locking applied research into protected silos. The result is potentially a "zero-sum game" mentality. This contrasts to the more cooperative (but still highly competitive) spirit of "growing the pie" together that we generally see with basic science and which we saw in the early days of the personal computer, Internet applications, and even smartphone platforms such as Google's Android. Of course, most CRISPR scientists openly shared and published their basic research.[44] And although the U.S. Patent and Trademark Office already has granted hundreds of patents related to CRISPR, patent holders usually offered free licenses to academic researchers, even those still under litigation.

Ethical and social issues might also hinder widespread use of gene editing, especially if more "rogue" and potentially dangerous misuses of CRISPR occur. The debates are clearly more serious than what we discussed in Chapter 6 regarding the abuse of social media platforms. The broader controversy involving CRISPR centers on how much genetic engineering we, as a society, should allow. Experts already disagree about the safety of genetically altered plants and animals that contribute to the human food supply.[45] Scientists can deploy similar technology to change human embryos and cells, and we might someday control how this is done to treat genetic diseases or potential disabilities. But should we allow parents to edit their children's genes—for example, to prevent diseases like HIV that they might or might not contract, or to select for blue versus brown eyes, or a higher IQ?[46]

In sum, platform dynamics has been influencing industries and technologies outside of personal computers, Internet applications, and smartphones. Again, though, it is not so clear how to use the power of the platform wisely and safely, and what types of government monitoring and self-regulation are most appropriate. These issues seem likely to become even fiercer topics of debate as CRISPR and other gene-editing technologies evolve into more widely used platforms for medical, food, and other applications.

FINAL THOUGHTS

Industry-wide platforms and global ecosystems for innovations and transactions have already changed many aspects of our personal and working lives. Many more changes and new technologies will come. We are referring to more than technologies like voice-powered AI assistants and self-driving cars, or quantum computing and gene editing. More broadly, the explosion of transaction platforms has enabled nearly every type of exchange imaginable in today's world. Platform entrepreneurs have made "anything as a service" possible. We are heading into a future where we will buy and own fewer products (cars, bikes, vacation homes, household tools, consumer electronics, etc.), and we will contract for more services directly with each other. We will likely manage this sharing through peer-to-peer transaction platforms and technologies such as blockchain, to ensure secure and transparent exchanges. To a large degree, transaction platforms originated in ancient bazaars as well as nineteenth-century advertising businesses like the Yellow Pages and shopping catalogues. However, no one predicted such a rise in the popularity, diversity, and global reach of modern transaction platforms, which initially appeared as applications that made personal computers and smartphones more valuable as innovation platforms.

One ongoing challenge for all platform companies is the centralization of power. Yes, the Internet once promised to deliver a "flat world," where distributed computing and communication networks provided equal access to digital information and economic opportunities. While this is partly true, the opposite trend has also emerged. Platform dynamics has led to more centralization of economic and social activity in a relatively small number of companies, and they seem to be getting increasingly large and powerful with each passing day. In response, we see growing demands from both users and governments to regulate or break up some of the biggest platforms. This movement brings to mind how the muckrakers at the turn of the twentieth century called for the dissolution of Standard Oil and other monopolies.

Today, there are growing calls for governments to rein in platform businesses and for entrepreneurs, managers, and boards of directors at the leading platform companies to take more responsibility for their social, political, and economic power. Purely "open" platforms, with no rules overseeing access, actions, or content, have made some platforms seem like the lawless American Wild West, where "might" dominated "right." Consequently, we believe that platform companies need to respond to these calls by self-regulating and curating. They need to set limits for who can do what on the platform. Both self-regulation and curation are central to good governance and will become more important in the future, even though they may weaken network effects, financial returns, and growth opportunities for some platform businesses.

We encourage platform managers and entrepreneurs to have great ambitions. We hope this book can help them. However, different rules should apply once a platform business gains a certain size and influence, or achieves the ability to link markets in heretofore unseen ways, such as through new types of data-driven economies of scale and scope. It is the joint responsibility of leaders from government, society, and business to figure out the new rules and make sure competition remains transparent and fair to the extent possible. If not, platform businesses that openly abuse their power are likely to fail in the long run, or at least fail to achieve their potential to do good things. There is also the constant danger of individuals misusing their access to these global platforms. Governments, universities, and companies need to work together, and work harder, to figure out how to curb platform abuses.

Our call for self-regulation and curation also has implications for the kinds of leaders and managers that platform companies will need in the future. It takes courage to make decisions that raise costs, reduce advertising revenue, or suppress network effects and growth potential. Nonetheless, the present reality requires platform companies to expand their strategic visions and definitions of success. Misusing platform power and technology is not a clever way to build an enduring ecosystem or contribute to a stable society, which is good for business. We must measure success in terms that go beyond sales, profits, and market values, although these metrics remain essential to a sustainable business model. We hope that company executives and boards of directors at the top platform companies, as well as leaders in government and academia, will recognize that times have changed. We need to choose a next generation of leaders with a better understanding of how platforms and digital technologies can impact society and the global economy.

In this book, we tried not to exaggerate the importance of platform businesses, present and future. Nor did we try to overly simplify what a platform company must do in order to survive and thrive. Rather, we applied some cold logic and hard data—and several decades of experience. Our goal has been to help managers and entrepreneurs build platform businesses that can stand the test of time and win their share of battles with both digital and conventional competitors.

The bottom line is that platforms have the potential for both good and evil. This is why we say that platforms are *double-edged swords*. Every major company we cited in this book has been the subject of government investigations, local regulatory oversight, and intense media scrutiny. No one has been spared. Microsoft, Alphabet-Google, Apple, Intel, Facebook, Cisco, Qualcomm, Uber, Airbnb, Alibaba, Tencent, and many other firms, small and large, have faced legal, taxation, or regulatory challenges.

At the same time, the data suggests that industry platforms offer a more efficient way to organize the innovation process and many other types of economic activity. Platforms have already delivered revolutionary change. But we now live in a world where the "business of platforms" has become intimately tied to digital competition, innovation, and power—for better and for worse. It is up to us whether platforms in the future improve the world or undermine it. We are optimistic but cautious.

APPENDIX TABLE 1-1: **PLATFORM COMPANIES IN THE DATA ANALYSIS, 1995–2015**

18 INNOVATION PLATFORMS	COUNTRY	INDUSTRY
Qihoo 360	China	Internet software & services
SAP	Europe	Application software
Nintendo	Japan	Home entertainment software
Sony	Japan	Consumer electronics
ARM	U.K.	Semiconductors
Kakao	S. Korea	Internet software & services
Apple **(Hybrid)**	U.S.A.	Hardware, storage, peripherals
Cisco	U.S.A.	Communications equipment
IBM	U.S.A.	IT consulting & other services
Intel	U.S.A.	Semiconductors
Microsoft **(Hybrid)**	U.S.A.	Systems software
Nvidia	U.S.A.	Semiconductors
Oracle	U.S.A.	Systems software
Qualcomm	U.S.A.	Semiconductors
Red Hat	U.S.A.	Systems software
Salesforce **(Hybrid)**	U.S.A.	Application software
VMware	U.S.A.	Systems software
Workday	U.S.A.	Application software

25 TRANSACTION PLATFORMS	COUNTRY	INDUSTRY
Alibaba **(Hybrid)**	China	Internet software & services
Baidu	China	Internet software & services
JD.com	China	Internet retail
Tencent **(Hybrid)**	China	Internet software & services
NetEase	China	Internet software & services
Rakuten	Japan	Internet retail
Yahoo Japan	Japan	Internet software & services
Naver	S. Korea	Internet software & services
Mail.ru Group	Russia	Internet software & services
Yandex N.V.	Russia	Internet software & services
Amazon **(Hybrid)**	U.S.A.	Internet retail
Expedia	U.S.A.	Internet retail
Facebook **(Hybrid)**	U.S.A.	Internet software & services
Google **(Hybrid)**	U.S.A.	Internet software & services
Groupon	U.S.A.	Internet retail
LendingTree	U.S.A.	Thrifts & mortgage finance
LinkedIn **(Hybrid)**	U.S.A.	Internet software & services
PayPal	U.S.A.	Data processing & outsourced services
Priceline	U.S.A.	Internet retail
TripAdvisor	U.S.A.	Internet retail
Twitter **(Hybrid)**	U.S.A.	Internet software & services
Yahoo	U.S.A.	Internet software & services
Yelp	U.S.A.	Internet software & services
Zillow	U.S.A.	Internet software & services
eBay	U.S.A.	Internet software & services

APPENDIX TABLE 4-1: FAILED PLATFORMS: OVERALL DURATION

Average: 4.9 years; median: 3 years. Total Number of Firms: 209

Duration by category

CATEGORY	AVERAGE (YRS.)	MEDIAN (YRS.)	NO. OF FIRMS	TYPE
Social media/networks/online communities	6.4	5	26	Mixed (T, H)
Mobile OS	10.2	10	5	Innovation
ISP/web portal/search engines	9.5	9	21	Mixed (T, H)
Information/content sites/news aggregators	5.6	4	7	Transaction
Media streaming/online broadcasting	6	6	4	Mixed (T, H)
Ride sharing (air and car)	3.7	2	12	Transaction
Ride sharing (excluding air)	4.2	2	9	Transaction
Car sharing	3.1	3	7	Transaction
On-demand economy (delivery, services, etc.)	2.9	2	29	Transaction
Online marketplaces	3.8	3	16	Transaction
B2B industry marketplaces	2.2	2	41	Transaction
Online marketing/advertising platforms	6.1	5	9	Transaction
Career sites	6	4.5	4	Transaction
Web browsers	2.9	3	14	Innovation
Other	6.5	4	14	Mixed (T, H, I)

APPENDIX TABLE 4-2: **DURATION BY FAILED PLATFORM TYPE**

TYPE	AVERAGE	MEDIAN	NO. OF FIRMS
Transaction	4.5	3	174
Hybrid	7.4	6	14
Innovation	5.0	4	21
Stand-alone	3.7	2	116
Acquired	7.4	6	49
Part of larger company/ consortium	4.6	2	44

NOTES

PREFACE AND ACKNOWLEDGMENTS

1. Annabelle Gawer and Michael A. Cusumano, *Platform Leadership: How Intel, Microsoft, and Cisco Drive Industry Innovation* (Boston: Harvard Business School Press, 2002).

2. Annabelle Gawer and Michael A. Cusumano, "How Companies Become Platform Leaders," MIT Sloan Management Review 49, no. 2 (Winter 2008): 28–35.

3. For a discussion of platform envelopment, see Thomas Eisenmann, Geoffrey Parker, and Marshall Van Alstyne, "Strategies for Two-Sided Markets," *Harvard Business Review*, October 2006, 92–101.

4. David B. Yoffie and Michael A. Cusumano, *Strategy Rules: Five Timeless Lessons from Bill Gates, Andy Grove, and Steve Jobs* (New York: HarperBusiness, 2015).

CHAPTER 1: PLATFORM THINKING: INTRODUCTION

1. Michael W. Miller, "High-Tech Saga: How Two Computer Nuts Transformed Industry Before Messy Breakup," *Wall Street Journal*, August 27, 1986.

2. For accounts of this story, see Stephen Manes and Paul Andrews, *Gates: How Microsoft's Mogul Reinvented an Industry—and Made Himself the Richest Man in America* (New York: Doubleday, 1993), 150–63; and Michael A. Cusumano and Richard W. Selby, *Microsoft Secrets* (New York: Free Press/Simon & Schuster, 1995), 137, 158–59.

3. This information comes from a 1994 magazine interview with Bill Gates cited in Cusumano and Selby, *Microsoft Secrets*, 159.

4. David B. Yoffie and Michael A. Cusumano, *Strategy Rules: Five Timeless Lessons from Bill Gates, Andy Grove, and Steve Jobs* (New York: HarperBusiness, 2015), 98–100.

5. Manes and Andrews, *Gates*, 245–46.

6. For details, see "Did Apple not originally allow anyone to develop software for the Macintosh?" Stack Exchange Retrocomputing, https://retrocomputing.stackexchange.com/questions/2513 /did-apple-not-originally-allow-anyone-to-develop-software-for -the-macintosh/2520?utm_medium=organic&utm_source=google _rich_qa&utm_campaign=google_rich_qa (accessed May 21, 2018).

7. Yoffie and Cusumano, *Strategy Rules*, 114.

8. Mathew Rosenberg and Sheera Frenkel, "Facebook's Role in Data Misuse Sets Off a Storm on Two Continents," *New York Times*, March 18, 2018; and Katrin Benhold, "Germany Acts to Tame Facebook, Learning from Its Own History of Hate," *New York Times*, May 19, 2018.

9. Politico Staff, "Full Text: Mark Zuckerberg's Wednesday Testimony to Congress on Cambridge Analytica," *Politico*, April 11, 2018, https:// www.politico.com/story/2018/04/09/transcript-mark-zuckerberg -testimony-to-congress-on-cambridge-analytica-509978 (accessed May 15, 2018).

10. See "List of Unicorn Start-Up Companies," *Wikipedia*, https:// en.wikipedia.org/wiki/List_of_unicorn_start-up_companies (accessed May 21, 2018).

11. Brian X. Chen, "Google's File on Me Was Huge. Here's Why It Wasn't as Creepy as My Facebook Data," *New York Times*, May 16, 2018.

12. See Lina Khan, "Amazon's Antitrust Paradox," *Yale Law Journal* 126, no. 3 (January 2017): 710–805; and "How Many Products Does Amazon Sell?—January 2018," ScrapeHero, https://www.scrapehero .com/many-products-amazon-sell-january-2018/ (accessed May 17, 2018).

13. See, for example, David B. Yoffie and Eric Baldwin, "Apple, Inc. in 2015" (Boston: Harvard Business School Publishing, Case #9-715-456).

14. Our definition of the term "platform" has evolved over the years from an initial focus on what today we would call industry innovation platforms, as in Annabelle Gawer and Michael A. Cusumano, *Platform*

Leadership: How Intel, Microsoft, and Cisco Drive Industry Innovation (Boston: Harvard Business School Press, 2002). This book follows the broader definition used in Annabelle Gawer, ed., *Platforms, Markets, and Innovation* (Cheltanham: Edward Elgar, 2009); and Michael A. Cusumano, *Staying Power: Six Enduring Principles for Management Strategy and Innovation in an Uncertain World* (Oxford: Oxford University Press, 2010). See also Michael A. Cusumano, "The Evolution of Platform Thinking," *Communications of the ACM* 53, no. 1 (January 2010): 32–34.

15. Geoffrey Parker, Marshall Van Alstyne, and Sangeet Paul Choudary, *Platform Revolution: How Platform Markets Are Transforming the Economy and How to Make Them Work for You* (New York: W. W. Norton, 2016).

16. David S. Evans and Richard Schmalensee, *Matchmakers: The New Economics of Multisided Platforms* (Boston: Harvard Business Review Press, 2016).

17. Annabelle Gawer and Michael A. Cusumano, "How Companies Become Platform Leaders," *MIT Sloan Management Review* 49, no. 2 (Winter 2008): 28–35; and Cusumano, *Staying Power*, 64.

18. Network effects are sometimes called "network externalities" (in truth, they are slightly different) or "demand-side economies of scale," although it can be difficult to determine which is the demand side. To learn more, see S. J. Liebowitz and Stephen E. Margolis, "Network Externality: An Uncommon Tragedy," *Journal of Economic Perspectives* 8, no. 2 (Spring 1994): 133–50.

19. There were several influences on our earliest treatment of network effects or "bandwagon dynamics," as described in Michael A. Cusumano, Richard S. Rosenbloom, and Yiorgos Mylonadis, "Strategic Maneuvering and Mass Market Dynamics: The Triumph of VHS Over Beta," *Business History Review* 66, no. 1 (Spring 1992): 51–94. The most important influences in the economics literature were Michael Katz and Carl Shapiro, "Network Externalities, Competition, and Compatibility," *American Economic Review* 75, no. 3 (June 1985):

424–40; "Technology Adoption in the Presence of Network Externalities," *Journal of Political Economy* 94, no. 4 (August 1986): 822–41; and Paul David, "CLIO and the Economics of QWERTY," *American Economic Review* 75, no. 2 (May 1985): 332–37. Also see Joseph Farrell and Garth Saloner, "Standardization, Compatibility, and Innovation," *Rand Journal of Economics* 16, no. 1 (Spring 1985): 70–83; and "Installed Base and Compatibility: Innovation, Product Preannouncements, and Predation," *American Economic Review* 76, no. 5 (December 1986): 940–55.

20. David S. Evans, "How Catalysts Ignite: The Economics of Platform-Based Start-ups," in Gawer, ed., *Platforms, Markets, and Innovation*, 99–128.

21. Innovation platforms are what we previously referred to as "industry platforms" in Gawer and Cusumano, *Platform Leadership*; and other articles and books, as noted earlier. They are similar to what Evans, Hagiu, and Schmalensee called "software platforms" in various writings. See David S. Evans, Andrei Hagiu, and Richard Schmalensee, *Invisible Engines: How Software Platforms Drive Innovation and Transform Industries* (Cambridge, MA: MIT Press, 2006); and Evans and Schmalensee, *Matchmakers*.

22. Evans and Schmalensee have previously referred to what we call transaction platforms as "matchmakers" as well as "transaction systems." For use of the latter term in particular, see David S. Evans and Michael Noel, "Defining Antitrust Markets When Firms Operate Two-Sided Platforms," *Columbia Business Law Review* 2005, no. 3 (January 2005): 667–702. A U.S. Supreme Court opinion used the term "transaction platform" in a case involving American Express, which focused on the legality of efforts to dissuade merchants from steering customers to other credit cards with lower fees. Several lower court cases litigated this matter. See Supreme Court of the United States, *Ohio et al. v. American Express Co. et al.* (2018). Our thanks to Richard Schmalensee for this reference.

23. To do some statistical analysis and control for industry differences,

we also selected all the firms in the Forbes Global 2000 from the same industries as the platform companies and then compared this industry control group of 100 firms (1,018 yearly observations) to the 43 platforms (374 yearly observations). Several other comparisons were highly significant (at the 99 percent statistical confidence level).

24. For our first paper on the data analysis, see Michael A. Cusumano, Annabelle Gawer, and David B. Yoffie, "Platform vs. Non-Platform Company Performance: Some Exploratory Data Analysis," Platform Research Symposium, Boston University, July 2018. The final analysis contained in this book was performed by Ankur Chavda while a doctoral student at MIT. The earlier database was constructed, cleaned, and analyzed by other research assistants at Harvard University (Daniel Nightingale and Damjan Korac) and the University of Surrey (Georges Xydopoulos).

25. Amazon, Inc., "Form 10K" (annual). Data cited is from 2017. Page 26 shows Amazon Web Services profit data.

26. On these platform market drivers, see Thomas Eisenmann, Geoffrey Parker, and Marshall Van Alstyne, "Strategies for Two-Sided Markets," Harvard Business Review, October 2006, 92–101; and Parker, Van Alstyne, and Choudary, Platform Revolution.

CHAPTER 2: WINNER TAKE ALL OR MOST: MORE THAN NETWORK EFFECTS

1. Andrei Hagiu and Simon Rothman also pointed out the limits of network effects. They cautioned platform companies not to focus on fast growth and, instead, create a solid base of trust with consumers and regulators. See Andrei Hagiu and Simon Rothman, "Network Effects Aren't Enough," Harvard Business Review, April 2016.

2. For our conceptualization of the four market drivers, we are indebted to Thomas Eisenmann, Geoffrey Parker, and Marshall Van Alstyne, "Strategies for Two-Sided Markets," Harvard Business Review, October

2006, 92–101. Also see Geoffrey Parker, Marshall Van Alstyne, and Sangeet Paul Choudary, *Platform Revolution: How Platform Markets Are Transforming the Economy and How to Make Them Work for You* (New York: W. W. Norton, 2016).

3. "Track Gauge in the United States," *Wikipedia*, https://en.wikipedia.org /wiki/Track_gauge_in_the_United_States (accessed April 26, 2018).

4. For one source on the history, see AT&T, "Evolution of the SBC and AT&T Brands: A Pictorial Timeline," http://www.att.com/Common /files/pdf/logo_evolution_factsheet.pdf (accessed April 26, 2018).

5. The concept of network externalities was apparently first introduced in the 1908 Bell Telephone annual report by the CEO, Theodore Vail, according to "Network Effect," *Wikipedia*, https://en.wikipedia.org /wiki/Network_effect (accessed April 26, 2018). The most influential early technical paper on the economics of network externalities in the communications industry is Jeffrey Rohlfs, "A Theory of Interdependent Demand for a Communications Service," *Bell Journal of Economics and Management Science* 5, no. 1 (Spring 1974): 16–37. In this and other papers, the concept of network externalities was used to justify pricing the service low enough (below cost, for example), especially to new users, to achieve universal coverage, that is, with old users (especially in cities) subsidizing new users (especially in rural areas), on the assumption that everyone in the network potentially benefits from each additional user.

6. Michael DeGusta, "Are Smart Phones Spreading Faster than Any Technology in Human History?" *MIT Technology Review*, May 9, 2012.

7. See "Telephone Directory," *Wikipedia*, https://en.wikipedia.org/wiki /Telephone_directory (accessed April 26, 2018).

8. We describe the concept of "free but not free" in Michael A. Cusumano and David B. Yoffie, *Competing on Internet Time: Lessons from Netscape and Its Battle with Microsoft* (New York: Free Press/Simon & Schuster, 1998), 100.

9. For the history of the Yellow Pages, see https://en.wikipedia.org/wiki /Yellow_pages (accessed April 26, 2018).

10. Evan D. White and Michael F. Sheehan, "Monopoly, the Holding Company, and Asset Stripping: The Case of the Yellow Pages," *Journal of Economic Issues* 26, no. 1 (March 1992): 159–82.

11. Michael J. de la Merced, "AT&T Sells Majority Stake in Yellow Pages to Cerberus," *New York Times*, April 9, 2012.

12. To offer your product or service as a "core" or an essential ingredient in a solution to an industry-wide problem is a strategy that, in previous writings, we have called "coring." This is useful for markets where no platform yet exists. See Annabelle Gawer and Michael A. Cusumano, "How Companies Become Platform Leaders," *MIT Sloan Management Review* 49, no. 2 (Winter 2008): 28–35.

13. Thumbtack Editors, "How Do the Yellow Pages Still Make Money?" *Thumbtack Journal*, October 7, 2015, https://www.thumbtack.com /blog/how-do-the-yellow-pages-still-make-money/ (accessed October 30, 2018).

14. Christopher Hinton, "R.H. Donnelly Files for Bankruptcy," Marketwatch.com, May 29, 2009.

15. Thumbtack Editors, "How Do the Yellow Pages Still Make Money?"

16. Michael E. Porter, *Competitive Strategy: Techniques for Analyzing Industries and Competitors* (New York: Free Press, 1980).

17. See Timothy Bresnahan, Joe Orsini, and Pai-Ling Yin, "Demand Heterogeneity, Inframarginal Multihoming, and Platform Market Stability: Mobile Apps," Stanford University Working Paper, September 15, 2015.

18. See Eisenmann, Parker, and Van Alstyne, "Strategies for Two-Sided Markets"; and Michael A. Cusumano, *Staying Power: Six Enduring Principles for Management Strategy and Innovation in an Uncertain World* (Oxford: Oxford University Press, 2010), 61–62.

19. See "Open Handset Alliance," *Wikipedia*, https://en.wikipedia.org /wiki/Open_Handset_Alliance (accessed October 19, 2018). For further discussion of this example and "tipping," see Gawer and Cusumano, "How Companies Become Platform Leaders."

20. Shira Ovide and Daisuke Wakabayashi, "Apple's Share of Smartphone

Industry Profits Soars to 92%," *Wall Street Journal*, July 12, 2015; and Patrick Seitz, "Apple Took 92% of Smartphone Profits in Q4," *Investors Business Daily*, February 7, 2017, http://www.investors.com/news /technology/click/apple-took-92-of-smartphone-industry-profits-in-q4/.

21. Upwork, "Fortune 500 Enterprises Shift Their Contingent Workforce to Upwork Platform Saving Both Time and Money," press release, February 6, 2018, https://www.upwork.com/press/2018/02/06 /fortune-500-enterprises/.

22. Dylan Minor and David B. Yoffie, "Upwork: Creating the Human Cloud" (Boston: Harvard Business School Publishing, HBS Case #9-718-402, July 6, 2018), 1.

23. Form S-1, UPWORK INC., https://www.sec.gov/Archives/edgar /data/1627475/000119312518267594/d575528ds1.htm (accessed September 11, 2018).

24. See David B. Yoffie, ed., *Competing in the Age of Digital Convergence* (Boston: Harvard Business School Press, 1997).

25. See David Gelles, "Facebook's Grand Plan for the Future," *Financial Times*, December 3, 2010; and Annabelle Gawer, "What Managers Need to Know About Platforms," *European Business Review*, July 20, 2011.

26. Brittany Darwell, "Facebook Platform Supports More Than 42 Million Pages and 9 Million Apps," *Adweek*, April 27, 2012, https:// www.adweek.com/digital/facebook-platform-supports-more-than-42 -million-pages-and-9-million-apps/ (accessed May 22, 2018).

27. Matt Turck, "The Power of Data Network Effects," blog posted January 4, 2016, http://mattturck.com/the-power-of-data-network -effects/ (accessed December 21, 2017).

28. Andrew Del-Colle, "How Waze Conquered Mapping with Thousands of Volunteers," *Popular Mechanics*, May 19, 2015.

29. Alexis C. Madrigal, "The Perfect Selfishness of Mapping Apps," *Atlantic*, March 15, 2018.

30. See, for example, Google chairman Eric Schmidt's testimony to congress in September 2011, https://www.cnet.com/news/eric -schmidts-written-testimony-to-congress/ (accessed August 4, 2018).

31. Jamie Condliffe, "Instagram Now Looks Like a Bargain," *New York Times*, June 27, 2018.

32. Henry Blodgett, "Everyone Who Thinks Facebook Is Stupid for Buying WhatsApp for $19 Billion Should Think Again . . ." *Business Insider*, February 20, 2014.

33. Evan Spiegel, "Let's Chat,"Snap Inc., May 9, 2012, https://www.snap .com/en-US/news/post/lets-chat/ (accessed October 30, 2018).

34. See Adi Suja, "Top 15 Niche Online Businesses for Inspiration," *ecommerce platforms*, June 28, 2018, https://ecommerce-platforms.com /articles/top-niche-ecommerce-stores (accessed August 11, 2018).

35. Betsy Morris and Deepa Seetharaman, "The New Copycats: How Facebook Squashes Competition from Start-ups," *Wall Street Journal*, August 9, 2017.

36. Kurt Wagner and Rani Molla, "Why Snapchat Is Shrinking," *Recode*, August 7, 2018, https://www.recode.net/2018/8/7/17661756/snap -earnings-snapchat-q2-instagram-user-growth (accessed August 13, 2018).

37. Lina Khan, "Amazon's Antitrust Paradox," *Yale Law Journal* 126, no. 3 (January 2017): 780–83.

38. Ibid., 710–805.

39. Venkat Venkatraman, *The Digital Matrix: New Rules for Business Transformation through Technology* (Canada: Lifetree Media, 2017).

40. Michael A. Cusumano, "Amazon and Whole Foods: Follow the Strategy (and the Money)," *Communications of the ACM* 60, no. 10 (October 2017): 24–26.

CHAPTER 3: STRATEGY AND BUSINESS MODELS: INNOVATION, TRANSACTION, OR HYBRID

1. See Jonathan Wareham, Paul Fox, and Josep Lluis Cano Giner, "Technology Ecosystem Governance," *Organization Science* 25, no. 4 (July–August 2014); and Geoffrey Parker, Marshall Van Alstyne, and Sangeet Paul Choudary, *Platform Revolution: How Platform Markets*

Are Transforming the Economy and How to Make Them Work for You (New York: W. W. Norton, 2016).

2. David B. Yoffie, Liz Kind, and David Ben Shimol, "Numenta: Inventing and (or) Commercializing AI" (Boston: Harvard Business School Publishing, Case #9-716-469, July 2018).

3. Also see Cade Metz, "Jeff Hawkins Is Finally Ready to Explain His Brain Research," *New York Times*, October 14, 2018.

4. David S. Evans and Richard Schmalensee, *Matchmakers: The New Economics of Multisided Platforms* (Boston: Harvard Business Review Press, 2016).

5. Annabelle Gawer and Michael A. Cusumano, "How Companies Become Platform Leaders," *MIT Sloan Management Review* 49, no. 2 (Winter 2008): 28–35.

6. Thales Teixeira and Morgan Brown, "Airbnb, Etsy, Uber: Acquiring the First Thousand Customers" (Boston: Harvard Business School Publishing, Case #9-516-094, January 2018).

7. David S. Evans, "How Catalysts Ignite: The Economics of Platform-Based Start-ups," in Annabelle Gawer, ed., *Platforms, Markets, and Innovation* (Cheltenham: Edward Elgar Publishing Limited, 2009), 99–128.

8. Stuart Dredge, "WhatsApp Messaging App to Charge iPhone Users an Annual Subscription," *Guardian*, July 17, 2013. Also Alex Hern, "WhatsApp Drops Subscription Fee to Become Fully Free," *Guardian*, January 18, 2016.

9. Elaine Pofeldt, "Freelance Giant Upwork Shakes Up Its Business Model," *Forbes*, May 3, 2016.

10. For this latest data and analysis of Uber driver churn rates, recruitment costs, and other expenses, see CB Insights, "How Uber Makes Money" (2018), available at https://drive.google.com/file/d/1tOp8MorFS0q _DI22nU2WFyYq-4UTXQY/view (accessed December 14, 2018).

11. Steven Hill, "What Dara Khosrowshahi Must Do to Save Uber," *New York Times*, August 30, 2017. Also Ben Thompson, "Uber's Bundles," Stratechery.com, August 28, 2018.

12. Kirsten Korosec, "Uber Freight's App for Truck Drivers Is Getting an Upgrade," *Techcrunch*, October 11, 2018.

13. See David S. Evans, Andrei Hagiu, and Richard Schmalensee, *Invisible Engines: How Software Platforms Drive Innovation and Transform Industries* (Cambridge, MA: MIT Press, 2006). Also Evans and Schmalensee, *Matchmakers*; and Parker, Van Alstyne, and Choudary, *Platform Revolution*.

14. Michael A. Cusumano, "The Bitcoin Ecosystem," *Communications of the ACM* 57, no. 10 (October 2014): 22–24.

15. "Start-up of the Week: Deliveroo," *Wired*, April 2, 2015.

16. Sarah Butler, "Deliveroo Boss Doubled His Pay Ahead of Riders' Protest," *Guardian*, November 11, 2016.

17. Adam Satariano, "Deliveroo Takes a Kitchen-Sink Approach to Food Apps," *Bloomberg Businessweek*, February 17, 2018.

18. Stephanie Strom, "OpenTable Began a Revolution. Now It's a Power Under Siege," *New York Times*, August 29, 2017.

19. Google, "Google Ads," https://ads.google.com/home/ (accessed October 30, 2018).

20. Slinger Jansen and Michael A. Cusumano, "Defining Software Ecosystems: A Survey of Software Platforms and Business Network Governance," in Slinger Jansen, Sjaak Brinkemper, and M. A. Cusumano, eds., *Software Ecosystems: Analyzing and Managing Business Networks in the Software Industry* (Cheltanham: Edward Elgar, 2013), 13–28.

21. Sascha Ega, "5 Reasons Why Google Sold Motorola, and 5 Reasons Why Lenovo Bought It," *PCMag.com*, January 30, 2014.

22. Edoardo Maggio, "Google Acquires HTC Team in $1.1 Billion Agreement to Beef Up Hardware Division," *Business Insider*, September 20, 2017.

23. Janet Wagner, "Overly Restrictive API Policies Kill Innovation," *ProgrammableWeb*, 2014, https://www.programmableweb.com/news/overly-restrictive-api-policies-kill-innovation/analysis/2014/07/16 (accessed June 14, 2017).

24. Sharon Gaudin, "Twitter Apologizes to, Tries to Woo Back, Developers," *ComputerWorld*, October 21, 2015.

25. Uber, "What Does the Background Check Include?" https://help
    .uber.com/h/1bde7f02-9eb0-4111-bf29-6c984e2146ad (accessed
    June 14, 2017). Also Farhad Manjoo, "Uber Wants to Rule the
    World. First It Must Conquer India," *New York Times*, April 14,
    2017.

26. Li Yuan, "Customer Died. Will That Be a Wake-up Call for China's
    Tech Scene?" *New York Times*, August 29, 2018; and Sui-Lee Wee,
    "Didi Suspends Carpooling Service in China After 2nd Passenger is
    Killed," *New York Times*, August 26, 2018.

27. Uber, "Community Guidelines," https://www.uber.com/legal
    /community-guidelines/us-en/ (accessed July 3, 2017).

28. Airbnb, "Community Commitment," http://blog.atairbnb.com/the
    -airbnb-community-commitment/ (accessed July 5, 2017).

29. David B. Yoffie and Dylan Minor, "Upwork: Creating the Human
    Cloud" (Boston: Harvard Business School Publishing, Case #9-717-
    475, May 2017).

30. Sheera Frenkel, "Facebook Will Use Artificial Intelligence to Find
    Extremist Posts," *New York Times*, June 15, 2017; and TripAdvisor,
    "Review Moderation and Fraud Detection FAQ," https://www
    .tripadvisor.co.uk/vpages/review_mod_fraud_detect.html (accessed
    July 3, 2017).

31. Airbnb, "Updated Terms of Service," https://www.airbnb.co.uk/terms
    (accessed July 3, 2017).

32. Annabelle Gawer and Michael A. Cusumano, *Platform Leadership:
    How Intel, Microsoft, and Cisco Drive Industry Innovation* (Boston:
    Harvard Business School Press, 2002).

33. Chuck Jones, "Apple's App Store Generated Over $11 Billion in
    Revenue for the Company Last Year," *Forbes*, January 6, 2018.

34. Kevin Roose, "Facebook Emails Show Its Real Mission: Making Money
    and Crushing Competition," *New York Times*, December 5, 2018.

35. Georgia Wells, "Snapchat Zigs Where Facebook Zags," *Wall Street
    Journal*, June 14, 2018.

36. Expedia Affiliate Network, "eps rapid," http://developer.ean.com/

(accessed July 5, 2017); and "API," https://www.ean.com/solutions /api (accessed July 5, 2017).

37. "The Hidden Cost of Building an Android Device," *Guardian,* January 23, 2014.

38. Chinese smartphone makers were an exception. Since Google did not operate in China, platform companies such as Tencent, Xiaomi, Huawei, and Baidu created alternative app stores for use mainly within their country. See http://technode.com/2017/06/02/top-10-android -app-stores-china-2017/ (accessed September 29, 2017) as well as the individual company websites.

39. Our thanks to Valeria Xiao Jia for researching WeChat's business model.

40. Rachel King, "IBM Courts Coders with Watson," *New York Times,* November 11, 2016.

41. Rajiv Lal and Scott Johnson, "GE Digital" (Boston: Harvard Business School Publishing, Case #N9-517-063, February 2017); and Steve Lohr, "GE Makes a Sharp Pivot on Digital," *New York Times,* April 19, 2018.

42. Nathaniel Popper and Steve Lohr, "Blockchain: A Better Way to Track Porkchops, Bonds, Bad Peanut Butter?" *New York Times,* March 4, 2017.

43. Christopher Mims, "The Lesson of Yahoo: Don't Lose Your Focus," *Wall Street Journal,* July 27, 2016.

CHAPTER 4: COMMON MISTAKES:
MISPRICING, MISTRUST, MISTIMING—AND HUBRIS

1. Exostar, "About Us," https://www.exostar.com/company/ (accessed July 20, 2018).

2. Marshall W. Van Alstyne, Geoffrey G. Parker, and Sangeet Paul Choudary, "6 Reasons Platforms Fail," *Harvard Business Review,* March 31, 2016.

3. Ellen Huet, "Sidecar Puts Passengers Aside, Pivots to a Mostly-Deliveries Company," *Forbes,* August 5, 2015.

4. Douglas MacMillan, "Sidecar Succumbs to Uber and Lyft in Car-Hailing Wars," *Wall Street Journal*, December 29, 2015. Also Sunil Paul, "Why We Sold to GM," *Medium* (blog post), January 20, 2016, https://medium.com/@SunilPaul/why-we-sold-to-gm-83a29058af5a #.okepk6jjy (accessed October 30, 2018).

5. Carolyn Said, "Could Sidecar's Patent Trip Up Uber, Lyft?" *SFGate*, May 16, 2015, http://www.sfgate.com/business/article/Could-Sidecar -s-patent-trip-up-Uber-Lyft-6267124.php#photo-7985861 (accessed October 30, 2018).

6. "Sidecar Connects Drivers and Passengers One Ride at a Time," *Sidecar*, http://www.side.cr/sidecar-connects-drivers-and-passengers -one-ride-at-a-time/ (accessed October 30, 2018).

7. Zusha Elinson, "Cab Companies Want to Put the Brakes on Rideshare Services," *NBC Bay Area*, September 4, 2012, https://www .nbcbayarea.com/news/local/Cab_companies_want_to_put_the _brakes_on_rideshare_services-168425826.html (accessed October 30, 2018).

8. Heather Somerville, "Sidecar Ends Donation Fares," *Silicon Beat*, November 15, 2013.

9. Ryan Lawler, "Lyft Off: Zimride's Long Road to Overnight Success," *TechCrunch*, August 29, 2014.

10. Ryan Lawler, "Look Out, Lyft: Uber CEO Travis Kalanick Says It Will Do Ride Sharing, Too," *TechCrunch*, September 12, 2012.

11. Luz Lazo, "Uber Turns 5, Reaches 1 Million Drivers and 300 Cities Worldwide. Now What?" *Washington Post*, June 4, 2015. Also Youngme Moon, "Uber: Changing the Way the World Moves" (Boston: Harvard Business School Publishing, Case #316-101, November 2015); and Andrew J. Hawkins, "Uber Covers 75 Percent of the US, but Getting to 100 Will Be Really Hard," *Verge*, October 23, 2015.

12. "Lyft CEO: We Have Over 100,000 Drivers Across the Country," *Bloomberg Technology*, March 6, 2015.

13. Scott Van Maldegiam, "Sidecar: The Ins and Outs," *Rideshare Guy*, February 25, 2015.

14. Sunil Paul, "So Long Sidecar and Thanks," *Medium* (blog), December 29, 2015, https://medium.com/@SunilPaul/so-long -sidecar-and-thanks-74c8a0955064#.3zka094ou (accessed October 30, 2018).

15. Paul, "Why We Sold to GM."

16. Huet, "Sidecar Puts Passengers Aside."

17. Michael Romano, vice president of investor relations for Lightspeed Venture Partners, quoted in Heather Somerville, "Sidecar to Stop Ride, Delivery Services at End of Year," Reuters, December 29, 2015.

18. Brian Solis, analyst with Altimeter Group, quoted in Huet, "Sidecar Puts Passengers Aside."

19. Quoted in Huet, "Sidecar Puts Passengers Aside."

20. Emma G. Fitzsimmons, "Uber Hit with Cap as New York City Takes Lead in Crackdown," *New York Times*, August 8, 2018.

21. Greg Bensinger and Maureen Farrell, "Uber Joins Lyft in Race to Tap Investors," *Wall Street Journal*, December 7, 2018.

22. See Robert Burgelman, Robert Siegel, and Henry Lippincott, "PayPal in 2015: Reshaping the Financial Services Website," Stanford GSB No. E-572, November 2015.

23. eBay Inc., *Annual Report 2002* (Form 10-K), March 31, 2003, 21–22.

24. Quoted in Jeffrey Ressner and Bill Powell, "Why eBay Must Win China," *Time*, September 5, 2005.

25. Helen H. Wang, "How eBay Failed in China," *Forbes*, September 12, 2010.

26. Porter Erisman, *Alibaba's World: How a Remarkable Chinese Company Is Changing the Face of Global Business* (New York: Palgrave Macmillan, 2015).

27. Mark Greeven, Shengyun Yang, Tao Yue, Eric van Heck, and Barbara Krug, "How Taobao Bested eBay in China," *Financial Times*, March 12, 2012.

28. See Liu Shiying and Martha Avery, *Alibaba: The Inside Story Behind Jack Ma and the Creation of the World's Biggest Online Marketplace* (New York: Collins Business, 2009), 124–25.

29. Ressner and Powell, "Why eBay Must Win China." Also Erisman, *Alibaba's World*.

30. Wang, "How eBay Failed in China."

31. Ressner and Powell, "Why eBay Must Win China."

32. Mylene Mangalinden, "Hot Bidding: In a Challenging China Market, EBay Confronts a Big New Riva," *Wall Street Journal*, August 12, 2005, A1. See also Jason Dean and Jonathan Cheng, "Yahoo Is Set to Announce Alibaba Deal," *Wall Street Journal*, August 11, 2005.

33. Wang, "How eBay Failed in China."

34. Tania Branigan, "China: Ambitious Alibaba Takes on the World," *Guardian*, September 14, 2010.

35. "eBay's Deal with Tom Online Offers Some Timely Lessons for Managers of Global Online Companies," *Knowledge@Wharton*, February 14, 2007, http://knowledge.wharton.upenn.edu/article /ebays-deal-with-tom-online-offers-some-timely-lessons-for-managers -of-global-online-companies/ (accessed October 30, 2018). Also Erisman, *Alibaba's World*.

36. Bruce Einhorn, "How eBay Found a Secret Way into China," *Bloomberg Businessweek*, April 14, 2011; and *Knowledge@Wharton*, "eBay's Deal with Tom Online."

37. See Shiying and Avery, *Alibaba*, 117–28.

38. Mure Dickie, "China's Crocodiles Ready for a Fight," *Financial Times*, July 14, 2004.

39. Einhorn, "How eBay Found a Secret Way into China."

40. Ma employed a variation on this quote a number of times; this version is quoted in Dickie, "China's Crocodiles Ready for a Fight."

41. James Kobielus, "Netscape's Code Giveaway Won't Kill Microsoft," *Network World*, March 23, 1998.

42. Andy Eddy, "Netscape's Helpers," *Network World*, June 22, 1998.

43. Charles Herold, "NEWS WATCH: BROWSERS: Netscape Unveils Mozilla 1.0, Another Window on the Web," *New York Times*, July 4, 2002.

44. "New Browser Wins Over Net Surfers," *BBC News*, November 24,

2005, http://news.bbc.co.uk/2/hi/technology/4037833.stm (accessed October 30, 2018).

45. Eric Lai and Gregg Keizer, "IE Still Top Dog in Corporate Browser Kennel," *ComputerWorld*, January 14, 2008.

46. Russel Kay, "Browsing the Browsers," *ComputerWorld*, November 8, 2004.

47. Michael Gartenberg, "Business Must Be Cautious with Firefox," *ComputerWorld*, January 24, 2005.

48. U.S. CERT, "Vulnerability Note VU#713878," June 9, 2004, https://www.kb.cert.org/vuls/id/713878 (accessed October 30, 2018).

49. Dan Tynan, "The 25 Worst Tech Products of All Time," *PCWorld*, May 26, 2006.

50. Todd Bishop, "Internet Explorer GM: 'We Messed Up,'" Microsoft Blog, *Seattle PI*, March 20, 2006, http://blog.seattlepi.com/microsoft/2006/03/20/internet-explorer-gm-we-messed-up/ (accessed October 30, 2018).

51. Measuring browser market share can be challenging. The two major market research sites that measure browser share use different methods: one measures total page views, while the other measures unique daily site visits. The difference is that if a user visits, say, the *New York Times* website and reads four different stories, that user would account for four page views but only one unique site visit. Page views measures the total web traffic carried by a given browser, while unique site visits is a rough proxy for number of users using a particular browser. When measuring unique daily site visits, IE remained the market-share leader by a narrow margin in 2016, leading Chrome 43 percent to 39 percent, with Firefox a distant third at just over 10 percent. In terms of page views, Chrome has a huge lead, with over 60 percent share, while Firefox and IE battled for second place, with 15.7 percent and 13.7 percent, respectively.

52. Steven Levy, "Inside Chrome: The Secret Project to Crush IE and Remake the Web," *Wired*, September 2, 2008.

53. Megan Geuss, "Which Browser Should You Use?" *PCWorld*, February 26, 2012.

54. Ann Bednarz, "Browser Wars," *Network World*, November 2, 2011.

55. All quoted in "Google Cell Platform No Threat, Rivals Say: Move Seen to Give Search Engine Leg Up on Mobile Advertising," *Ottawa Citizen*, November 6, 2007.

56. Jay Yarow, "Here's What Steve Ballmer Thought About the iPhone Five Years Ago," *Business Insider*, June 29, 2012.

57. Peter Bright, "Windows Phone 7: The Ars Review," *ArsTechnica*, October 22, 2010.

58. Sascha Segan, "Microsoft's Windows Phone 7 OS," *PCMag*, October 20, 2010.

59. Joshua Topolsky, "Windows Phone 7 Review," *Engadget*, October 20, 2010.

60. Dieter Bohn and Chris Ziegler, "Windows Phone 8 review," *Verge*, October 29, 2012.

61. Bright, "Windows Phone 7."

62. See Sam Oliver, "Nokia Ditches Symbian, Embraces Microsoft Windows Phone for New Handsets," *AppleInsider*, February 11, 2011.

63. Pete Cunningham, quoted in Kevin J. O'Brien, "Together, Nokia and Microsoft Renew a Push in Smartphones," *New York Times*, February 11, 2011.

64. O'Brien, "Together, Nokia and Microsoft Renew a Push in Smartphones."

65. See Katie Marsal, "IDC Predicts Windows Phone Will Top Apple's iOS in Market Share by 2015, *AppleInsider*, March 29, 2011.

66. Joey deVilla, "The Windows Phone Predictions that IDC, Gartner and Pyramid Research Probably Hope You've Forgotten," *Global Nerdy*, May 7, 2012.

67. Matt Rosoff, "The Research Firm That Once Thought Microsoft Would Beat the iPhone Has Given Up on Windows Phone," *Business Insider*, December 7, 2015.

68. Segan, "Microsoft Windows Phone 7 OS."

69. Topolsky, "Windows Phone 7 Review."

70. Jenna Wortham and Nick Wingfield, "Microsoft Is Writing Checks to Fill Out Its App Store," *New York Times*, April 5, 2012.

71. Ibid.

72. Alexandra Chang, "Review: Microsoft Windows Phone 8," *Wired*, October 29, 2012.

73. "Snapchat," *Windows Central*, May 3, 2016.

74. Ewan Spence, "Ruthless Microsoft's Smart Decision to Kill Windows Phone," *Forbes*, January 30, 2016.

75. Andrew S. Grove, *Only the Paranoid Survive: How to Exploit the Crisis Points that Challenge Every Company* (New York: Random House, 1996).

CHAPTER 5: OLD DOGS AND NEW TRICKS:
BUILD, BUY, OR BELONG TO A PLATFORM

1. Michael A. Cusumano, *Staying Power: Six Enduring Principles for Management Strategy and Innovation in an Uncertain World* (Oxford: Oxford University Press, 2010), 57.

2. Avery Hartmans, "Airbnb Now Has More Listings Worldwide Than the Top Five Brands Combined," *Business Insider*, August 10, 2017.

3. Julie Weed, "Blurring Lines, Hotels Get into the Home-Sharing Business," *New York Times*, July 2, 2018.

4. Andrei Hagiu and Julian Wright, "Do You Really Want to Be an eBay?" *Harvard Business Review*, March 2013; Andrei Hagiu and Julian Wright, "Controlling Versus Enabling," *Management Science*, forthcoming.

5. David B. Yoffie, one of the coauthors of this book, is a member of the board of directors of HTC.

6. Lina Khan, "Amazon's Antitrust Paradox," *Yale Law Journal* 126, no. 3 (January 2017): 710–805.

7. Brad Stone, *The Everything Store: Jeff Bezos and the Age of Amazon* (New York: Little, Brown and Company, 2014): 301–5.

8. Michael A. Cusumano and David B. Yoffie, *Competing on Internet Time: Lessons from Netscape and Its Battle with Microsoft* (New York: Free Press/Simon & Schuster, 1998).

9. P. H. Huang, M. Ceccagnoli, C. Forman, and D. J. Wu, "Appropriability Mechanisms and the Platform Partnership Decision: Evidence from Enterprise Software," *Management Science* 59, no. 1 (January 2013): 102–21.

10. Anna Hensel, "How This Entrepreneur Turned e-Commerce Giants into Customers," *Inc.*, August 12, 2015.

11. Burt Helm, "How This Company Makes $70 Million Selling Random Stuff on Amazon," *Inc.*, March 2016.

12. Rebecca Jarvis, John Kapetaneas, and Kelly McCarthy, "This NY Company Is Changing the e-Commerce Game with Changing Prices on Amazon," *ABC News*, June 2, 2016.

13. Helm, "How This Company."

14. Ibid.

15. Jarvis, Kapetaneas, and McCarthy, "This NY Company."

16. Helm, "How This Company."

17. Jarvis, Kapetaneas, and McCarthy, "This NY Company."

18. Karen Cheung, "HK Uber Drivers Fined HK$7,000, Licenses Suspended for 12 Months," *HKFP*, January 22, 2016, https://www .hongkongfp.com/2016/01/22/uber-drivers-fined-hk7000-licences -suspended-for-12-months/ (accessed July 20, 2016).

19. "Uber Clarifies Some Issues over Forced Exit from Hungary," *Portfolio*, July 18, 2016.

20. Shirley Leung, "All Hail Uber, Anywhere but Logan," *Boston Globe*, July 19, 2016.

21. Scott McCartney, "You Can't Take an Uber Home from These Airports," *Wall Street Journal*, July 6, 2016.

22. Jody Rosen, "The Knowledge, London's Legendary Taxi-Driver Test, Puts Up a Fight in the Age of GPS," *New York Times Style Magazine*, November 10, 2014.

23. U.K. Department of Transport, "Taxis, Private Hire Vehicles and Their Drivers," updated August 25, 2015, https://www.gov.uk/government /statistical-data-sets/taxi01-taxis-private-hire-vehilces-and-their -drivers#table-taxi0101 (accessed May 3, 2016).

24. Sam Knight, "How Uber Conquered London," *Guardian*, April 27, 2016.

25. Quoted in Knight, "How Uber Conquered London."

26. Kiki Loizou, "Hail Me on My Taxi App, Guv'nor," *Sunday Times* (London), August 12, 2012.

27. Toby Green, "Hail and Hearty Hailo Grows," *Evening Standard* (London), September 23, 2013. On taxi ridership, see London Chamber of Commerce and Industry, "The London Taxi Trade—a Report by the London Chamber of Commerce," June 2007, 3–4.

28. Louise Armitstead, "Hailo Is Just Waiting for That Tricky Second Album," *Daily Telegraph* (London), November 4, 2013; Annabel Palmer, "The Unlikely Bedfellows Driving a Cab Revolution," *City A.M.*, November 25, 2013.

29. "Hailo Taxi App Offices Vandalised as London Black Cab Drivers' Anger Grows," *Guardian*, May 22, 2014.

30. David Hellier, "London's Black-Cab Drivers Use Rival App to Compete with Upstart Uber," *Guardian*, September 5, 2015; Sam Shead, "Taxi App Gett Has Acquired London's Radio Taxis for 'Several Million Pounds' to Help It Take on Uber," *Business Insider*, March 30, 2016.

31. Prashant S. Rao and Mike Isaac, "Uber Loses License to Operate in London," *New York Times*, September 22, 2017.

32. Julia Kollewe and Glyn Topham, "Uber Apologises After London Ban and Admits 'We Got Things Wrong,'" *Guardian*, September 25, 2017; Rao and Isaac, "Uber Loses License to Operate in London."

33. Mark Kleinman, "Uber Lines Up Banker to Chair UK Unit amid London Ban Appeal," *SkyNews*, October 26, 2017.

34. Sean O'Kane and James Vincent, "Uber Wins the Right to Keep Operating in London," *Verge*, June 26, 2018.

35. "Walmart Tops 2002 Ranking of the Fortune 500," Time-Warner press release, April 1, 2002, http://www.timewarner.com/newsroom/press-releases/2002/04/01/Walmart-tops-2002-ranking-of-the-fortune-500 (accessed June 29, 2017).

36. See "Fortune Global 500," *Fortune,* http://fortune.com/global500/ (accessed July 1, 2017).

37. "Retail e-Commerce Sales in the United States from 2016–2022," *Statistica,* https://www.statista.com/statistics/272391/us-retail -e-commerce-sales-forecast/ (accessed October 30, 2018).

38. Laura Stevens and Sara Germano, "Nike Thought It Didn't Need Amazon—Then the Ground Shifted," *Wall Street Journal,* June 28, 2017.

39. Helm, "How This Company."

40. Amazon, "Amazon.com Announces First Quarter Sales Up 43% to $51.0 Billion," company press release, April 26, 2018.

41. Reuters, "Amazon's Third-Party Sellers Had Record-Breaking Sales in 2016," *Fortune,* January 4, 2017.

42. "Amazon.com: Third-Party Sellers Drive Profitability," *Seeking Alpha,* April 1, 2016.

43. Nandita Bose, "Walmart Completes Acquisition of Jet.com," Reuters, September 19, 2016.

44. David Collis, Andy Wu, Rembrand Koning, and Huaiyi Cici Sun, "Walmart Inc. Takes on Amazon.com" (Boston: Harvard Business School Publishing, Case #9-718-481, May 31, 2018), 23.

45. Nancee Halpin, "Walmart Reportedly in Talks to Acquire Jet.com," *Business Insider,* August 6, 2016.

46. Krystina Gustafson, "Wal-Mart: This Is Why Jet.com Is Worth $3.3 Billion," CNBC, August 8, 2016, http://www.cnbc.com/2016 /08/08/Wal-mart-this-is-why-jetcom-is-worth-33-billion.html.

47. Leena Rao, "Jet.com, the Online Shopping Upstart, Drops Membership Fee," *Fortune,* October 7, 2015.

48. See "The Jet Marketplace," https://jetsupport.desk.com/customer/en /portal/articles/2412295-the-jet-marketplace (accessed June 29, 2017).

49. Issie Lapowsky, "Crushing Amazon Would Be Nice, but Jet.com Also Wants to Boost Small Merchants," *Wired,* February 16, 2015.

50. Paul R. La Monica," Walmart Is killing Target and making Amazon sweat," *CNN Money*, November 16, 2017. See also Walmart, "Walmart U.S. Q3 Comps(1) Grew 2.7% and Walmart U.S. E-commerce Sales Grew 50%, Company Reports Q3 FY18 GAAP EPS of $0.58; Adjusted EPS(2) of $1.00," Walmart press release, November 16, 2018, https://news.walmart.com/2017/11/16/walmart-us-q3-comps-1-grew-27-and-walmart-us-e-commerce-sales-grew-50-company-reports-q3-fy18-gaap-eps-of-058-adjusted-eps-2-of-100 (accessed March 10, 2018).

51. Matthew Boyle, "Walmart Whistle-Blower Claims Cheating in Race with Amazon," *Bloomberg*, March 15, 2018, https://www.bloomberg.com/news/articles/2018-03-15/walmart-whistle-blower-claims-retailer-cheated-to-catch-amazon (accessed March 16, 2018).

52. Q4 2018 Wal Mart Stores Inc Earnings Call, February 20, 2018. Transcript available at https://corporate.walmart.com/media-library/document/q4fy18-earnings-webcast-transcript/_proxyDocument?id=00000161-d2c0-dfc5-a76b-f3f01e430000 (accessed March 10, 2018).

53. Phil Wahba, "Walmart's Jet.com Launches Its Own Private Brand to Woo Millennials," *Fortune*, October 23, 2017.

54. Boyle, "Walmart Whistle-Blower Claims."

55. Corinne Abrams, Sarah Nassauer, and Douglas MacMillan, "Walmart Takes on Amazon with $15 Billion Bid for Stake in India's Flipkart," *Wall Street Journal*, May 4, 2018; and Vindu Goel, "Walmart Takes Control of India's FlipKart in E-Commerce Gamble," *New York Times*, May 9, 2018.

56. See Andrei Hagiu and Elizabeth Altman, "Finding the Platform in Your Product," *Harvard Business Review*, July–August 2017.

57. Clay Christensen, *The Innovator's Dilemma: When New Technologies Cause Great Firms to Fail* (1997; repr., Boston: Harvard Business Review Press, 2015).

58. John Greenough, "GE Makes Wind Energy More Efficient—AT&T

Distracted Driving—Cloud Infrastructure Growth," *Business Insider Intelligence*, May 20, 2015.

59. Barb Darrow, "GE Preps Industrial-Strength Cloud of Its Own," *Fortune*, August 5, 2015.

60. Laura Winig, "GE's Big Bet on Data and Analytics," *MIT Sloan Management Review*, February 2016.

61. Rajiv Lal and Scott Johnson, "GE Digital" (Boston: Harvard Business Review Publishing, Case #517-063, February 2017), 5.

62. See Thomas Kellner, "Everything You Always Wanted to Know About Predix, but Were Afraid to Ask," GE Reports, October 4, 2014, http://www.ge.com/reports/post/99494485070/everything-you-always-wanted-to-know-about-predix/ (accessed October 30, 2018).

63. Lal and Johnson, "GE Digital," 6.

64. Barb Darrow, "GE Is Building Its Own Cloud: Outsiders Wonder Why," *Fortune*, August 6, 2015.

65. Barb Darrow, "New GE Chief Confirms Narrower Focus for Industrial Cloud," *Fortune*, September 20, 2017.

66. Barb Darrow, "Here's Why GE Shelved Plans to Build Its Own Amazon-Like Cloud," *Fortune*, September 6, 2017; Anna Hensel, "How This Entrepreneur Turned E-Commerce Giants into Customers," *Inc. 5000*, August 21, 2015; and Alwyn Scott, "GE Is Shifting the Strategy for Its $12 Billion Digital Business," *Business Insider*, August 28, 2017.

67. Winig, "GE's Big Bet," 6.

68. Thomas Kellner, "Ready for Prime Time: Intel Joins GE as It Opens Predix, Its Digital Platform for the Industrial Internet, to All Users," GE Reports, February 22, 2016, http://www.gereports.com/ready-for-prime-time-ge-opens-predix-its-digital-platform-for-the-industrial-internet-to-everyone/ (accessed October 30, 2018).

69. Mark Bernardo, "Introducing Predix Kits, the Newest Addition to Our Developer Toolkit," *Predix Developer Network Blog*, July 26, 2018, https://www.predix.io/blog/article.html?article_id=1948 (accessed October 30, 2018).

70. Danny Palmer, "GE Opens Paris 'Digital Foundry' in International Industrial IoT Push,' *ZD Net,* June 14, 2016; and Adrian Bridgewater, "GE Builds 'Digital Foundry' Locations, Where Physics + Analytics Intersect," *Forbes,* October 22, 2016.

71. Lal and Johnson, "GE Digital," 6.

72. Winig, "GE's Big Bet."

73. "Siemens and General Electric Gear Up for the Internet of Things," *Economist,* December 3, 2016.

74. Quoted in Winig, "GE's Big Bet."

75. Siemens, "MindSphere—The Internet of Things (IoT) Solution," https://www.siemens.com/global/en/home/products/software/mindsphere.html (accessed October 30, 2018).

76. Siemens and SAP, "Delivering an Open Cloud for Industrial Customers," https://cloudplatform.sap.com/success/siemens.html (accessed October 30, 2018).

77. "The Industrial IoT: 125+ Start-ups Transforming Factory Floors, Oil Fields, and Supply Chains," *CB Insights,* May 5, 2017.

78. Scott, "GE Is Shifting the Strategy."

79. Ibid.

80. John Flannery, "Our Future Is Digital," *LinkedIn* (blog post), September 15, 2017; https://www.linkedin.com/pulse/our-future-digital-john-flannery/ (accessed October 30, 2018).

81. Scott, "GE Is Shifting the Strategy."

82. ThomsonReuters Street Events, "General Electric Co Investor Update—Edited Transcript," November 13, 2017, https://www.ge.com/investor-relations/sites/default/files/GE-USQ_Transcript_2017-11-13.pdf (accessed March 15, 2018).

83. General Electric, *2017 Annual Report,* https://www.ge.com/investor-relations/ar2017/ceo-letter (accessed October 30, 2018).

84. Thomas Grysta and David Benoit, "GE Ousts CEO John Flannery in Surprise Move After Missed Targets," *Wall Street Journal,* October 1, 2018.

CHAPTER 6: DOUBLE-EDGED SWORDS:
HARNESS PLATFORM POWER, BUT DON'T ABUSE IT

1. Interview from Henry Blodget, "Mark Zuckerberg on Innovation," *Business Insider,* October 1, 2009.

2. Full testimony text can be found here: https://www.judiciary.senate .gov/imo/media/doc/04-10-18%20Zuckerberg%20Testimony.pdf.

3. Farhad Manjoo, "The Frightful Five Want to Rule Entertainment. They Are Hitting Limits," *New York Times,* October 11, 2017.

4. Lina M. Khan, "Amazon's Antitrust Paradox," *Yale Law Journal* 126, no. 3 (January 2017): 710–805.

5. Cao Li, Alexandra Stevenson, and Sui-Lee Wee, "As Chinese Investors Panic over Dubious Products, Authorities Quash Protests," *New York Times,* August 9, 2018.

6. See Michael A. Cusumano and David B. Yoffie, *Competing on Internet Time: Lessons from Netscape and Its Battle with Microsoft* (New York: Free Press/Simon & Schuster, 1998). See also Andrew I. Gavil and Harry First, *The Microsoft Antitrust Cases: Competition Policy for the Twenty-First Century* (Cambridge, MA: MIT Press, 2014); and William Page and John E. Lopatka, *The Microsoft Case: Antitrust, High Technology, and Consumer Welfare* (Chicago: University of Chicago Press, 2009).

7. Sharon Pian Chan, "Long Antitrust Saga Ends for Microsoft," *Seattle Times,* May 11, 2011.

8. See European Commission, Competition, "Microsoft Case: The Commission's Investigation," http://ec.europa.eu/competition /sectors/ICT/microsoft/investigation.html (accessed October 30, 2018).

9. In 2006, the Commission slapped Microsoft with another fine, this time of €280 million ($350 million), claiming that Microsoft was not complying quickly enough and that it charged too much for accessing the interface information. See David Gow, "EU Fine Microsoft €280m," *Guardian,* July 12, 2006. In 2008, the Commission ruled that Microsoft continued to charge "unreasonable rates" and

ordered the company to pay another €899 million ($1.12 billion), later reduced to €860 million ($1.07 billion). See Jon Brodkin, "Microsoft's Hefty Antitrust Fine Upheld by European Court," *Ars Technica*, June 27, 2012.

10. Chan, "Long Antitrust Saga Ends for Microsoft."

11. Cusumano and Yoffie, *Competing on Internet Time.*

12. European Commission, "Antitrust: Commission Welcomes General Court Judgment in Microsoft Compliance Case," press release, June 27, 2012, http://europa.eu/rapid/press-release_MEMO-12-500 _en.htm?locale=en; and "Online Platforms," Digital Single Market, Policy, May 4, 2018, https://ec.europa.eu/digital-single-market/en /online-platforms-digital-single-market (accessed October 30, 2018).

13. European Commission, "Antitrust: Commission Sends Statement of Objections to Google on Android Operating System and Applications," press release, April 20, 2016, http://europa.eu/rapid /press-release_IP-16-1492_en.htm (accessed October 30, 2018).

14. Ibid.

15. "Trust," *Merriam Webster*, https://www.merriam-webster.com /dictionary/trust (accessed June 21, 2018).

16. Glenn Harlan Reynolds, "When Digital Platforms Become Censors," *Wall Street Journal*, August 18, 2018. See also Jack Nicas, "Alex Jones and Infowars Content Is Removed from Apple, Facebook and YouTube," *New York Times*, August 6, 2018.

17. Nicholas Thompson and Fred Vogelstein, "Inside the Two Years that Shook Facebook—and the World," *Wired*, February 12, 2018.

18. Ibid.

19. John Reed, "Hate Speech, Atrocities, and Fake News: The Crisis of Democracy in Myanmar," *Financial Times*, February 21, 2018; on Sri Lanka, see Amanda Taub and Max Fisher, "Where Countries Are Tinderboxes and Facebook Is a Match," *New York Times*, April 21, 2018.

20. Thompson and Vogelstein, "Inside the Two Years."

21. Ibid.

22. Rob Price, "Facebook Is Asking Users to Pick Which News Outlets Are 'Trustworthy'—and Will Demote the Losers in Your Feed," *Business Insider,* January 19, 2018.

23. Issie Lapowsky, "Facebook's Election Safeguards Are Still a Work in Progress," *Wired,* March 29, 2018.

24. Nicholas Thompson, "Mark Zuckerberg Talks to *Wired* about Facebook's Privacy Problem," *Wired,* March 21, 2018.

25. Reynolds, "When Digital Platforms Become Censors."

26. Ibid.

27. "Top Facebook Executive Defended Data Collection in 2016 Memo—and Warned That Facebook Could Get People Killed," *BuzzFeed News,* https://www.buzzfeednews.com/article/ryanmac /growth-at-any-cost-top-facebook-executive-defended-data #.iuq17wEa9 (accessed August 20, 2018).

28. Hannah Kuchler, "Inside Facebook's Content Clean-up Operation," *Financial Times,* April 24, 2018; and "Transcript of Mark Zuckerberg's Senate Hearing," *Washington Post,* April 10, 2018.

29. Jen Kirby, "9 Questions About Facebook and Data Sharing You Were Too Embarrassed to Ask," *Vox,* April 10, 2018.

30. Kevin Roose, "How Facebook's Data Sharing Went from a Feature to a Bug," *New York Times,* March 19, 2018.

31. Thompson, "Mark Zuckerberg Talks."

32. Reynolds, "When Digital Platforms Become Censors."

33. Elaine Pofeldt, "Are We Ready for a Workforce That Is 50% Freelance?" *Forbes,* October 17, 2017.

34. Ibid.

35. Noam Scheiber, "Gig Economy Business Model Dealt a Blow in California Ruling," *New York Times,* April 30, 2018.

36. Sarah Kessler, "The Gig Economy Won't Last Because It Is Being Sued to Death," *Fast Company,* February 17, 2015.

37. Andrei Hagiu and Julian Wright, "The Status of Works and Platforms in the Sharing Economy," June 20, 2018, http://andreihagiu.com/wp -content/uploads/2018/07/Liquidity-constraint-06202018.pdf

(accessed September 11, 2018); and Andrei Hagiu and Rob Biederman, "Companies Need an Option Between Contractor and Employee," *Harvard Business Review*, August 21, 2015.

38. Kia Kokalitcheva, "Lyft to Pay $12.3 Million as Part of a Proposed Labor Lawsuit Settlement," *Fortune*, January 27, 2016.

39. Jeff John Roberts, "Is a Maid an Employee? Looking for a Third Way in the On-Demand Economy," *Fortune*, February 10, 2016.

40. Ibid.

41. Josh Eidelson, "U.S. Labor Board Complaint Says On-Demand Cleaners Are Employees" *Bloomberg*, August 30, 2017.

42. Sarah Butler, "Deliveroo Boss Doubled His Pay Ahead of Riders' Protest," *Guardian*, November 11, 2016.

43. Nic Hart and Alice Head, "Gig Economy Update—CAC Rules in Favour of Deliveroo in Worker Status Test Case," *Steptoe UK Employment Law Alert*, November 23, 2017.

44. Sarah Butler, "Deliveroo Wins Right Not to Give Riders Minimum Wage or Holiday Pay," *Guardian*, November 14, 2017.

45. Robert Wood, "FedEx Settles Independent Contractor Mislabeling Case for $228 Million," *Forbes*, June 16, 2015.

46. Kimball Norup, "Another FedEx Worker Misclassification Case Settled for $227 Million," *TalentWave*, May 9, 2017.

47. Jeffrey S. Horton Thomas and Steven P. Gallagher, "Say Goodbye to Independent Contractors: The New 'ABC' Test of Employee Status," *HR Defense*, May 7, 2018.

48. Benjamin Edelman, "Uber Can't Be Fixed—It's Time for Regulators to Shut It Down," *Harvard Business Review*, June 2017.

49. The law applies to "platform operators," which are defined as every natural or legal person offering professionally—whether remunerated or not—a public online communication service relying on: (1) listing or ranking through data processing the content, goods or services offered or uploaded by third parties; or (2) connecting multiple parties for the sale of a good, the provision of a service, or the exchange or sharing of content, a good, or a service. French

Law: Loi N° 2016-1321 du 7 Octobre 2016 pour une République Numérique, Article 49, https://www.legifrance.gouv.fr/eli/loi /2016/10/7/ECFI1524250L/jo/texte (accessed October 30, 2018).

50. European Commission, "Online Platforms."

51. Laura Stevens, "Why a Trump-Led Antitrust Case Against Amazon Is a Long Shot," *Wall Street Journal*, March 31, 2018.

52. Lina M. Khan, "Amazon's Antitrust Paradox," *Yale Law Journal* 126, no. 3 (2017): 710–805.

53. Linda Qiu, "Does Amazon Pay Taxes? Contrary to Trump Tweet, Yes," *New York Times*, August 16, 2017.

54. Ibid.

55. Daniel Keyes, "How e-Tailers Can Steal Amazon's Customers at the Last Moment," *Business Insider Intelligence*, June 1, 2018 (accessed June 22, 2018).

56. Emma Woollacott, "YouTube Hires More Moderators as Content Creators Complain They're Being Unfairly Targeted," *Forbes*, December 5, 2017.

57. Sam Levin, "Google to Hire Thousands of Moderators After Outcry Over YouTube Abuse Videos," *Guardian*, December 5, 2017.

58. Susan Wojcicki, "Expanding Our Work Against Abuse of Our Platform," *YouTube Official Blog*, December 4, 2017, https://youtube. googleblog.com/2017/12/expanding-our-work-against-abuse -of-our.html (accessed October 30, 2018).

59. Ibid.

60. Alex Hern, "YouTube to Manually Review Popular Videos Before Placing Ads," *Guardian*, January 17, 2018.

61. Amar Toor, "EU Close to Making Facebook, YouTube, and Twitter Block Hate Speech Videos," *Verge*, May 24, 2017.

62. Catherine Supp, "Commission Backs Away from Regulating Online Platforms over Hate Speech," *Euractiv*, January 19, 2018.

63. European Commission, "Results of Commission's Last Round of Monitoring of the Code of Conduct Against Online Hate Speech,"

January 2018, http://ec.europa.eu/newsroom/just/item-detail
.cfm?item_id=612086 (accessed October 30, 2018).

64. David B. Yoffie and Mary Kwak, "Playing by the Rules: How Intel
Avoids Antitrust Litigation," *Harvard Business Review*, June 2001,
119–22.

CHAPTER 7: LOOKING FORWARD: PLATFORMS AND THE FUTURE

1. Georgia Wells, "Snapchat Zigs Where Facebook Zags," *Wall Street
Journal*, June 14, 2018.

2. Khari Johnson, "Everything Amazon's Alexa Learned to Do in
2017," *Venture Beat*, December 29, 2017; Paul Cutsinger, "2017 Alexa
Skills Kit Year in Review: More Than 100 New Products, Programs,
Features, and Tools" January 5, 2018, https://developer.amazon.com
/blogs/alexa/post/829a615b-301f-407c-96e7-6956fb988570/2017
-alexa-skills-kit-year-in-review-more-than-100-new-products
-programs-features-and-tools (accessed May 2, 2018); and Monica
Chin, "Amazon Is Killing the Skill (as We Know It)," *Tom's Guide*,
September 13, 2018.

3. Jake Swearingen, "Amazon Could Give the Echo Dot Away and Still
Make Money," *New York Magazine*, January 3, 2018.

4. James Stables, "Google Assistant Aces Accuracy Study—but Alexa Is
Catching Up Fast," *Ambient*, April 30, 2018.

5. Rob Verger, "Someday, You Might Subscribe to a Self-Driving Taxi
Service, Netflix-Style," *Popular Science*, March 15, 2018.

6. Ibid.

7. Phil LeBeau, "General Motors Plans to Take On Ride-Sharing Services
with Self-Driving Cars by 2019," CNBC, November 30, 2018, https://
www.cnbc.com/2017/11/30/gm-to-take-on-ride-sharing-services
-with-self-driving-cars-by-2019.html (accessed June 2018).

8. Caitlin Huston, "Driverless Cars Could Cost 35 Cents per Mile for the
Uber Consumer," *Marketwatch*, September 19, 2016, https://www

.marketwatch.com/story/demand-for-driverless-cars-could-boost
-uber-to-2016-09-19 (accessed June 2018).

9. Christopher Mims, "How Self-Driving Cars Could End Uber," *Wall Street Journal*, May 7, 2017.

10. Max Chafkin, "Uber's First Self-Driving Fleet Arrives in Pittsburgh This Month," *Bloomberg*, August 18, 2016.

11. See Lyft, "The Open Autonomous Era," https://take.lyft.com/open
-platform/ (accessed June 2018).

12. Mike Isaac, "Lyft Adds Ford to Its List of Self-Driving Car Partners," *New York Times*, September 27, 2018, https://www.nytimes
.com/2017/09/27/technology/lyft-ford-self-driving-cars
.html?mcubz=0 (accessed June 2018).

13. John Zimmer, "The Third Transportation Revolution: Lyft's Vision for the Next Ten Years and Beyond," *Medium*, September 18, 2016, https://medium.com/@johnzimmer/the-third-transportation
-revolution-27860f05fa91 (accessed June 2018).

14. Isaac, "Lyft Adds Ford."

15. This section is based on Michael A. Cusumano, "The Business of Quantum Computing," *Communications of the ACM* 61, no. 10 (October 2018): 20–22.

16. Jason Palmer, "Here, There, and Everywhere: Quantum Technology Is Beginning to Come into Its Own," *Economist*, May 20, 2018.

17. "List of Companies Involved in Quantum Computing or Communication," *Wikipedia*, https://en.wikipedia.org/wiki/List_of
_companies_involved_in_quantum_computing_or_communication (accessed May 26, 2018).

18. Veritasium, "How Does a Quantum Computer Work?" YouTube, June 17, 2013, https://www.youtube.com/watch?v=g_IaVepNDT4 (accessed May 30, 2018).

19. Alan MacCormack, Ajay Agrawal, and Rebecca Henderson, "D-Wave Systems: Building a Quantum Computer" (Boston: Harvard Business School Publishing, Case #604-073, 2004).

20. Quentin Hardy, "A Strange Computer Promises Great Speed," *New York Times*, March 21, 2013; and Lev Grossman, "Quantum Leap," *Time*, February 17, 2014.

21. Cade Metz, "Yale Professors Race Google and IBM to the First Quantum Computer," *New York Times*, November 13, 2017.

22. Xanadu, "Strawberry Fields," https://www.xanadu.ai/software/ (accessed May 28, 2018).

23. Simon Bisson, "Inside Microsoft's Quantum Computing World," *InfoWorld*, October 17, 2017; and Allison Linn, "The Future Is Quantum: Microsoft Releases Free Preview of Quantum Development Kit," December 11, 2017, https://blogs.microsoft.com/ai/future -quantum-microsoft-releases-free-preview-quantum-development-kit/ (accessed May 27, 2018).

24. Brian Wang, "D-Wave Adiabatic Quantum Computer Used by Harvard to Solve Protein Folding Problems," *Next Big Future*, August 16, 2012.

25. Michael Brooks, "Quantum Computers Buyers' Guide: Buy One Today," *New Scientist*, October 15, 2014.

26. Sara Castellanos, "Companies Look to Make Quantum Leap with New Technology," *Wall Street Journal*, May 6, 2017; and Jack Ewing, "BMW and Volkswagen Try to Beat Google and Apple at Their Own Game," *New York Times*, June 22, 2017.

27. "List of Companies Involved in Quantum Computing or Communication."

28. Owen Matthews, "How China Is Using Quantum Physics to Take Over the World and Stop Hackers," *Newsweek*, October 30, 2017.

29. Steve Brachman, "U.S. Leads World in Quantum Computing Patent Filings with IBM Leading the Charge," *IP Watchdog*, December 4, 2017.

30. Richard Gray, "Why Gene Therapy Will Create So Many Jobs," *BBC .com*, October 15, 2018, http://www.bbc.com/capital/story/20181003 -why-gene-therapy-will-create-so-many-jobs/ (accessed October 22, 2018).

31. Our special thanks to Samantha Zyontz, a Ph.D. student at the MIT
     Sloan School of Management, for her assistance in understanding
     and writing up this discussion of CRISPR. We also acknowledge
     assistance from Gigi Hirsch and David Fritsche of the MIT Center for
     Biomedical Innovation.

32. Carl Zimmer, "Breakthrough DNA Editor Born of Bacteria," *Quanta*,
     February 6, 2015.

33. McKinsey & Company, "Realizing the Potential of CRISPR," January
     2017, https://www.mckinsey.com/industries/pharmaceuticals-and
     -medical-products/our-insights/realizing-the-potential-of-crispr
     (accessed June 6, 2018).

34. Michael Specter, "How the DNA Revolution Is Changing Us,"
     National Geographic, August 2016.

35. Gina Kolata and Pam Belluck, "Why Are Scientists So Upset About the
     First Crispr Babies?" *New York Times*, December 5, 2018.

36. Samantha Zyontz, "Running with (CRISPR) Scissors: Specialized
     Knowledge and Tool Adoption," Technological Innovation,
     Entrepreneurship, and Strategic Management Research Seminar, MIT
     Sloan School of Management, October 22, 2018.

37. See AddGene, "CRISPR Plasmids and Resources," https://www
     .addgene.org/crispr/ (accessed October 19, 2018).

38. See Antonio Regalado, "Start-up Aims to Treat Muscular Dystrophy
     with CRISPR," *MIT Technology Review*, February 27, 2017; and Editas
     Medicine, "Our Pipeline," http://www.editasmedicine.com/pipeline
     (accessed June 14, 2018).

39. Amirah Al Idrus, "Feng Zhang and David Liu's Base-Editing CRISPR
     Start-up Officially Launches with $87 Million," *FierceBiotech.com*,
     May 14, 2018.

40. Kashyap Vayas, "New CRISPR-based Platform Could Soon Diagnose
     Diseases from the Comfort of Your Home," *Science*, April 29, 2018; and
     Megan Molteni, "A New Start-up Wants to Use CRISPR to Diagnose
     Disease," *Wired*, April 26, 2018.

41. "CRISPR Company Cofounded by Jennifer Doudna Comes Out of

Stealth Mode," *Genome Web*, April 26, 2018, https://www.genomeweb
.com/business-news/crispr-company-cofounded-jennifer-doudna
-comes-out-stealth-mode#.WxgKnVVKicM (accessed June 6, 2018).

42. David Cyranoski, "CRISPR Alternative Doubted," *Nature*, August 11,
2016, 136–37.

43. Labiotech editorial team, "The Most Important Battle in Gene
Editing: CRISPR Versus TALEN," Labiotech, March 13, 2018,
https://labiotech.eu/features/crispr-talen-gene-editing/ (accessed
October 22, 2018); and Michael Boettcher and Michael T. McManus,
"Choosing the Right Tool for the Job: RNAi, TALEN, or CRISPR,"
Molecular Cell 58, no. 4 (May 21, 2015): 575–85, https://www.ncbi
.nlm.nih.gov/pmc/articles/PMC4441801/ (accessed October 23,
2018).

44. Eric Lander, "The Heroes of CRISPR," *Cell*, January 14, 2016.

45. Carl Zimmer, "What Is a Genetically Modified Crop? A European
Ruling Sows Confusion," *New York Times*, July 27, 2018.

46. Erika Check Hayden, "Should You Edit Your Children's Genes?"
Nature, February 23, 2016.

INDEX